ABOUT THE AUTHORS

Karen Gayton Swisher (Standing Rock Sioux) is the former director of the Center for Indian Education at Arizona State University in Tempe. She is the recipient of the G. Mike Charleston Research Award for Outstanding Scholarship from the American Indian/Alaska Native Education Special Interest Group of the American Educational Research Association; the Early Career Contribution Award from the Committee on the Role and Status of Minorities in Educational Research Development from the American Educational Research Association; the Sioux Award for Accomplishments in Professional Career, the highest honor of the University of North Dakota Alumni Association; and the Special Contributions Award from the National Indian Education Association. A former school teacher and principal, and currently chair of the Teacher Education Department at Haskell Indian Nations University in Lawrence, Kansas, Dr. Swisher has authored many published articles in American Indian/Alaska Native education.

AnCita Benally (Navajo) earned a B.A. in history at Brigham Young University, and a M.A. in history from Arizona State University in Tempe, where she is a doctoral student in the Department of History. Born in Pinon, Arizona, Ms. Benally spoke only Navajo until the age of five and comes from a strong storytelling tradition. Steeped in the Navajo language and culture, she has taught Indian and Navajo history to high school students on the Navajo Reservation and has taught the Navajo language at Arizona State University.

NATIVE NORTH AMERICAN FIRSTS

NATIVE NORTH AMERICAN FIRSTS

Karen
Gayton
Swisher, EdD

AnCita
Benally

Foreword by
BILLY MILLS

GALE

DETROIT · NEW YORK · TORONTO · LONDON

Karen Gayton Swisher and AnCita Benally, *Editors*

Gale Research Staff

Sharon Malinowski, Melissa Walsh Doig, *Editors*
Dawn Barry, Jeffrey Lehman, *Contributing Editors*
Mark D. Graham, *Editor Assistant*
Linda S. Hubbard, *Managing Editor, Multicultural Team*

Susan Trosky, *Permissions Manager*
Margaret A. Chamberlain, *Permissions Specialist*

Mary Beth Trimper, *Production Director*
Evi Seoud, *Assistant Production Manager*
Shanna Heilveil, *Production Assistant*

Cynthia Baldwin, *Product Design Manager*
Tracy Rowens, *Designer*
Randy Bassett, *Image Database Supervisor*
Robert Duncan, Michael Logusz, *Imaging Specialists*
Pamela Reed, *Photography Coordinator*

⊚™This book is printed on acid-free paper that meets the minimum requirements of American National Standard for Information Sciences— Permanence Paper for Printed Library Materials, ANSI Z39.48-1984.

Library of Congress Catalog Card Number 97-22999
A CIP record is available from the British Library

ISBN 0-7876-0518-2

Printed in the United States of America.

Library of Congress Cataloging-in-Publication Data

Native North American firsts : 500 years of extraordinary achievement / Karen Gayton Swisher and AnCita Benally [editors]. — 1st ed.
    p. cm.
    Includes bibliographical references and index.
    ISBN 0-7876-0518-2 (acid-free paper)
        1. Native Americans.   I. Swisher, Karen Gayton. II. Benally, AnCita.
    E77.S96 1997   97-22999
    970',00497—DC21   CIP

10 9 8 7 6 5 4 3 2 1

DEDICATION

This volume of firsts is dedicated to our families and friends for their support; to all American Indians and Alaska Natives whose firsts will forever go unrecognized; and to young people, so that they will know they have many role models and that they too can achieve greatness.

CONTENTS

FOREWORD

Among the Dakota, Lakota, and Nakota people there are four virtues or values that guide one's behavior: bravery, fortitude, wisdom, and generosity.

According to Royal B. Hassrick, who wrote *The Sioux,* bravery was the foremost virtue for both men and women. He noted that "to be considered full of courage, to have a strong heart, was an honor of extreme importance and worth great effort. Acclaim was accorded only to those who had proven themselves." One whose life is strictly guided by these virtues often stands out as a leader. This person—a leader—is one who often takes risks that bring distinction as the first to accomplish a task or deed, to take care of his or her people, or to reach out to help someone in need.

A leader is challenged to assume responsibility, display the power of giving, follow the virtue of humility and center one's life around a core of spirituality. To do this is the mark of a warrior, and a warrior does not talk about the tasks or deeds accomplished; instead, it is left for others to speak for him or her.

When I won a gold medal at the 1964 Olympic Games in the 10,000 meter run and became the first, and still the only, American to ever win this event, my Lakota elders gave me my Indian name, Makoce Teh'la (Loves-His-Country). I earned warrior status. They danced my deeds—I was honored.

This book speaks for the hundreds of individuals and groups who have gained preeminence in a particular area of endeavor. Many of the men and women included in this book of firsts are not only the first American Indians to gain distinction, but the first Americans as well.

They are our mentors and our heroes. They are the ordinary men and women achieving extraordinary things. This book allows us to learn about them, to learn from them, and to admire them. For this, we dance their deeds—they are honored.

Billy Mills

Olympic Gold Medalist

National Spokesperson,
Running Strong for American Indian Youth

PREFACE

As the first Americans, the indigenous people of this country and continent, American Indians and Alaska Natives have distinguished themselves in many ways and in various fields. Contributions of indigenous peoples have been noted in the area of arts, sciences, humanities, and sports. Foods, plants, place names, games, medicine, ecology, and astronomy are but a few broad categories in which the influence of indigenous people and events can be found.

The relative importance of events differs, based on one's perspective. Being first is a concept liberally attributed to the dominant culture of this country and may not be considered significant to indigenous people. We agree with Joseph B. Oxendine's observations in *American Indian Sports Heritage:* "Indians had little interest in numbers or in record keeping for its own sake." We must also consider that in many indigenous cultures, humility is a value that is strictly adhered to, so it is inappropriate for individuals to speak of, or bring attention to, her/his deeds or accomplishments. We know there are many firsts by Native people that have gone unnoticed and unrecorded. Operating under the federal policies of assimilation, many Native people did not emphasize their ethnicity and culture, making verification of their Indian or Native identification difficult. As ethnic pride has taken hold in America and Canada during the last few decades, the volume of work recording notable accomplishments of indigenous people has increased. Since the 1970s there has been a renaissance among indigenous people in South America who identify themselves as Indians.

So why do a book of firsts? Living in two worlds is a metaphor accepted by Indians and non-Indians alike, so to be recognized as a first is part of living in one of two worlds in which accomplishments are measured by such efforts. It has been suggested that Indian people live in a complex world with multiple loyalties, wherein the strength of our cultures contributes to success in the world of the dominant culture. This philosophy explains the phenomenon of being Indian in a white world where differences in cultural values are evident.

As a monolithic group, nearly two million American Indians and Alaska Natives want to be recognized for their contributions to this country and the world. Although we have a unique relationship with the federal government and are sovereign nations within a nation, we are citizens of this country and the world. As such, it is important that Indian people be the ones to define what being first means to us. As authors of this book, we are individuals who cannot speak for all Indian people; nevertheless, we present a perspective that until recently has remained unrecognized.

Our research began with myriad handbooks, chronologies, almanacs, biographies, newspapers, and newsletters devoted to Indians of the Americas, including North, Central, and South America; our search was not limited to American Indians and Alaska Natives of the United States of America. We were able to find a considerable number of entries about Canadian First Nations people and events that closely paralleled the American Indian and Alaska Native entries, probably because of the common British/Anglo colonization experiences. We were unable to find as much material about the indigenous peoples of Central and South America. Time was an issue in this research, so we concentrated our energy on American Indians and Alaska Natives. We distributed letters of request at conferences of indigenous people, advertised in prominent Native newspapers, and wrote letters to tribal headquarters.

The more obvious and well-known firsts in several categories were prominently recorded, but others were more obscure. Some entries were explicitly stated as "firsts," in other instances words such as "founded" or "established" met the criteria we set and we pursued other sources for verification. We quickly realized that some of the most significant people and events were not always the "first," therefore, someone as well-known as Sitting Bull is not included.

We struggled with including events that were not directly attributed to Indian people, but the results of which profoundly affected Indian lives and destiny. For example, translation of the Bible and Christian hymns into various Indian languages was apparently not through the initiative of Indian people but their involvement as interpreters; and the advent of these publications produced significant cultural effects. Legislation offers another example. While Indian people had no part in the design and drafting of the Dawes Act of 1887, the change it created in land allotment for many tribes targeted the core of Indian or indigenous identity—relationship to the land. This piece of legislation, while not a Native first, marked a point in history from which subsequent twentieth century firsts occurred in the contrived assimilation process.

We tried to be complete and accurate. We could not include some interesting firsts because of lack of corroboration or proof. For example, we could not verify that Frances Folsom, who was said to be Choctaw, and wife of Grover Cleveland, was in fact the first Native American First Lady.

Dates were also problematic. The authors who meticulously described the person or event often did not include dates. In some cases, we gave approximate dates plus enough other identifying information for readers to locate desired details. Decisions about which year in a span of years an event occurred were difficult to determine; e.g., during an administrative experience of four years. Occasionally we were mislead by wrong information, which once published seemed to persist in source after source. Variant spelling of names and/or places presented another problem that was difficult to reconcile.

As we researched the "firsts," we found many "lasts." For example, Ishi was the last of his people, but he served as a source for the first pieces of authentic information about his people. The people who were the last traditional chiefs of their nation were the role models for the first chairpersons, presidents, and governors in contemporary times. The last speaker of a language provoked realization that a rebirth or revitalization was necessary if the culture was to survive. In so many examples, the "last" often set the stage for other firsts or significant events.

Many of the firsts are well-documented in the history of this country; however, many more are obscurely situated in books, newsletters, local newspapers, local histories, or the collective minds of those who know. We were unable to access many of these hidden treasures of information. Indian Country is a vast land and when time is limited, communication becomes difficult. We are thankful for the many people who responded to our calls, letters, announcements at conferences, and advertisements in newspapers and newsletters. We realized that word of mouth—the oral tradition—is still a vibrant source of information dissemination. We hope that this book of firsts will challenge our readers to identify those we missed or overlooked. It is an accomplishment that, in the words of one respondent, is "long overdue."

Karen Gayton Swisher, Ed.D., Lawrence, Kansas
AnCita Benally, Tempe, Arizona

ACKNOWLEDGEMENTS

The combined efforts of many individuals created *Native North American Firsts*. First of all, we thank those who responded to our call for information, provided photographs, and suggested sources of rich information. Many tribal governments responded with firsts that we might never have discovered. For example, to Amelia Flores, Archivist and Librarian for the Colorado River Indian Tribes, our special thanks for all the information she provided. Many others simply responded to support our efforts. We are deeply thankful to Patricia A. Etter, Curator, and Jacqueline M. Torres, Library Specialist, Archives and Manuscripts of the Labriola National American Indian Data Center in the Hayden Library at Arizona State University. Pat and Jacquie provided us with unlimited time, space, and assistance; we could not have accomplished this monumental task in just over one year's time without them. Thanks also to Chris Marin, Curator of Chicano Research Collection. We appreciate the support of the Hayden Library, including the use of the Labriola Center and the Luhrs Reading Room. The extensive holdings of the Labriola Center are impressive and should be considered by anyone doing research about American Indian and Alaska Native histories and cultures.

The Center for Indian Education at Arizona State University and the Teacher Education Department at Haskell Indian Nations University provided a home base for our efforts over the past year. Thanks to Laura E. Williams (Winnebago/Japanese), Secretary, and Octaviana Trujillo (Yaqui), Assistant Professor and Director of Computer Use, for giving and receiving information about the project. Haskell Indian Nations University Library proved an invaluable source of information and we are thankful to President Bob G. Martin (Cherokee), Dean of Instruction, Deborah Wetsit (Assiniboine), and Patricia Lorenta (Wichita), Secretary in the Teacher Education Department, for their support. Thanks go to the Haskell Foundation Director, Fran Day (Cherokee), and Bobbi Rayhder, Archivist, for information regarding the American Indian Athletic Hall of Fame, and for finding photographs.

Our special thanks and gratitude to our initial partner and assistant Kathy Kingfisher (Cherokee), a doctoral student in history at Arizona State University, for research assistance and photograph location; Myla Vicente Carpio (Jicarilla Apache/Laguna Pueblo), a doctoral student in history at Arizona State University, and Tarajean Yazzie (Navajo), now a doctoral student at Harvard University, for computer and database technical assistance; Marcia Lein Schiff at AP/Wide

World Photos for responding so positively and quickly in finding photographs. We appreciate the work of Duane Champagne (Turtle Mountain Chippewa) in developing many of the current reference books about indigenous peoples of the Americas.

To our editors Melissa Walsh Doig and Sharon Malinowski, we give special thanks for keeping us focused on deadlines and details and trying to remain calm and positive when we were doubtful. Thanks also to Peg Bessette for introducing us to the project.

ILLUSTRATION CREDITS

The photographs and illustrations appearing in Native North American Firsts were received from the following sources:

Cover: Charles Curtis (courtesy of Courtesy of AP/Wide World Photos); Maria Tallchief (courtesy of The Bettmann Archive/Newsphotos); Billy Mills (courtesy of AP/Wide World Photos).

Timeline of Important Native North American Events: *p. xxxiv:* Nineteenth-century engraving of Massasoit (courtesy of The Bettmann Archive/ Newsphotos); *p. xxxvi:* Kateri Tekakwitha (courtesy of The Bettmann Archive/ Newsphotos); *p. xxxvii:* Jim Thorpe (courtesy of Archive Photos); *p. xxxviii:* Charles Curtis (courtesy of AP/Wide World Photos); *p. xxxix:* Maria Tallchief (courtesy of Archive Photos); *p. xl:* James Gladstone (courtesy of AP/Wide World Photos); *p. xli:* Chief Joseph (courtesy of Library of Congress); *p. xlii:* Navarre Scott Momaday (courtesy of The Bettmann Archive/Newsphotos); *p. xliii:* Loretta Lynn (courtesy of Archive Photos); *p. xliv:* Rigoberta Menchu (courtesy of AP/Wide World Photos); *p. xlv:* Charles J. Chaput (courtesy of AP/Wide World Photos).

Art, Crafts, and Design: *p. 1:* Nampeyo (courtesy of National Archives and Records Administration); *p. 5:* Pueblo artists Julian and Maria Montoya Martinez (courtesy of AP/Wide World Photos); *p. 11:* Navajo sandpainting rug woven by Altnabah (courtesy of Museum of Northern Arizona); *p. 12: Moonrise,* by R. C. Gorman (courtesy of R. C. Gorman Gallery); p. 12: *R. C. Gorman (courtesy of R. C. Gorman Gallery).*

Business and Economics: *p. 17:* Oil painting of Joseph Brant (courtesy of The Bettmann Archive/Newsphotos).

Civic Leadership: *p. 21:* Annie Dodge Wauneka (courtesy of AP/Wide World Photos); *p. 22:* Louis R. Bruce Jr. (courtesy of The Bettmann Archive/Newsphotos); *p. 26:* Tribal leaders Peterson Zah, Josiah Moore, and Vernon Masayesva (courtesy of Arizona State University).

Cultural History: *p. 30:* Depiction of Hiawatha (courtesy of The Bettmann Archive/Newsphotos); *p. 33:* Nineteenth-century engraving of Massasoit (courtesy of The Bettmann Archive/Newsphotos); *p. 35:* Drawing of Sacajawea (courtesy of The Bettmann Archive/Newsphotos); *p. 40:* Chief Joseph (courtesy of Library of Congress); *p. 41:* Navajo Code Talker Dan Akee receives a medal in a 1989 ceremony in Phoenix, Arizona (courtesy of AP/Wide World Photos).

Education: *p. 44:* Carlisle Indian School (courtesy of National Archives and Records Administration); *p. 45:* Henry Roe Cloud (courtesy of Haskell Foundation); *p. 46:* Archie Phinney (courtesy of AP/Wide World Photos).

Government: *p. 53:* Charles Curtis (courtesy of AP/Wide World Photos); *p. 54:* Charles Curtis (courtesy of AP/Wide World Photos); *p. 55:* Ben Reifel (courtesy of AP/Wide World Photos); *p. 57:* Ben Nighthorse Campbell (courtesy of AP/Wide World Photos); *p. 58:* Joseph R. Garry (courtesy of AP/Wide World Photos); *p. 60:* Larry Echohawk (courtesy of Larry Echohawk); *p. 61:* Debora Norris (courtesy of Debra Norris); *p. 61:* Sally Gonzales (courtesy of Sally Gonzales); *p. 62:* James Gladstone (courtesy of AP/Wide World Photos).

Tribal Government: *p. 69:* Alice Brown Davis (courtesy of AP/Wide World Photos); *p. 69:* Henry Chee Dodge (courtesy of AP/Wide World Photos); *p. 70:* Red Cloud (courtesy of National Archives and Records Administration); *p. 74:* Betty Mae Jumper (courtesy of AP/Wide World Photos); *p. 76:* Wilma Mankiller (courtesy of AP/Wide World Photos); *p. 77:* Marge Anderson (courtesy of Haskell Foundation); *p. 79:* Robert L. Bennett (courtesy of The Bettmann Archive/Newsphotos); *p. 81:* Wilma Victor (courtesy of AP/Wide World Photos); *p. 82:* Ada Deer (courtesy of AP/Wide World Photos).

Language: *p. 88:* Cherokee syllabary in phonetic transcription and translation (courtesy of University of Oklahoma Press).

Law and the Judiciary: *p. 92:* Quannah Parker (courtesy of The Bettmann Archive/Newsphotos); *p. 94:* Nora Guinn (courtesy of Charles J. Guinn); *p. 95:* John Echohawk (courtesy of AP/Wide World Photos).

Literature: *p. 103:* Sarah Winnemucca (courtesy of The Granger Collection); *p. 107:* Navarre Scott Momaday (courtesy of The Bettmann Archive/Newsphotos); *p. 108:* Leslie Marmon Silko (courtesy of Robyn Stoutenburg).

Military: *p. 127:* Company "A" Apache Scouts (courtesy of National Archives and Records Administration); *p. 128:* Alchesay (courtesy of National Archives and Records Administration); *p. 129:* Curley Crow (courtesy of National Archives and Records Administration); *p. 131:* Thomas N. Almojuela (courtesy of Colleen Almojuela); *p. 134:* Ely Samuel Parker (courtesy of Library of Congress); *p. 136:* Troup I, 114th Cavalry Regiment (courtesy of Haskell Foundation); *p. 137:* Major General Clarence L. Tinker (courtesy of Haskell Foundation); *p. 138:* Colin Powell with Navajo Code Talkers and their families (courtesy of AP/Wide World Photos); *p. 139:* Lt. Ernest Childers (courtesy of National Archives and Records Administration); *p. 140:* Grace Thorpe (courtesy of AP/Wide World Photos); *p. 141:* Ira Hayes (courtesy of AP/Wide World Photos).

Performing Arts: *p. 145:* Maria Tallchief (courtesy of Archive Photos); *p. 146:* Louis W. Ballard (courtesy of The Bettmann Archive/Newsphotos); *p. 147:* The American Indian Dance Theater performs an Eagle Dance (photo by Don Perdue; courtesy of Hanay Geiogamah); *p. 149:* Will Sampson (courtesy of Archive Photos); *p. 150:* Chief Dan George (courtesy of AP/Wide World Photos); *p. 151:* Jay Silverheels (courtesy of AP/Wide World Photos); *p. 153:* Ed Lee Natay with Ray Boley (courtesy of Canyon Records); *p. 155:* Loretta Lynn (courtesy of Archive Photos).

Religious Life: *p. 165:* Rev. Peter Jones, by David Octavius Hill (courtesy of Amon Carter Museum, Fort Worth, Texas); *p. 168:* Kateri Tekakwitha (courtesy of

The Bettmann Archive/Newsphotos); *p. 169:* Statue of Kateri Tekakwitha (courtesy of AP/Wide World Photos); *p. 177:* Charles J. Chaput (courtesy of AP/Wide World Photos).

Indian Rights and Activism: *p. 187:* Standing Bear (courtesy of The Granger Collection); *p. 189:* Gertrude Bonnin (courtesy of The Bettmann Archive/Newsphotos); *p. 192:* LaDonna Harris (courtesy of The Bettmann Archive/Newsphotos); *p. 193:* Dennis Banks (courtesy of The Bettmann Archive/Newsphotos); *p. 194:* Clyde Bellecourt (courtesy of The Bettmann Archive/Newsphotos); *p. 195:* Dennis Banks (courtesy of AP/Wide World Photos); *p. 196:* Russell Means (courtesy of AP/Wide World Photos); *p. 197:* Russell Means (courtesy of AP/Wide World Photos); *p. 198:* Russell Means and K. Frizzell (courtesy of AP/Wide World Photos); *p. 199:* Russell Means with Dennis Banks and other AIM members (courtesy of The Bettmann Archive/Newsphotos); *p. 201:* Rigoberta Menchu (courtesy of AP/Wide World Photos).

Sports: *p. 211:* Walter Perry Johnson (courtesy of AP/Wide World Photos); *p. 212:* Walter Perry Johnson (courtesy of AP/Wide World Photos); *p. 217:* Ellison J. "Tarzan" Brown (courtesty AP/Wide World Photos); *p. 217:* Wilson "Buster" Charles (courtesy of Haskell Foundation); *p. 218:* Lewis Tewanima (courtesy of AP/Wide World Photos); *p. 219:* Jim Thorpe (courtesy of Archive Photos); *p. 220:* Billy Mills (courtesy of Billy Mills); *p. 221:* Billy Mills (courtesy of Billy Mills).

ADVISORY BOARD

CALENDAR OF FIRSTS

JANUARY

FEBRUARY

MARCH

APRIL

MAY

JUNE

JULY

AUGUST

SEPTEMBER

OCTOBER

NOVEMBER

DECEMBER

TIMELINE

ca. 300 B.C.E.   Maya invent concept of zero and put it to practical use.

ca. 1000   Mixtec of southern Mexico develop an efficient system of centralized government.

1150   Earliest known Hopi village is established.

1168   Aztec begin eighty-year migration to the Valley of Mexico.

1200   Mano Capac initiate the Inca empire centered at Cuzco.

1492   Taino first encounter Europeans when Christopher Columbus arrives at Watling Islands.

ca. 1500s   Deganiwidah and Hiawatha found the League of Iroquois Nations.

1587   Christening of Hatteras guide Manteo is the earliest recorded Protestant service in the New World.

1595   Pocahontas is received as royalty by English royalty.

1609   El Inca is the first person of Indian ancestry to write extensively on Native history and culture.

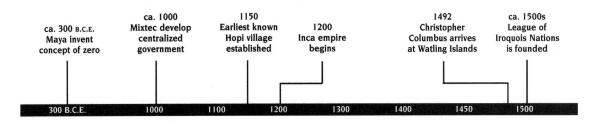

Massasoit

1621	Wampanoag and the pilgrims of Plymouth celebrate the first Thanksgiving feast.
1642	First Indian-English dictionary, *A Key into the Language of America,* is published.
1663	Mohegan scholar and first American Indian to graduate from Harvard University produces the earliest known written work by a Native North American.
ca. 1680s	Pope successfully leads the Pueblo Revolt against religious persecution by Spanish occupiers of the Southwest.
1681	Mahican leader initiates one of the first efforts of pan-Indian unity.
1683	French missionaries provide first description of Ojibwa sport of baggataway (lacrosse).
1706	Abenaki leader is believed to be the only American Indian knighted by a European monarch.
1715	Iroquois Confederacy forms into the Indian League of Nations.
1720	First permanent Indian school is established in Williamsburg, Virginia.
1772	Mohegan writer Samson Occom publishes first literary work by a Native American.
1775	Continental Congress decrees its jurisdiction over American Indian nations.
1778	The first treaty between the United States and an Indian nation is negotiated.

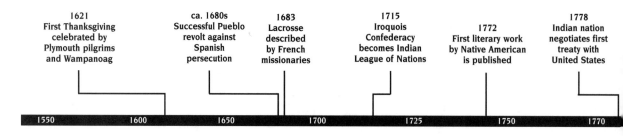

1621 First Thanksgiving celebrated by Plymouth pilgrims and Wampanoag	ca. 1680s Successful Pueblo revolt against Spanish persecution	1683 Lacrosse described by French missionaries	1715 Iroquois Confederacy becomes Indian League of Nations	1772 First literary work by Native American is published	1778 Indian nation negotiates first treaty with United States

1550　　1600　　1650　　1700　　1725　　1750　　1770

1786   First federal Indian reservation is established.

1804   Shoshoni guide and interpreter Sacajawea is the only woman to accompany the Lewis and Clark expedition through Louisiana territory.

1820s   Sequoyah develops and introduces a modified version of traditional Cherokee syllabary.

1824   The Bureau of Indian Affairs is created by the Department of War.

1827   Cherokee Nation adopts its first modern constitution, organizing a constitutional tribal government, and establishing itself as an independent and sovereign entity.

1828   *The Cherokee Phoenix* is the first American Indian newspaper in North America.

1830   The U.S. Congress passes the Indian Removal Act, which legally removes American Indian tribes from their lands.

1832   The U.S. Supreme Court recognizes sovereignty of American Indian nations.

1834   The Cherokee were divested of their lands in the "Trail of Tears."

1840   A four-nation alliance between the Cheyenne, Kiowa, Arapaho, and Comanche nations is established.

1842   The Choctaw Academy is the first Indian school established by an Indian tribe.

1854   The Five Civilized Tribes (Cherokee, Chickasaw, Choctaw, Creek, and Seminole) confederate.

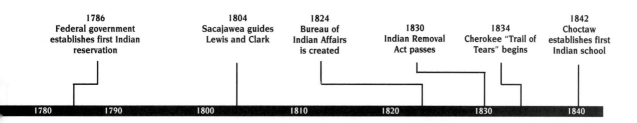

Kateri Tekakwitha

1861   Zapotec politician Pablo Benito Juarez becomes president of Mexico—the first Native to govern a nation.

1865   Cherokee trailblazer Jesse Chisholm opens the Chisholm Trail from Texas to Kansas.

1867   The Medicine Lodge Peace Treaty negotiations convene and create the Indian Territory in present-day Oklahoma.

1868   American Indians are specifically denied the right to vote by the Fourteenth Amendment.

1869   Pawnee scout "Mad Bear" is the first American Indian to be awarded the Medal of Honor.

1870   Lumbee and African American politician Hiram M. Revels from Mississippi is the first person of American Indian ancestry to be elected a U.S. senator.

1870s White sport hunters and amateurs begin a campaign of wanton destruction of the American bison.

1879   Carlisle Indian School is founded in Pennsylvania.

1881   American Indians are forbidden to practice their religions.

1882   Indian Rights Association is organized by non-Indian reformers concerned over the administration of U.S. Indian policy and the plight of American Indian peoples.

1884   Mohawk religious figure Kateri Tekakwitha is the first Native American to be venerated by the Roman Catholic church.

1885   President Ulysses S. Grant signs a law withdrawing federal troops guarding Indian Territory, opening the way for white settlers to squat on American Indian land.

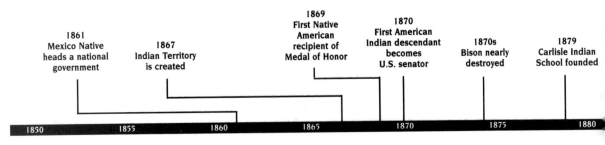

1861
Mexico Native
heads a national
government

1867
Indian Territory
is created

1869
First Native
American
recipient of
Medal of Honor

1870
First American
Indian descendant
becomes
U.S. senator

1870s
Bison nearly
destroyed

1879
Carlisle Indian
School founded

1850   1855   1860   1865   1870   1875   1880

1887 The Dawes (General Allotment) Act authorizes the subdivision of American Indian lands among tribal members and the sale of surplus land to whites.

1894 *The Ghost Dance,* filmed by Thomas A. Edison Films, is the first motion picture to focus on an American Indian subject.

ca. 1895 Datsolalee revives and elevates Washo basketry to a high art form.

1897 Penobscot athlete Louis Sockalexis is the first known American Indian athlete to sign with a major league baseball team.

1907 Onondaga runner Thomas Longboat is the first Native American to win the Boston Marathon in a record-breaking effort.

1911 Society of American Indians is founded—the first Indian organization to have exclusively Native American membership.

1912 Sac-Fox athlete Jim Thorpe is the first Native American to win gold medals at the Olympics in Sweden.

1914 Maya soprano Ada Navarrate is the first Native American to enter the international opera world.

1916 Ishi, the last member of his Yahi-Yana tribe, provides information about his traditions, religious ways, and language.

1917 For the first time in fifty years the birthrate among American Indians exceeds the death rate.

1918 The first Native American language is used in U.S. military communications.

1918 The Native American Church, the first American Indian church, is organized and incorporated.

Jim Thorpe

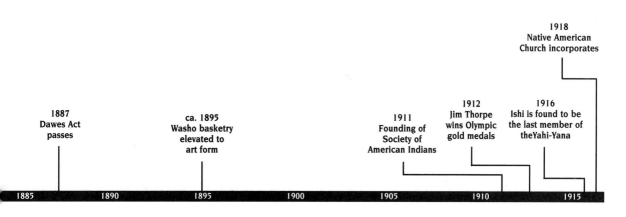

1887
Dawes Act
passes

ca. 1895
Washo basketry
elevated to
art form

1911
Founding of
Society of
American Indians

1912
Jim Thorpe
wins Olympic
gold medals

1916
Ishi is found to be
the last member of
theYahi-Yana

1918
Native American
Church incorporates

1885   1890   1895   1900   1905   1910   1915

Charles Curtis

1919   San Ildefonso Pueblo potter Maria Montoya Martinez revives indigenous pottery making and transforms it into an art form.

1921   The Haskell unit of the Kansas National Guard, the first and only all-American Indian National Guard, is organized by the Indian Service.

1924   The Indian Citizenship Act is passed.

1926   Gertrude Bonnin co-founds Congress of American Indians as the only nationally organized reform group with exclusively Indian membership.

1926   Nez Percé anthropologist Archie Phinney makes one of the most significant contributions to the preservation and understanding of his tribal culture.

1927   First novel by an American Indian woman is published.

1928   "Meriam Report" details American Indian problems.

1929   Kansa-Kaw/Osage politician Charles D. Curtis is the first person of American Indian ancestry to become vice president of the United States.

1931   Cherokee playwright Rollie Lynn Riggs' *Green Grow the Lilacs* is named one of the ten best plays on Broadway and is later adapted by Rodgers and Hammerstein into the musical *Oklahoma!*

1933   Santee Dakota Sioux leader Charles Alexander Eastman receives the first Indian Achievement Award.

1936   Congress passes Indian Arts and Crafts Board legislation to protect spurious imitations of Indian art and to control exploitation.

1938   The sacred Midipadi Bundle is returned to the Hidatsa people marking the first successful efforts to repatriate Native American sacred objects to their rightful caretakers.

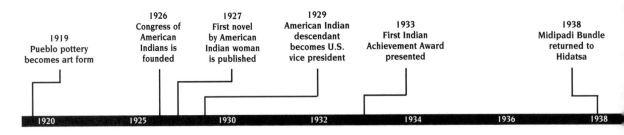

1919
Pueblo pottery
becomes art form

1926
Congress of
American
Indians is
founded

1927
First novel
by American
Indian woman
is published

1929
American Indian
descendant
becomes U.S.
vice president

1933
First Indian
Achievement Award
presented

1938
Midipadi Bundle
returned to
Hidatsa

1920   1925   1930   1932   1934   1936   1938

1939   Seneca "Chet" Ellis is the first American Indian to win boxing championships at the national and international levels.

1939   Paiute baseball player Walter Perry Johnson is one of the first men inducted into the Baseball Hall of Fame.

1940   For the first time in U.S. history, American Indians register for the military draft.

1940s   "No Indians Allowed" policies are declared an infringement on Native civil rights.

ca. 1942   Osage ballerina Maria Tallchief is the first American to dance with the Paris Opera.

1942   The Navajo language is the first Native American language in the United States to be used as a codified military means ofcommunication.

1942   Kiowa soldier Pascal Cleatur Poolaw becomes the most decorated American Indian soldier in U.S. military history.

1944   National Congress of American Indians is founded.

1945   Pima Marine Ira Hayes is the only American Indian in the famous photograph of six U.S. Marines raising the American flag at Mt. Suribachi on Iwo Jima Island, symbolically declaring victory over the Japanese.

1948   Sioux leaders suggest the creation of the Crazy Horse Memorial, the world's largest sculpture in stone.

ca. 1950s   Oglala Lakota Sioux Alice New Holy Blue Legs revives the art of quilling.

1950   The Canadian government extends the right to vote in federal elections to the Inuit people.

Maria Tallchief

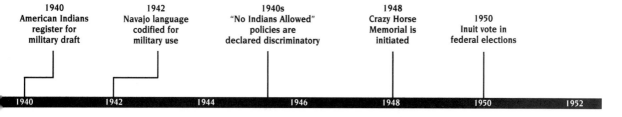

| 1940 American Indians register for military draft | 1942 Navajo language codified for military use | 1940s "No Indians Allowed" policies are declared discriminatory | 1948 Crazy Horse Memorial is initiated | 1950 Inuit vote in federal elections |

| 1940 | 1942 | 1944 | 1946 | 1948 | 1950 | 1952 |

James Gladstone

1950	*Broken Arrow* is the first film to treat American Indians as multi-dimensional.
1951	First professional pitcher in American League baseball history throws two no-hitters.
1953	First Miss American Indian selected at All-Indian Days festivities.
1954	First foreign government honors American Indian art.
1958	Blood politician James Gladstone is appointed Canada's first Native senator.
1958	Cherokee descendant Keely Smith is the first woman of Native American descent to win a Grammy award.
1960	Quawpaw/Cherokee composer Louis W. Ballard writes the first modern Canadian Indian ballet, *Koshare*.
1961	Mohawk writer Emily Pauline Johnson is the first Canadian author whose image appears on a Canadian postage stamp.
1961	Brulé Lakota Sioux politician Benjamin Reifel is the first Native American since Charles Curtis to win a seat in the U.S. Congress.
1962	Institute of American Indian Arts established
1962	Powhatan/Cherokee entertainer Wayne Newton is the first Native American featured on televised variety shows.
1963	Navajo tribal leader Annie Dodge Wauneka is the first Native American to receive the Presidential Medal of Freedom.

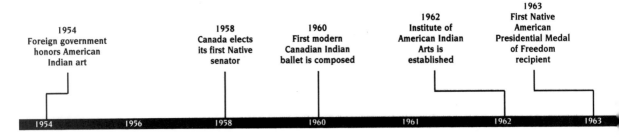

1954
Foreign government honors American Indian art

1958
Canada elects its first Native senator

1960
First modern Canadian Indian ballet is composed

1962
Institute of American Indian Arts is established

1963
First Native American Presidential Medal of Freedom recipient

1954 1956 1958 1960 1961 1962 1963

Chief Joseph

1964   Oglala Lakota Sioux runner Billy Mills wins an Olympic gold medal for the 10,000 meter race, setting the world's record.

1966   Alaska Federation of Native Associations is organized.

1967   The Navajo Tribal Council grants members of the Native American Church the right of religious freedom—the first time that a non-Navajo religion is granted such a right.

1967   Union of Ontario Indians formed.

1967   First ballet especially for Indian ballerinas is composed.

1968   American Indian Movement (AIM) is founded by Dennis Banks and others as the first group to use demonstrations to raise public awareness of the plight of American Indians in modern society.

1968   U.S. Post Office issues the first commemorative stamp recognizing a Native American leader—Nez Percé leader Chief Joseph.

1968   Interior Salish Okanagen Leonard Marchand is the first Native elected to the Canadian House of Commons.

1969   First American Indian commissioner appointed to Indian Claims Commission.

1969   First tribally chartered and controlled community college is founded.

1969   First Native studies program in Canada is established.

1969   National Indian Education Association is established.

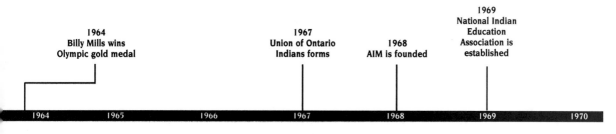

1964
Billy Mills wins
Olympic gold medal

1967
Union of Ontario
Indians forms

1968
AIM is founded

1969
National Indian
Education
Association is
established

1964   1965   1966   1967   1968   1969   1970

N. Scott Momaday

1969   Kiowa/Cherokee author N. Scott Momaday becomes the first American Indian to receive the Pulitzer Prize, for his novel *House Made of Dawn*.

1969   Alcatraz Island takeover occurs in San Francisco to protest injustices and to force issues of Indian rights into the open.

1970   First convocation of American Indian scholars takes place at Princeton University.

1970   Squamish actor "Chief" Dan George is the first Canadian Indian nominated for an Oscar for best supporting actor for an American film—*Little Big Man*.

1971   Alaska Native Claims Settlement Act passes, settling the debate over Alaskan Native land rights.

1971   The Native American Rights Fund, the first legal organization, is established by American Indians for the exclusive purpose of defending and prosecuting Indian rights cases.

1971   The National Tribal Chairmen's Association, the first organization seeking to unite sitting tribal leaders, is formed.

1972   Quawpaw/Cherokee composer Louis W. Ballard is the first musician to receive the Indian Achievement Award of the Indian Council Fire.

1972   Activists protest in Washington, D.C., in the "Trail of Broken Treaties" march.

1973   The Menominee Indian Tribe of Wisconsin is the first terminated tribe to regain its reservation status.

1973   Activists stage an armed takeover of the 1890 Wounded Knee massacre site on the Pine Ridge Reservation.

1975   American Indian Film Festival opens.

1971 Alaska Native Claims Settlement Act passes	1972 First musician to receive Indian Achievement Award	1973 Wounded Knee occupied by activists	1975 American Indian Film Festival Opens	
1971	1972	1973	1974	1975	1976	1977

1975   Creek actor Will Sampson is the first American citizen of
        Native American ancestry to be nominated for an Oscar
        for an American film—*One Flew Over the Cuckoo's Nest*.

1976   Navajo potter Alice Cling Williams begins a renaissance
        in Navajo pottery.

1978   U.S. Supreme Court upholds the right of Santa Clara Pueblo
        to determine who is rightly a member of the tribe.

1978   The Native American Religious Freedom Act is passed.

1979   First Canadian station offers Native language programming.

1979   Mohawk actor Jay Silverheels is the first American Indian
        awarded a star on the Hollywood Walk of Fame.

1980   Superstar Loretta Lynn is named Entertainer of the Decade,
        becoming the most honored woman artist of Native American
        descent in the country/western music business.

1981   Choctaw ballerina Rosella Hightower is the first
        American and the first Native American to direct the
        Paris Opera Ballet.

1982   Hopi educator Frank Dukepoo founds the National Native
        American Honor Society.

1983   *I'd Rather Be Powwowing* is the first television documentary
        produced by an all-Indian crew.

1983   First anthologies of Native American writers and artists are
        published by Beth Brant and Joseph Bruchac.

1983   First person of indigenous ancestrey elected to
        Brazilian Congress.

Loretta Lynn

1978
Pueblo
determination
of tribal
membership
upheld

1979
Native language
programming
begins in Canada

1981
First American
directs Paris Opera

1983
Brazil elects first person of indigenous
ancestrey to Congress

1978   1979   1980   1981   1982   1983   1984

Rigoberta Menchu

1985	Wilma Mankiller becomes first female Cherokee Nation principal chief.
1986	Abenaki priest Donald E. Pelotteis the first Native American to be ordained bishop in the Roman Catholic church.
1986	The first national memorial honoring Native American veterans is dedicated at Arlington National Cemetery in Washington, D.C., by the Vietnam Era Veterans.
1987	The first radio news service covering Native American issues is established.
1988	For the first time in modern history American Indian leaders meet with the president of the United States.
1990	First organization devoted to training Native Americans in the film industry is established.
1991	Navajo Nation initiates Peacemaker Courts.
1992	Northern Cheyenne politician Benjamin Nighthorse Campbell is the first American Indian elected to the U.S. Senate since Charles Curtis.
1992	The first Indian Boys and Girls Club is founded.
1992	Marge Anderson is the first and only woman elected as chief executive of the Mille Lacs Band Ojibwa.
1992	K'iche' Maya activist Rigoberta Menchu is the first Indian and youngest Nobel Peace Prize recipient.
1992	Fort Sill Chiricahua Apache sculptor Allan Houser becomes the first American Indian to receive the National Medal of Arts.

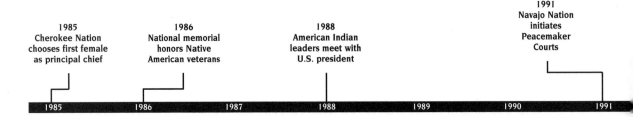

1985
Cherokee Nation
chooses first female
as principal chief

1986
National memorial
honors Native
American veterans

1988
American Indian
leaders meet with
U.S. president

1991
Navajo Nation
initiates
Peacemaker
Courts

1985 1986 1987 1988 1989 1990 1991

1993   Menominee leader Ada Deer is the first American Indian woman to be confirmed as assistant secretary of Indian Affairs.

1993   First film festival to showcase American Indian and Canadian Native work opens.

1993   First national Native newspaper is published in Canada.

1993   First Native vice president of Bolivia is elected.

1994   Oglala Lakota Sioux Robert D. Ecoffey becomes the first Native American to hold the office of U.S. marshall in the Justice Department.

1995   First Native American painting soars into space aboard space shuttle *Endeavor.*

1996   First woman is inducted into American Indian Athletic Hall of Fame.

1997   Prairie Band Potawatomi bishop Charles J. Chaput is the first American Indian named archbishop in the Roman Catholic church.

Charles Chaput

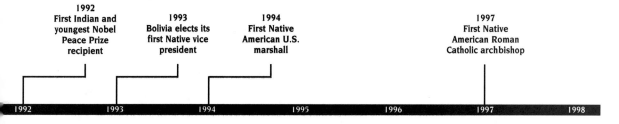

1992
First Indian and youngest Nobel Peace Prize recipient

1993
Bolivia elects its first Native vice president

1994
First Native American U.S. marshall

1997
First Native American Roman Catholic archbishop

1992   1993   1994   1995   1996   1997   1998

ART, CRAFTS, AND DESIGN

1640 The origin of floral designs of the Northeast Indian peoples has been traced to the period when French Ursuline nuns devoted time to teach converts to embroider. Floral designs spread, and each tribe developed their own distinctive style. Floral designs are still unique to Native peoples of the Northeast and the Great Lakes area.

Sources: Champagne, ed., *Chronology of Native North American History,* p. 59.

ca. 1895 Nampeyo (Hopi/Tewa; ca. 1860–1942) led the Sityatki Revival Movement, a renaissance of pottery designs among Hopi potters. In 1895 J. Walter Fewkes arrived in Hopiland to excavate Sityatki, and Nampeyo's husband began working with him. She often accompanied them to the excavation site, where she began studying ancient designs on pottery shards. Nampeyo borrowed pencils and paper and drew the designs she saw. At the same time she began experimenting with different types of clay, which she started using to shape pots like the ancient ones found at Sityatki. Nampeyo became so skilled that Fewkes

Nampeyo popularized Hopi pottery by adding elements of the past to her creations.

became concerned that her pots might be mistaken for the originals. However, her pots and designs did not imitate the old ones, but rather adapted and modernized them. Nampeyo was the first person to include modified ancient designs on her pots. In 1903 and 1907 she worked at Fred Harvey's Hopi House demonstrating her methods. In 1910 she was featured at the U.S. Land and Irrigation Exposition in Chicago. She died July 20, 1942; her granddaughters have continued the pottery making tradition she began.

Sources: Dockstader, *Great North American Indians*, p. 187–89; Malinowski, ed., *Notable Native Americans*, pp. 285–86; Waldman, *Who Was Who in Native American History*, p. 244.

ca. 1895 Datsolalee (Washo; ca. 1835–1925), the most noted Washo basket weaver, revived and innovated Washo basketry to a high art form. In 1851 the Northern Paiute defeated the Washo and imposed two penalties: the Washo could own no horses and they could weave no baskets. It was an economic disaster for the Washo who had little other than their basketry with which to earn income. In 1895 Datsolalee defied the ban and sold glass bottles covered with weaving to The Emporium Company, owned by Abram and Amy Cohn. They asked for more baskets and Datsolalee obliged, beginning a revival of basketry. Her baskets combined creative and unusual designs with technical mastery so fine that there could be thirty-six stitches per inch with geometric designs perfectly spaced apart. Datsolalee experimented with colors, designs, and basket shapes; and she worked with such designs as the incurving spheroid degikup basket form, two-color design, and expanded pattern areas.

Datsolalee was born about 1835 and is believed to have met Captain John C. Fremont on his expedition through the Carson Valley in January 1844. With the help of her husband Charley Kizer, an exceptional craftsman himself, Datsolalee began the Washo basket revival. In time, her baskets received national attention. In 1919 she traveled to the St. Louis Exposition to exhibit her baskets and demonstrate her weaving techniques, breaking tribal custom that forbade instruction to anyone outside one's family. She died December 5, 1925. During her lifetime she received little remuneration, but in 1930 one basket was bought for $10,000. Today her baskets are valued in the hundreds of thousands of dollars. The Washo tribe owns none of her baskets.

Sources: Champagne, ed., *The Native American Almanac*, pp. 1039–40; Johansen and Grinde, *The Encyclopedia of Native American Biography*, p. 99; Malinowski, ed., *Notable Native Americans*, pp. 108–109.

ca. late-1800s Amos Bad Heart Bull (Oglala Sioux; 1869–1913), also known as Eagle Lance, was an artist as well as a tribal historian. Helen Blish, who photographed his pictographs before they were interred, called him "the Herodotus of his people." He was the first Native American to develop ledger drawings. Bad Heart Bull's father was band historian for the Oglala; as keeper of the winter count, he was entrusted to create a hide chronicle on which each year's most significant event would be recorded. When he died at an early age, this honor fell to his son who became keeper of the winter count. With the help of his uncles Bad Heart Bull learned about important tribal events and began drawing them in a ledger book. His art work recorded battles, including the Battle of the Little Bighorn, the Ghost Dance, the massacre at Wounded Knee, as well as daily life among his people. He spent over two decades drawing the detailed pictures that include captions explaining tribal history that spanned more than sixty years.

Devising technical innovations, Bad Heart Bull created unique historical records, which are considered artistic masterpieces. He drew with black pen, indelible pencil, blue, yellow, green, and brown crayons, and red ink; at times, he used brush strokes so fine they can be seen only under magnification. The drawings provide multiple perspectives of the same event using panoramic views, a view from above, topographic views, and close-ups of a participant from a crowd scene near-view insert. He also used foreshortening and stylized profile renditions.

Upon Bad Heart Bull's death the ledger book went to his sister Dolly Pretty Cloud. She kept it until her death in 1947, at which time the family interred the drawings with her. In 1959 the University of Nebraska Press wanted to publish the drawings and unsuccessfully petitioned the family to disinter them. However, the pictures had been photographed in 1927 by Hartley Burr Alexander and his student Helen Blish. The 415 drawings were published in *A Pictographic History of the Oglala Sioux*, and they have appeared in every documentary about the Ghost Dance, Wounded Knee, the Battle of the Little Bighorn, and the deaths of Crazy Horse and Sitting Bull. Today there is a revival of ledger drawings and this type of art has been recognized as the first modern Indian art.

Sources: *Biographical Dictionary of Indians of the Americas*, Vol. 1, p. 34; Dockstader, *Great North American Indians*, p. 25; Johansen and Grinde, *The Encyclopedia of Native American Biography*, p. 20; Malinowski, ed., *Notable Native Americans*, pp. 21–22.

ca. late-1800s Ledger drawings are considered the first modern Indian art form. Done primarily by men, the drawings depict both the commonplace and momentous events in which they participated—usually war, hunting, and ceremonial occurrences. The drawings were done on bound ledger books acquired through trade or war, or supplied by soldiers and traders who commissioned the drawings. Sometimes the drawings were taken from dead warriors. Pencils, crayons, and water colors were the usual media employed in this visual history as seen and remembered by American Indians. Original ledger drawings from the early period are highly prized, and currently there is a revival of this art form among many young Plains Indian artists. Amos Bad Heart Bull was the most prominent of the early ledger artists.

See also: Art, Crafts, and Design, ca. late-1800s (Amos Bad Heart Bull).

Sources: Davis, ed., *Native America in the Twentieth Century*, pp. 417, 419; "Ledger Drawing Tour Begins," *Indian Country Today*, Vol. 16, No. 19 (November 4–11, 1996), p. C-3.

ca. 1900 The first Hopi illustrations of Kachinas was commissioned by J. Walter Fewkes. It was the first non-indigenous media of traditional representations done by Native people. The action was condemned by Hopi traditionalists who disapproved not only of the commercialization of religious topics, but also because thereafter they would become subject to public viewing by strangers.

Sources: Champagne, ed., *Chronology of Native North American History*, p. 250.

1906 Angel DeCora Dietz (Winnebago; ca.1871–1919) was first director of the Leupp Art Department at Carlisle Indian School, where she developed an intensive art program. It was not only the first art program established specifically for Indians, but it also sought to include tribal designs and other art forms. DeCora

Dietz believed firmly that Indian students were gifted for pictorial art and sought to provide training for them, despite opposition from Richard Pratt—founder of Carlisle Indian School. DeCora Dietz encouraged students to use Western art media to promote tribal designs in their artistic expressions. She wanted to encourage students to be the recorders of their tribal cultures. Her views coincided with the development of the San Ildefonso School of Indian artists in the Southwest in 1910. This period, considered a renaissance period in Indian art, resulted in the inclusion of art programs as part of the Indian New Deal when the Indian Arts and Crafts Department was established in 1935. DeCora Dietz was active in other aspects of Indian affairs as well and was an active supporter of the Society of American Indians. In addition she authored many articles and two autobiographical sketches. She was one of the first major figures to encourage the development of Indian artists.

Sources: Bataille, ed., *Native American Women,* pp. 78–82; *Biographical Dictionary of Indians of the Americas,* Vol. 1, p. 189; Malinowski, ed., *Notable Native Americans,* pp. 125–26.

1919 Maria Montoya Martinez (San Ildefonso Pueblo; ca. 1887–1980) and her husband Julian (d. 1943) were the first Indian potters to revive a unique technique in which designs were etched onto the glossy black background of pots. It became the Martinez trademark and the innovations led to a revival in indigenous pottery making, which transformed it into an art form. In 1907 Julian began working at the Pajarito Plateau excavation sites. Edgar Hewett, the project director, asked him to copy pottery and wall designs and to recreate pots from the pottery shards that were found. After experimenting with different clays, firing, and polishing techniques, Maria and Julian developed thinner, harder, and more highly polished pots like those made by the ancients. Together they continued to innovate designs and pottery styles with Maria making the pots and Julian painting and etching the designs. No design was duplicated with the exception of the Avanyu, a mythical water serpent. By 1919 they had developed their famous black on black pots. In 1923 Maria began signing her pots and then began to offer classes to teach others from their village to create similar pots.

In 1934 Maria became the second individual and the first Indian woman to win the Indian Achievement Award from the Indian Council Fire. In 1954 she received the Craftsmanship Medal, the nation's highest honor for craftsmanship. Julian died in 1943, and in 1956 Maria formed a partnership with her son Popovi Da, and with him, made several additional discoveries and innovations. In 1957 they revived polychrome, and then discovered gunmetal firing, both of which had a lasting impact. They also discovered firing sienna and the two-firing process of black and sienna. In 1954, they, along with Santa Clara Pueblo muralist Pablita Velarde and Apache sculptor Allan Houser, received the French government's Palmes d'Academiques for outstanding contributions to art. It was the first time a foreign government had recognized Indian art. In 1959 Maria Martinez received the Jane Addani Award, one of the highest honors ever granted to an American woman. Maria and Julian's impact on Pueblo pottery was the most far-reaching and influential of any other potter, transforming it from a craft to an art.

Sources: Dockstader, *Great North American Indians,* pp. 169–71; Malinowski, ed., *Notable Native Americans,* pp. 263–64; Spivey, Richard L., "Maria Martinez," *american indian art,* Vol. 21, No. 1 (Winter 1995), p. 80.

Opposite page:
Pueblo artists Julian and Maria Montoya Martinez revitalized indigenous pottery-making techniques.

1920s Lucy Parker Telles (Miwok/Paiute), an innovative basket weaver, was the first Miwok to use new and different weaving techniques. In using red and black colors together, she created designs never before done by Miwok, such as realistic floral, butterfly, and hummingbird motifs, lids for baskets, and flat-topped high-shouldered baskets. Other weavers had begun weaving baskets as decorative art pieces, but Telles was the first to begin using other than traditional techniques and designs. In 1929 she began a basket that, at thirty-six inches in diameter and twenty inches high, would take her four years to complete and would earn her first prize at the Panama Pacific Exposition in San Francisco in 1939.

Sources: Bataille, ed., *Native American Women,* pp. 257–58.

1931 Artist Awa Tsireh (San Ildefonso Tewa; ca. 1895–1955), also known as Alfonso Roybal and Cattail Bird, won the first award at the "Exposition of Indian Tribal Arts." This major exhibit was first shown in New York City in 1931.

Sources: *Biographical Dictionary of Indians of the Americas,* Vol. 1, p. 33; Dockstader, *Great North American Indians,* pp. 23–24.

1934 Maria Montoya Martinez (San Ildefonso Pueblo; ca. 1887–1980), wife of Julian Martinez, became the first woman, and only the second individual, to win the American Indian Achievement Award. Martinez went on the develop a silver overcast finish to the Martinez's trademark black finish pottery.

> *See also: Art, Crafts, and Design, 1919.*

Sources: *Biographical Dictionary of Indians of the Americas,* Vol. 1, p. 397.

1936 The Indian Arts and Crafts Board legislation was enacted by the U.S. Congress in an attempt to protect spurious imitations of Indian art and to control exploitation. The legislation specifically encourages Indian peoples to commercialize certain aspects of their cultural traditions.

Sources: Dennis, *The American Indian, 1492–1976,* p. 54.

1939 The Sioux Museum and Crafts Center was created through joint sponsorship by the federal government and the town of Rapid City, South Dakota. The museum is administered by the Indian Arts and Crafts Board.

Sources: Dennis, *The American Indian, 1492–1976,* p. 55.

ca. 1940s Lorencita Bird (San Juan Pueblo; d. 1995), a renowned textile designer, studied with Dorothy Dunn, who encouraged her to develop her artistic abilities. She began by painting the daily events of her pueblo as well as ceremonial gatherings. Under the tutelage of Mabel Morrow, she developed the Pueblo-style embroidery and weaving for which she became known. Professionally, she taught at Sherman Institute in California and the Santa Fe and Albuquerque Indian Schools. A major portion of her work was done after her retirement from teaching in the early 1970s. She taught many students the art of weaving and embroidery creating mantas, kilts, sashes and other clothing articles. Throughout her artistic career she won many awards beginning in the 1940s. She died in May of 1995.

Sources: Romero, Allison Bird. "Lorencita Bird," *american indian art,* Vol. 21, No. 1 (Winter 1995), p. 48.

1948 Soapstone carving, introduced to the Inuit of Hudson Bay by non-Native James Houston, became one of the most important art media for Canadian and Alaska Natives, particularly the Inuit. Regional styles developed and Native artists became highly creative and adept at working with soapstone. Today, soapstone carving is associated with Native art.

Sources: Champagne, ed., *Chronology of Native North American History,* p. 316.

1948 Allan Houser (Fort Sill Chiricahua Apache; 1914–1994) designed and sculpted the nation's first Native American public monument, *Comrade in Mourning,* which was dedicated in 1949. The monument, a memorial to Indian servicemen who died during World War II, was Houser's first monument. In 1992, Houser became the first American Indian to receive the National Medal of Arts, the nation's highest art achievement award, from President George Bush. Although known as a great artist, Houser was also a dedicated teacher. A former student of Dorothy Dutton at the Santa Fe Indian School, he taught and trained many contemporary Indian artists of the latter half of the twentieth century. He was also known as a designer and sculptor of monuments, including: *Coming of Age,* commissioned by the Denver Art Museum, 1977; *Chiricahua Apache Family,* for the Fort Sill Apache Tribal Center; and the 1985 *Offering of the Pipe,* for the U.S. Mission to the United Nations in New York City. Shortly before his death in 1994, he dedicated his final monument to the people of the United States, *May We Have Peace.* In 1954, along with Santa Clara Pueblo muralist Pablita Velarde and Pueblo potter Maria Martinez, he received the French government's Palmes d'Academiques for outstanding contributions to art. It was the first time a foreign government had recognized Indian art. Included among his many other honors are the Honored One recognition as the finest Native American artist at the Red Earth Festival in Oklahoma City, and the Ellis Island National Medal of Freedom.

Sources: Hirschfelder, *Artists and Craftspeople,* p. 33; King, Jeanne Snodgrass. "Allan Houser," *american indian art,* Vol. 21, No. 1 (Winter 1995) p. 68; Malinowski, ed., *Notable Native Americans,* pp. 202–203.

1948 Crazy Horse Memorial, the world's largest sculpture in stone, was suggested by Sioux leaders; and sculptor Korczak Ziolkowski was chosen to create the sculpture. After the completion of Mount Rushmore (on which Ziolkowski worked), Sioux leaders declared that Indians had great leaders too and that they should be remembered as well. The monument is located on top of Thunderhead Mountain in the Black Hills National Forest. When it was dedicated five survivors of the Battle of the Little Bighorn were in attendance. The monument includes plans for a university and a medical school. Ziolkowski died in 1982, but his wife and children continue the project. The face of Crazy Horse is expected to be completed by 1998. Offers from government agencies to fund the project have consistently been refused. All costs are paid through private donations.

Sources: Champagne, ed., *Chronology of Native North American History,* p. 317; Leitch, *Chronology of the American Indian,* p. 222.

1949 An artist devoted to the preservation of his culture, Fred Kabotie (Hopi; 1900–?) was the first Hopi to receive the Indian Achievement Award. The award is given by the Indian Council Fire of Chicago. In addition to being the first Hopi to receive the honor, Kabotie was also the first Southwest Indian to receive the award. He is considered to be the first professional Hopi artist. Kabotie preserved many traditional Hopi designs by reproducing them in his paintings. Kabotie combined his desire to record his culture with his goal to preserve genuine Hopi designs and established the Hopi Silvercraft Cooperative Guild.

Sources: *Biographical Dictionary of Indians of the Americas,* Vol. 1, p. 327; Champagne, ed., *Chronology of Native North American History,* p. 250; King, Jeanne Snodgrass, "Fred Kabotie," *american indian art,* Vol. 21, No. 1 (Winter 1995) p. 74; Malinowski, ed., *Notable Native Americans,* pp. 222–23; "Mr. & Mrs. Charles Sheaffer Scrapbook," LAB MSS-2, Labriola National American Indian Data Center, University Libraries, Arizona State University.

ca. mid-1900s Elsie Allen (Ukiah Pomo; 1899–1990) was the first Pomo basket weaver to teach Pomo basketry to individuals outside her family, including non-Indians. Pomo tradition forbade family members from teaching those outside the family. To break that tradition was highly unusual and teaching non-Pomos was even more unusual. Allen, however broke with tradition because she wanted to help preserve not only the basket making tradition but also her family's unique designs and style.

Sources: Bataille, ed., *Native American Women,* p. 5; Malinowski, ed., *Notable Native Americans,* pp. 5–6; McGill, Marsha Ann. "California Indian Women's Clubs: Past and Present," *News from Native California,* 4 (Spring 1990), pp. 22–23.

1950s Charles Loloma (Hopi; 1921–1991) dismantled barriers that restricted Indian jewelers to creating what the non-Indian public thought was Indian art. He developed the use of gold and stones other than turquoise to create a new kind of "Indian" jewelry. He combined contrasting colors of stones, of varying textures, heights, and sizes, and set them in gold and silver—a practice rarely done. His innovations enabled other Indian metal craftsman to experiment and create new styles of jewelry. He was also the first jewelry designer to add designs and stones to the inside of jewelry, where no one but the artist and the wearer would know about them; Loloma said that they were symbols of inner strength and beauty possessed by each person. He received many awards, including first prize seven years in a row at the Scottsdale National Indian Arts Exhibition. He has been featured in two films, the 1972 NET film, *Three Indians,* and the 1974 PBS film *Loloma.*

Sources: Hirschfelder, *Artists and Craftspeople,* pp. 69-74; Jacka, Lois Essary, "Charles Loloma," *american indian art,* Vol. 21, No. 1 (Winter 1995), p. 79; Malinowski, ed., *Notable Native Americans,* pp. 244–45.

ca. 1950s Artist, cartoonist, and illustrator Brummett Echohawk (Pawnee; 1922–) was perhaps the first American Indian to have his own comic strip. Echohawk's comic strip, *Little Chief,* appeared in the *Tulsa World* newspaper. Echohawk served in the U.S. Army from 1940 to 1945 and witnessed heavy combat in World War II. From 1945 to 1948 he attended the Chicago Art Institute.

Sources: *Biographical Dictionary of Indians of the Americas,* Vol. 1, p. 208; Gridley, ed., *Indians of Today,* p. 370.

ca. 1950s Alice New Holy Blue Legs (Oglala Lakota Sioux; 1925–) revived the art of designing with porcupine quills, called quilling, among the Sioux. She was raised by her grandmother after her mother died, and she grew up watching her grandmother quill. After the older woman's death, Blue Legs received instruction from her father, but she had to relearn the art through trial and error, trying to remember how her mother and grandmother designed with quills. She has since become an expert and now travels to teach youth the art of quilling. In 1985, she was the only Indian artist from South Dakota to win a cash award from the National Endowment for the Arts. That same year, she and her husband and daughters were the subject of a documentary film, *Lakota Quill Work*.

Sources: Bataille, ed., *Native American Women*, p. 30–31.

ca. 1950s Eunice Ben Kassi Carney (Gwich'in; 1909–?) was the last beadworker working in the old Gwich'in style. Born in 1909 in the Yukon Territory, she was sent to the Chouttle boarding school in southern Yukon after her father's death. When she returned to her mother, she could barely speak Gwich'in. Unable to communicate, they began beading together in the old Gwich'in style of skin sewing and beading. The unique style entails a delicate floral pattern with tracery tendrils, delicate motifs and alternate colors at the points of leaves and centers of outer edges of petals. Although she taught others this style of beading, Eunice Carney was the last beader who worked consistently with the old Gwich'in style.

Sources: Duncan, Kate C. (associate professor, School of Art, Arizona State University), Personal communication to AnCita Benally, May 27, 1997; Duncan, Kate C., "Eunice Carney," *american indian art*, Vol. 21, No. 1 (Winter 1995), p. 59.

1954 Pablita Velarde (Santa Clara Pueblo; 1918–) received, along with San Ildefonso potter Maria Montoya Martinez and Apache sculptor Allan Houser, the French government's Palmes d'Academiques for outstanding contributions to art. It was the first time a foreign government had recognized Indian art. Velarde is especially known for the murals she has created. She combines her personal knowledge and experience of Santa Clara Pueblo culture with meticulous research and study of petroglyphs and ancient ruins, careful historical scholarship, and ethnographic research. In 1939 she was commissioned by the U.S. Park Service to paint archaeological and ethnological murals that would reconstruct the life of ancient peoples, resulting in realistic murals that have had a powerful impact on visitors at Bandelier National Monument Visitor's Center. In addition to her art Velarde collaborated with her father to publish *Old Father, the Storyteller*, an illustrated book of Tewa tales, which was selected as one of the best Western books of 1960. In 1990 Velarde became the first Native American artist to receive the annual award of the Philadelphia Women's Caucus for Art.

Sources: Bataille, ed., *Native American Women*, p. 267; Hirschfelder, *Artists and Craftspeople*, pp. 53–60; Malinowski, ed., *Notable Native Americans*, pp. 441–42.

ca. 1954 Polingaysi Qoyawayma (Hopi), also known as Elizabeth White, was the first Hopi potter to create new forms using native materials. She used native clays that ranged from creamy white to buff pink to red in color. The designs she placed on her pots were in raised relief, most often an ear of corn or Kokopelli (the Humpback Flute Player). Other Hopi potters used non-native clays and paints to create new designs and techniques, but Polingaysi was the first to use solely native materials to create new designs.

Sources: Spivey, Richard L. "Polingaysi Qoyawayma," *american indian art*, Vol. 21, No. 1 (Winter 1995), p. 91.

1957 Oscar Howe (Yanktonai Dakota Sioux; 1915–1983) became the first recipient of the South Dakota Governor's Award for Creative Achievement. The award came after a long life of artistic achievements. Howe was instrumental in convincing major art galleries and patrons to accept art other than what they perceived as "Indian" art. His expressed opinion that Indian artists could and should be able to express themselves through other than traditionally perceived art forms and media allowed other artists to explore and innovate techniques and styles. Among his other numerous awards are: Artist Laureate of the Middle Border, 1954; Artist Laureate of South Dakota, 1960; and the Waite Phillips Trophy for outstanding contributions to American Indian Art from the Philbrook Art Center in Tulsa Oklahoma.

Sources: Day, John A., "Oscar Howe," *american indian art,* Vol. 21, No. 1 (Winter 1995), p. 71; Hirschfelder, *Artists and Craftspeople,* p. 44; Malinowski, ed., *Notable Native Americans,* pp. 203–204.

1958 Permanent versions of Navajo sandpaintings were produced for sale. Traditionalists vigorously opposed the reproductions of sacred subject matter, and they strongly disapproved of their commercialization.

Sources: Champagne, ed., *Chronology of Native North American History,* p. 332.

1962 Artist Mungo Martin (Kwakiutl; ca. 1879–1962) was the first Native American to be awarded the Canada Council medal for his many contributions to Canada's artistic, cultural, and intellectual life. He was the third highest ranking chief of the Kwakiutl in addition to being an artist. At a time when the Canadian government was legislating the extinction of Native religions and cultures, art, and languages, Martin was working to revive and maintain tribal traditions. He defied the prohibitions and continued to carve totems; and he taught and recorded the songs and stories of Kwakiutl traditions.

Gradually the political climate changed and in 1947 he was invited by the University of British Columbia to carve totems, beginning a revival of Northwest Coast Indian woodcarving. The revival included ceremonialism such as the potlatch. The first public potlatch held since its prohibition was done in 1953. It was a major event. In 1956 Martin raised the tallest totem pole in Victoria's Beacon Hill Park, a one-hundred-foot totem commissioned by Queen Elizabeth II, to stand in Windsor Great Park to mark the provincial centennial of British Columbia.

During the last ten years of his life, Martin sought to restore old poles and instructed young novices to learn the art of woodcarving. His most notable students were his son-in-law and his grandsons, Henry Hunt, Tony Hunt, and Richard Hunt, and their cousin Calvin Hunt. Upon his death in 1962, Martin was buried at sea by the Canadian navy and every flag in port was dropped to half-mast, an honor unprecedented for a Native American. Between 1970 and 1971 Martin's son-in-law and grandson raised a pole in his honor at Alert Bay, the first pole raising in that village in forty years. In 1991 the U'mista Cultural Center displayed the first international traveling exhibit, an exhibit of the greatest breadth ever arranged by a Canadian native cultural museum. The exhibit was entitled "Mungo Martin: A Slender Thread" in honor of his efforts and great accomplishments in being the slender thread that preserved Kwakiutl art and culture.

Sources: Champagne, ed., *Chronology of Native North American History,* p. 226; Dockstader, *Great North American Indians,* pp. 167–68; Malinowski, ed., *Notable Native Americans,* pp. 262–63.

1962 The Institute of American Indian Arts (IAIA) was established in Santa Fe, New Mexico. Playing a key role in training contemporary Native American artists, the institute was designed to provide training in traditional and contemporary art techniques. Some of the most prominent Indian artists assisted in establishing the art school and taught there as well, including such notable artists as Allan Houser and Charles Loloma.

Sources: Bodenstein, Susan, "The Institute of American Indian Arts," *Winds of Change*, Vol. 6, No. 1 (Winter 1991), pp. 10–13; Champagne, ed., *Chronology of Native North American History*, p.333.

Navajo sandpainting rug woven by Altnabah.

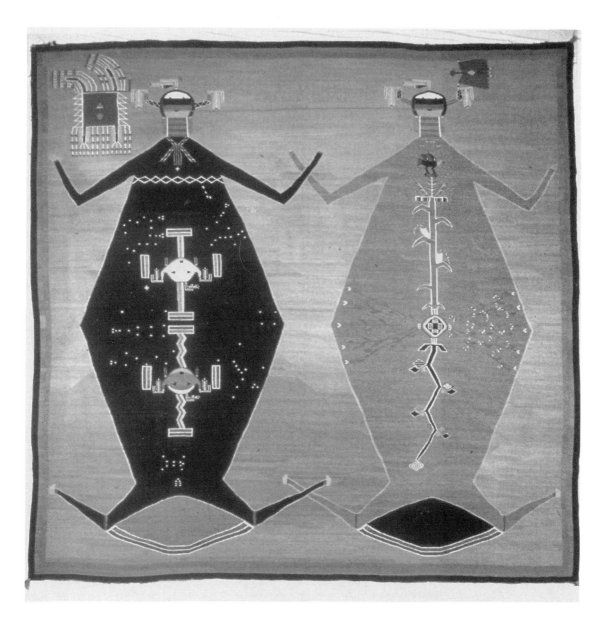

1963 The American Indian Arts Center opened in New York City to promote Indian art and to increase awareness of its availability and improve its commercial aspects.

Sources: Dennis, *The American Indian, 1492–1976*, p. 63.

1964 Helen Cordero (Cochiti Pueblo; 1915–) made the first storyteller doll. She was instrumental in developing the storyteller doll and turning it into a major art genre. The figurine is based on the memory of her grandfather's storytelling and on the tradition of small clay figures that women made as toys for their children. "The Singing Mothers," as they are called, was greatly discouraged by Spanish Catholic missionaries, and in time, the tradition almost died out. Cordero's innovation revived the art and created a new art form. She won first, second, and third prizes at the New Mexico State Fair in 1964 for her first storyteller dolls. Cordero's dolls have the trademarked closed eyes, open mouth, and tilted head, which she has said signifies the storyteller deep in thought as he/she tells his/her story. No two dolls are alike. In addition to the Storyteller, Cordero has also created "The Drummer," "The Singing Mother," nativity scenes, "The Night Crier," "The Children's Hour," and animal figures. From the memory of her grandfather as a storyteller, Cordero has created a flourishing art form among many artists within and outside the Cochiti tribe.

Sources: "Helen Cordero," *american indian art*, Vol. 21, No. 1 (Winter 1995), p. 63; Hirschfelder, *Artists and Craftspeople*, pp. 44-52; Malinowski, ed., *Notable Native Americans*, pp. 91-92.

1973 R. C. Gorman (Navajo; 1931–) became the only living artist to be honored in the "Masterworks of the American Indian" exhibit at the Metropolitan Museum in New York. In 1975 he became the first artist to be selected for a series on contemporary American Indian artists at the Museum of the American Indian.

Moonrise, by R. C. Gorman.

Gorman's works are easily recognized; he is the best-known American Indian contemporary artist. Son of Carl Nelson Gorman, an artist and former Navajo Code Talker, Gorman was born on the Navajo Reservation and was raised primarily by his grandmother. He studied art at Northern Arizona University, San Francisco State University, and Mexico City College. It was at the latter school that he received his greatest influence—the art work of Diego Rivera. Throughout his career, R. C. Gorman has won numerous awards and his work has been collected by museums all over the world.

Sources: Johansen and Grinde, *The Encyclopedia of Native American Biography,* pp. 151–52; Malinowski, ed., *Notable Native Americans,* p. 169–170.

1975 R. C. Gorman (Navajo; 1931–) became the first artist to be selected for a series on contemporary American Indian artists at the Museum of the American Indian.

R. C. Gorman.

See also: Art, Crafts, and Design, 1973.

Sources: Johansen and Grinde, *The Encyclopedia of Native American Biography,* pp. 151–52; Malinowski, ed., *Notable Native Americans,* pp. 169–70.

1976 Alice Cling Williams (Navajo; 1953–) began a renaissance in Navajo pottery. Traditionally Navajo pots were only utilitarian, but Williams experimented with pottery shape, design, and finish to develop a ceramic style that was attractive and marketable. She developed a smooth and polished pot that resembles the look of wood. Williams refined the method of applying pinon pitch, and of smoothing her finished pots with stone rather than a corn cob—the traditional method. Today she is perhaps the best-known Navajo potter, and she has won numerous awards for her designs.

Sources: Bataille, ed., *Native American Women,* p. 280.

1978 Joan Hill (Cherokee/Creek) participated in the first Painters Cultural Interchange with the People's Republic of China. Professors of the Central Art Academy in Beijing asked that color plates of her work be left in China as a traveling exhibition. She is the only known Native American artist to have her work exhibited in that country. She has received numerous honors and awards; her 355 awards include the Waite Phillips Special Artists Trophy from the Philbrook Museum, a commemorative medal from Great Britain, and the Grand Master Award from the Five Civilized Tribes. She does extensive historical research in order to assure authenticity and accuracy in the details of her acrylic paintings. Her work is based on her cultural heritage, particularly the stories she heard from her parents.

Sources: Bataille, ed., *Native American Women,* pp. 112–13; *Biographical Dictionary of Indians of the Americas,* Vol. 1, pp. 279–89; Gridley, *Indians of Today,* pp. 338–39.

1978 In June of 1978, Bill Reid (Haida; 1920–) carved a totem for his mother's village at Skidegate, which became the first pole raised in more than one hundred years.

Sources: Champagne, *The Native North American Almanac,* p. 1142.

1980 Kenojuak Ashevak (Inuit; 1927–), the best-known Inuit woman printmaker was the first Inuit woman artist to have her work commemorated on a stamp. Two of her prints have been used to design Canadian postage stamps. In 1970, a sixteen-cent stamp commemorating the centennial of the Northwest Territories used her most renowned work *The Enchanted Owl;* and in 1980, a seventeen-cent stamp used her 1961 print, *Return of the Sun.* She has won numerous awards for her artwork, which has been displayed prominently. Kenojuak has often collaborated with her husband Johnniebo, a hunter and artist himself. One work, a ninety-six-square-foot plaster was displayed at the Canadian Pavilion at Expo '70 in Osaka, Japan. In 1974 she became a member of the Royal Canadian Academy; and in 1982 she was appointed a Companion to the Order of Canada.

Sources: Bataille, ed., *Native American Women,* p. 15; Duncan, Kate C. (associate professor, School of Art, Arizona State University), Personal communication to AnCita Benally, May 22, 1997.

1980s Marie Lehi (San Juan Paiute) was a key figure in the revival of Paiute basketry. She was instrumental in reviving interest among the Paiute and in efforts to maintain the old styles and designs while initiating new designs. In 1992, she was one of only four artists throughout Arizona to receive the Arizona Indian Living Treasures Award.

Sources: McGreevy, Susan Brown, "Marie Lehi," *american indian art,* Vol. 21, No. 1 (Winter 1995), p. 76.

1985 Rhonda Holy Bear (Lakota Sioux/Cheyenne) received the Southwestern Indian Association on Indian Affair's fellowship for the Sioux dolls she creates. It was the first time an artist working with dolls was ever given the award. Holy Bear has spent much time in meticulous study and research in museums, private collections, and in storytelling to create her dolls. Her dolls are known for the intricate beading and stitching work, and the hidden additions included, such as tattoos and underclothing. She is well known for re-creating in miniature, war honor-dresses—dresses worn by women to honor their husbands and sons.

Sources: Hirschfelder, *Artists and Craftspeople,* pp. 124–39.

1985 Clifford Bahniptewa (Hopi) received the Anisfield-Wolf Book Award for race relations, becoming the only Hopi Indian to receive that award. He joined other distinguished recipients, including Martin Luther King Jr., Malcolm X, Julian Huxley, and Vine Deloria Jr. Bahnimptewa was a famed artist who specialized in painting Kachina dolls. At the persuasion of Don Hoel, he painted individual fifteen-by-twenty inch paintings of 286 Kachinas listed in Harold S. Colton's book, *Hopi Kachina Dolls.* The paintings were later sold to Dean Nichols and were published in book form. It was advertised as a single Hopi's interpretation of Kachinas; Bahniptewa did not receive the royalties promised him.

Sources: "Clifford Bahniptewa," *american indian art,* Vol. 21, No. 1 (Winter 1995), p. 40.

ca. late-1980s Melvin Olanna (Yupik/Inuit) established the Rural Alaska Native Arts Workshop in Shishmaref, a little village near Nome. Renamed the Melvin Olanna Carving Center, it is responsible for the great interest in whalebone sculpture in Shishmaref. Olanna, a renowned sculptor who has worked with alabaster and marble, bronze, whalebone, ivory, and wood, has carved walrus, seal, bears, and owls in addition to sculptures of people. Olanna learned to carve from Ronald Senungetuk and his style was influenced by teachers Allan Houser and Henry Moore. His great interest in encouraging young artists motivated him to establish an art workshop.

Sources: Duncan, Kate C. (associate professor, School of Art, Arizona State University), Personal communication to AnCita Benally, May 27, 1997; Duncan, Kate C., "Melvin Olanna," *american indian art*, Vol. 21, No. 1 (Winter 1995), p. 87.

1991 Rolland D. Lee (Navajo) was the youngest artist (at age fourteen) to ever exhibit his paintings in the Skylight Gallery of the Wheelwright Museum in Santa Fe, New Mexico. He is from Montezuma Creek, Utah. In addition to his artistic talents he was regional spelling bee champion for several years.

Sources: "Navajo Student Is Gallery's Youngest Artist," *Navajo Times*, March 21, 1991, p. 12.

1993 Sculptor Oreland C. Joe (Navajo/Ute) was the first "full-blooded" Native American member of the Cowboy Artists of America. He has received many awards for his unique style.

Sources: "The Navajos and Their Art," *Arizona Highways*, Vol. 70, No. 11 (November 1994), p. 30.

1995 A painting created by Don Montileaux (Lakota Sioux) flew aboard the March 1995 mission of the space shuttle *Endeavor*, becoming the first Native American artwork to travel in space.

Sources: *Airogram, American Indian Research Opportunities*, Vol. 2, No. 9 (December 1995), p. 1.

1996 Virgil "Smoker" Marchand (Colville Arrow Lakes Band Salish) was the first American Indian artist to have his work featured on the Hamilton Collection plates. His painting entitled *Trail Talk* was the first of the "Vision in the Mist" series. Marchand has designed logos for Indian organizations and governmental agencies, including the Colville Tribal Enterprises Corporation, the National Park Service in West Virginia, and the U.S. Bureau of the Census. He also designed the Colville Indian Agency Veterans Memorial in Nespelem.

Sources: "Hamilton Collection Ltd., Features Marchand, First Indian Artist for Goldplate," *Indian Country Today*, Vol. 16, No. 20 (November 11–18, 1996), p. B-5.

1996 An art exhibit entitled "Plains Indian Drawings 1865–1935: Pages from a Visual History," presented for the first time the most extensive study of ledger drawings as a separate and unique art genre. The exhibit was sponsored by the Drawing Center of New York and the American Federation of Arts. Ledger draw-ings were developed by the Lakota, Cheyenne, Kiowa, and Arapaho warriors in the late-nineteenth and early-twentieth centuries. They were drawings done on lined paper, depicting battle scenes, hunting scenes, and everyday tribal events, drawn by men who were asked to record their memories of events in which they participated. Today these ledger drawings represent important records of the social and political history of the Plains people.

See also: Art, Crafts, and Design, ca. late-1800s (Amos Bad Heart Bull).

Sources: "Ledger Drawing Tour Begins," *Indian Country Today*, Vol. 16, No. 19 (November 4–11, 1996), p. C-3.

BUSINESS AND ECONOMICS

1670 Cree and Ojibwa traders began their role as middlemen between European traders and Indian consumers, who lived farther from white trading centers. They travelled to Hudson's Bay Company (HBC) posts to trade rather than wait for the traders to come to them. This created a business rivalry between HBC and the French traders, which improved the quality and variety of goods at reasonable prices. Some Indian groups were induced to remain near the posts to provide services year-round, which created opportunities for intermarriage between indigenous women and white traders.

Sources: Champagne, ed., *Chronology of Native North American History,* p. 68.

ca. 1775 Sally Anise (Oneida) was the earliest known Indian woman to become successful in business. She acquired a land deed from the Oneida near Fort Stanwix, where she began a fur trading business in 1775. By 1778 she had bought a house and a lot in Detroit with her profits. The census of 1779 indicates that she also had acquired livestock and household luxuries. In time her business success allowed her to expand into the political sphere and she became a diplomat and an intermediary, participating in peace negotiations after the Battle of the Fallen Timbers. A number of times she acted on behalf of Mohawk leader and British army officer Joseph Brant as an intermediary between Indian tribes and the British government. The changing political circumstances caused her to lose her fortune; it took twenty years and many legal maneuverings to regain the Oneida land deed, but she prevailed and spent the last years of her life there.

Sources: Bataille, ed., *Native American Women,* pp. 2–3; Hamil, F. C., *Sally Anise, Fur Trader,* Detroit, Michigan: Algonquin Society, 1939; Tanner, Helen Hornbeck, *Atlas of Great Lakes Indian History,* Norman: University of Oklahoma Press, 1986.

1796 The United States formulated a policy that allowed Indian Trading Houses to be operated by the government in an attempt to curb French and Spanish influence on the Indian tribes. The policy was abolished in 1822.

Sources: Dennis, *The American Indian, 1492–1976,* p. 21.

1802 The United States formally passed a law forbidding the sale of liquor to Indians. Formerly, liquor sales had been strongly discouraged, but it had not been legislated. Today some Indian tribal governments maintain a form of this policy. It was not until 1953 that a congressional act removed the prohibition.

Sources: Dennis, *The American Indian, 1492–1976,* p. 22.

1806 The Office of Superintendent of Indian Trade was established. Responsibilities included the purchase of goods to be traded with the various Indian nations.

Sources: Dennis, *The American Indian, 1492–1976*, p. 22.

ca. late-1800s Wallace Altaha (White Mountain Apache) was described as the most successful Apache cattle rancher. With an acumen for business, he used what he had learned from his father about establishing, increasing, and improving the herd. While still a young man, he obtained a beef contract from the military at

Oil painting of Joseph Brant, a Mohawk leader and British army officer during the Revolutionary War.

Fort Apache. He acquired land close to the fort so that the cattle did not have to be driven far. By 1901, his brand R-14 was well recognized by the non-Indian ranching community. He supplied butchers from nearby towns like Globe, Winslow, Taylor, and Springerville, with R-14 cattle. Another herd he owned, the Spear R, grew to ten thousand head and he became more prosperous. In 1918 he sold $45,000 worth of beef, bought $25,000 worth of liberty bonds, and $5,000 worth of victory bonds. Such investments and profits made him the richest Indian cattleman in the country. He was especially well known in the Southwest. Personally, Altaha was generous with his success as well as with his skills and knowledge of cattle ranching. He helped several of his siblings start their own herds and make sizeable profits. Altaha died in 1936 having proved that full-blood Indians could succeed on their own terms, and could adapt without extended schooling or coddling by parents.

Sources: Iverson, Peter, "The Road to Reappearance: Indians and Cattle Ranching in the American West," *Tribal College,* Vol. 7, No. 2 (Fall 1995), pp. 23–26; Iverson, *When Indians Became Cowboys,* p. 102.

1912 The first public auction sale for oil leases on the Osage Reservation was held by the Osage Indians of Oklahoma. The first sale brought a bonus of $1 million or more on March 2, 1922. The largest bid on a tract was nearly $2 million. A total of 18,160 acre tracts were leased. A plaque under an elm tree called the "Million Dollar Elm" commemorates the auction at the Osage Agency, Pawhuska, Oklahoma.

Sources: Dennis, *The American Indian, 1492–1976,* p. 49.

1938 On December 6, 1938, the San Carlos Apache tribe voted to create a second herd known as IDT, or the "Social Security herd." The tribe had already successfully created one herd from which they were profiting and established this new herd to help those unable to obtain surplus heifers. The profits from these sales went toward helping elders, widows, and orphans.

Sources: Iverson, Peter, "The Road to Reappearance: Indians and Cattle Ranching in the American West," *Tribal College,* Vol. 7, No. 2 (Fall 1995), p. 23–26.

ca. 1960s Nunny Waano-Gano (Karok), a floral artist, was the first Native American to own her own FTD florist shop. Waano-Gano has won national and international awards for her floral arrangements. In addition she has appeared in a number of motion pictures with such notable actors as Shirley Temple, Gary Cooper, and Tyrone Power. A musician as well, playing the violin and piano, she joined her husband, artist Joe Waano-Gano (Cherokee), as members of an all-Indian cast that presented dramatic adaptations of Indian stories.

Sources: *Biographical Dictionary of Indians of the Americas,* p. 785; Gridley, ed., *Indians of Today,* p. 479.

1966 The Bureau of Indian Affairs (BIA) initiated the first "family-centered" residential training opportunity center when it signed a contract with Radio Corporation of America (RCA). The center is located in Philadelphia, Mississippi, next to the Choctaw Reservation. Many families completed the program and found employment because of this experiment.

Sources: Dennis, *The American Indian, 1492–1976,* p. 65.

1971 The Kicking Horse Regional Manpower Center, the first all-Indian job corps center was dedicated. It is sponsored by the Confederated Salish Kootenai Tribal Council of the Flathead Reservation. It includes all the usual job corps benefits as well as an Indian cultural enrichment program. In the first year it served students representing thirty-four Indian tribes and Alaska Native groups west of the Mississippi.

Sources: Dennis, *The American Indian, 1492–1976*, p. 87.

1973 Barney Old Coyote (Crow; 1923–) became the first American Indian to become president of the first national Indian bank. He founded the American Indian National Bank and received a charter for it, including Federal Deposit Insurance Corporation support. Old Coyote enlisted in the military at the age of seventeen and served for five years. He received several decorations, including the Air Medal and the Fourteen Oak Clusters award. Following an honorable discharge, he attended college and earned a B.A. degree. He served with the Bureau of Indian Affairs (BIA) for twenty-one years. In 1968 he received a Distinguished Service Award from the Department of the Interior. He has also worked in the field of education.

Sources: *Biographical Dictionary of Indians of the Americas*, Vol. 2, p. 785; Gridley, ed., *Indians of Today*, pp. 227–29; Malinowski, ed., *Notable Native Americans*, pp. 296–97.

1975 Council of Energy Resources Tribes (CERT) was established, composed of tribal leaders from twenty-five reservations with major deposits of natural energy resources. The group assists tribes in developing their land's energy and mineral resources, and promotes the welfare of tribal members through protection, control, and careful management of their oil, gas, shale, uranium, geothermal energy, and other resources.

Sources: Champagne, ed., *Chronology of Native North American History*, p. 402.

1985 The Jicarilla Apache Tribe became the first Indian tribe to offer tax-exempt municipal bonds to institutional investors. Revenue bonds worth $30.2 million were issued.

Sources: Champagne, ed., *Chronology of Native North American History*, p. 449.

CIVIC LEADERSHIP

1889 Joseph Juneau (Menominee) co-founded Juneau, Alaska, which was named after him. He was the son of Josette (Menominee/French) and Solomon Juneau, founder and first mayor of Milwaukee, Wisconsin. In 1880, Joseph Juneau, Richard Harris, and three Tlingit Indians discovered gold in what is Juneau, Alaska, today. A gold rush immediately began and within a year more than one hundred miners had arrived. In 1900 the site was incorporated.

Sources: Bataille, ed., *Native American Women,* p. 133; "Joseph Juneau," in *The American Indian;* Waldman, *Who Was Who in Native American History,* p. 177.

1903 Roberta Campbell Lawson (Delaware; d. 1940) was the first president of the first Women's Club organization in Nowata, Oklahoma. She achieved further distinction by becoming the first Native American woman to be elected president of the National Federation of Women's Clubs. Lawson became involved in women's clubs because it was one of the few avenues available to women who wanted to become publicly involved in civic matters. She served in numerous civic organizations and was known for her interest in women's issues, especially education. She promoted the improvement of political roles for women as well as better educational opportunities. She died in 1940.

Sources: Dockstader, *Great North American Indians,* pp. 145–46; Gridley, *American Indian Women,* pp. 88–93; "Self Guiding Tour for the National Hall of Fame for Famous Indians," p. 3.

1922 Ruth Muskrat Bronson (Cherokee; 1897–1982) was the first and only American Indian representative at the World's Student Christian Federation Annual Conference held in Beijing, China, in 1922. It was the first time an American Indian student took part in a world conference. She was one of ten American students chosen to represent the United States and was the only one of two people of color. (Dr. Willis King, an African American was the other; he was elected the first person of African descent to be elected to the Federation's General Committee.) In China Bronson was in great demand as a lecturer and she shared her knowledge and experiences of American Indian cultures. In 1923 Bronson enrolled at Mount Holyoke College, where she became the first Native American to attend, which made her aware of the ignorance her fellow students had about American Indians. This and her trip to China affected her outlook regarding assimilation, education, and self-determination for Indians. She recognized the value of Indian heritage and saw the need for unity among the various Indian tribes in the

United States. After graduation in 1925, Bronson began a distinguished career with the Bureau of Indian Affairs (BIA) serving in the Education Division.

Sources: Bataille, ed., *Native American Women,* pp. 42–44; Gridley, ed., *Indians of Today;* Harvey, Gretchen A., *Cherokee and American: Ruth Muskrat Bronson, 1897–1982* (dissertation), Tempe: Arizona State University, 1966.

1951 Annie Dodge Wauneka (Navajo; 1910–) was the first woman delegate elected to the Navajo Tribal Council; and in 1963, she became the first Native American to be presented with the presidential Medal of Freedom—the highest honor that the U.S. government can bestow on a citizen. As a public health advocate, Wauneka worked hard to bring tuberculosis under control on the Navajo reservation. She developed a Navajo-English medical dictionary, and hosted a radio show informing the Navajo of the benefits of Western medicine and how it complemented traditional healing practices. Her efforts led to a drastic reduction of tuberculosis among the Navajo. In addition, she advocated pre- and post-natal care, which resulted in an increased infant survival rate.

Annie Dodge Wauneka.

Wauneka learned her leadership skills from her father, Henry Chee Dodge, the first chairman of the Navajo Tribal Council. She accompanied him on his trips throughout the reservation and often assisted him in his duties. She was re-elected to the Council three times. In the 1950s she earned a B.S. in public health from the University of Arizona; and in 1976, she was awarded an honorary doctorate of public health from the same university. Among the many honors she has received are the 1976 Women of the Year selection by the *Ladies Home Journal,* the 1980 American Lung Association's Seventy-fifth Anniversary Hall of Fame selection; and in 1984, the Navajo Nation honored her with the Navajo Nation Medal of Honor. In 1989, she was selected as one of fifty heros by *Newsweek* magazine; and in 1991, she was presented the Allan Houser Lifetime Achievement Award along with Choctaw tribal leader Phillip Martin and Menominee rights activist Ada Deer.

Sources: Bataille and Sands, *American Indian Women, Telling Their Lives,* p. 178; Champagne, ed., *The Native North American Almanac,* pp. 1185–86; "Dr. Wauneka Receives Allan Houser Award," *Navajo Times,* Vol. 31, No. 16 (April 18, 1991), p. 1; "Dr. Wauneka to Be Honored for Working for Her People," *Navajo Times,* Vol. 27, No. 27 (July 6, 1989), p. 5; Gridley, ed., *Indians of Today,* pp. 381–82; Malinowski, ed., *Notable Native Americans,* pp. 453–54; "Newsweek Pays Tribute to Annie Dodge Wauneka," *Newsweek,* July 10, 1989, p. 5.

1953 Arlene Wesley James (Yakima) became the first Miss Indian America. The Miss Indian America pageant was part of the All Indian Days festivities in Sheridan, Wyoming.

Sources: Champagne, ed., *Chronology of Native North American History,* p. 325.

1961 Louis R. Bruce (Mohawk; 1906–1989) organized the first National Indian Conference on Housing. He was the third Native American to serve as commissioner of Indian Affairs. During the Great Depression, Bruce initiated a summer camp program that offered American Indian boys the opportunity to travel to New England to teach Indian lore and crafts, creating more than six hundred summer jobs for Indian youth. As a result of his work in this program, he was appointed to serve as New York state director for Indian projects in the National Youth Administration of the Works Progress Administration (WPA). Bruce ran his program with all American Indian staff.

Bruce also co-founded the National Congress of American Indians (NCAI) and served as its secretary. During his activities of serving the American Indian community, he led a career as a successful businessman, dairy producer, and political leader. One of Bruce's greatest interests was youth work. In 1957, he organized the first National American Indian Youth Conference in Washington, D.C. After his appointment in 1969 to commissioner of Indian Affairs, he endeavored to alter the Bureau of Indian Affairs (BIA) from a management agency to a service provider, and he sought to fill as many positions with Native Americans as he

Louis R. Bruce Jr. was active in American Indian youth programs.

could. Nevertheless, Indian activists of the American Indian Movement (AIM) criticized him and, in 1972, occupied BIA headquarters to protest the policies of the BIA. After the BIA takeover, Bruce and other top BIA officials were dismissed from office. For his career of service, Bruce was awarded the American Indian Achievement Award and the Freedoms Award.

Sources: Champagne, ed., *The Native North American Almanac*, p. 1021; Dennis, *The American Indian, 1492–1976*, p. 71; Malinowski, ed., *Notable Native Americans*, pp. 56–58.

Mid-1960s John Woodenlegs (Cheyenne) was the only American Indian member of President Lyndon Johnson's twenty-five-member National Advisory Commission on Rural Poverty. He was president of the Northern Cheyenne Native American Church from 1946 to 1959 and a leader of traditional Cheyenne ceremonies. From 1956 to 1968, he served as Chief of the Northern Cheyenne and president of the Northern Cheyenne Tribal Council. He was active in opposing federal termination policy of American Indian reservations and ending trust status. Such a termination met the United States' abandonment of responsibilities and obligations to Indian tribes as stated in treaties. A reservation terminated would lose treaty privileges and rights as well as the special status as separate political entities, distinct from the non-Indian American community. A prominent leader in Cheyenne society, Woodenlegs became a member of the Chiefs' Society in 1962 and affiliated with the War Dancers' Society. In 1974, he accomplished a great spiritual achievement by fasting on Bear Butte while the Buffalo Hat was being renewed from damage that occurred during a dispute among the Cheyenne in 1894. One of the holiest possessions of Cheyenne people, the Sacred Buffalo Hat now is ritually cared for and kept among the Northern Cheyenne in Montana.

Sources: *Biographical Dictionary of Indians of the Americas*, Vol. 2, p. 841; Hirshfelder and Molin, *The Encyclopedia of Native American Religions*, p. 329.

1966 Verna Patronella Johnston (Ojibwa; 1909–) opened the first boarding house for Indian students in Toronto, Canada. The purpose of the boarding house was to assist Indian youth in adapting to urban life. Johnston taught boarders how to interact with various governmental agencies and how to conduct themselves in the city while maintaining their Native identities. At the same time, she ran a craft training program, which caught the attention of Native leaders. As a result she traveled to more than 124 different reserves to speak on Indian reserve and urban life. She ran her boarding house until ill health forced her to close in 1973. In 1974, she recovered to become a voluntary consultant and housekeeper for Anduhyaun House, a hostel for Indian girls. In 1976, Johnston was named Indian Woman of the Year by the Native Women's Association of Canada.

Sources: Bataille, ed., *Native American Women*, p. 129; Vanderburgh, Rosamund M., *I Am Nokomis Too: The Biography of Verna Patronella Johnston*, Don Mills, Ontario: General Publishing, 1977.

1968 Presbyterian minister Reverend Roe B. Lewis (Pima) was the first Pima to be awarded the Indian Achievement Award, September 7, 1968. It was an award presented annually by the Indian Council Fire. Reverend Lewis was chosen for his outstanding service in educational counseling and the assistance he had given to American Indian youth in pursuing academic careers.

Sources: Champagne, ed., *Chronology of Native North American History*, p. 354.

1970 Hildreth Marie Twostars (Sioux) was the first American Indian woman to be selected South Dakota Merit Mother. She was bestowed that honor again in 1981. Active in the health field as an administrator for almost forty years, she has received numerous awards related to health issues. In 1970, at the first national meeting of American Indian in Fort Collins, Colorado, she was given the title "Mrs. Indian Seminar." Former president of the North American Indian Women's Association, she received the Jefferson Award for her outstanding public service in 1981. In 1983, she was given a certificate and plaque at the first Indian Women's Recognition Ceremony of the National Congress of American Indians.
Sources: Bataille, ed., *Native American Women,* p. 268.

1971 William Youpee (Dakota Sioux) was the founder and first president of the National Tribal Chairmen's Association.
Sources: *Biographical Dictionary of Indians of the Americas,* Vol. 2, p. 860.

1971 The Boy Scouts of America honored Virginia A. Stroud (Cherokee), the 1971 Miss Indian America, presenting her with the Young American Award. She was cited for her outstanding accomplishments and service. The annual Young American awards were given to young persons between fifteen and twenty-one years of age who had made exceptional achievements in various endeavors, including sports, arts, science, religion, and business. Stroud was one of six individuals to receive the 1971 award.
Sources: Dennis, *The American Indian, 1492–1976,* p. 88.

1973 Philip Fontaine (Sagkeeng Ojibwa; 1944–) established the first locally controlled First Nations school programs in Canada. In 1976, he founded the locally controlled, first Indian Child and Family Agency and the Sagkeeng Alcohol Treatment Center, which by special agreement were to be free of any control from the Manitoba provincial government. To convince the Department of Indian Affairs of the necessity to build new schools, Fontaine organized a successful boycott, to which the government surrendered quickly.

Fontaine was nationally more recognized for his role in the defeat of the Meech Lake Accord and in convincing the Canadian government to investigate Indian child abuse in church-operated schools. Had it not been defeated, the Meech Lake Accord would have recognized Quebec as a distinct separate society, with no consideration of First Nations. Fontaine's years of coalition building among the First Nations paid off in uniting Natives to force a rejection of the accord in 1990. First Nations' efforts resulted in greater awareness of the unique status of First Nations in Canada. Fontaine also brought much needed attention to the issue of Indian education. Until the 1950s and 1960s, Indian education was placed in the control of Catholic and Protestant missions. In 1990, Fontaine announced that he had been sexually abused by at least one Catholic priest in the residential school he attended. His announcement brought others to publicize their experiences of abuse. The issue of Indian child adoption by non-Natives was also brought to the forefront by Fontaine.

Working to unite all peoples of the First Nations to resolve issues common to all, at the same time, Fontaine has worked to solve problems within his tribal band group, serving as deputy federal coordinator of the Native Economic Development Program and as regional director for the Canadian Department of Indian Affairs in the Yukon region. He also served as vice-chief, representing Manitoba at the Assembly of First Nations, a nationwide organization parallel to the Euro-Canadian government.

Sources: Champagne, ed., *The Native North American Almanac*, p. 1056; Malinowski, ed., *Notable Native Americans*, pp. 149–51.

1978 Laura Somersal (Wappo) was given the first Woman of Achievement Award by the Sonoma County Commission on the Status of Women. In addition she was recognized for her work in her community by the Women of Color. Leading a varied life, Somersal was a tribal scholar, a nationally and internationally renowned basket weaver, a lecturer, a polyglot, and a linguist. In addition, she was dedicated to working toward the preservation of Wappo culture and artistry.

Sources: Bataille, ed., *Native American Women*, p. 242–43.

1980 Norbert S. Hill Jr. (Wisconsin Oneida; 1946–) received the Reginald H. Jones Distinguished Service Award from the National Action Council for Minorities in Engineering (NACME). Among Hill's achievements, he founded/co-founded the Annual Native American Career Conference, the All-Indian Long Distance Runners Training Camp, and the *Winds of Change* magazine.

Sources: Malinowski, ed., *Notable Native Americans*, pp. 197–98.

1987 Principal chief Wilma Mankiller (Cherokee; 1945–) was the first and only Native American woman named as *Ms.* magazine's Woman of the Year.

Sources: *Biographical Dictionary of Indians of the Americas*, Vol. 1, p. 391; Champagne, ed., *The Native North American Almanac*, pp. 1098–1099; Malinowski, ed., *Notable Native Americans*, pp. 256–58.

1987 Loralei DeCora (Winnebago/Miniconjou Sioux) helped found the Porcupine Clinic on the Pine Ridge Sioux Indian Reservation. It was the first entirely community-owned and operated clinic in the country to be established on an Indian reservation. In 1993 DeCora received the Robert Wood Johnson Community Health Leadership Award for her work to improve the health conditions on the Pine Ridge Indian Reservation. The award was given to assist her further in her work.

Sources: "Nurse Wins $100,000 Foundation Award for Community Health Aid," *Indian Country Today*, Vol. 12, No. 44 (April 28, 1993), p. B-1.

1990 Arizona state senator James Henderson (Navajo) was awarded the Human Kindness Award by Don Stewart, president of Feed My People International. Henderson received the award for his efforts to keep the food banks in northern Arizona open and running. He brought the problems of the food banks to the attention of the state officials, and has worked to keep attention focused on them. Cited as "a true American who goes above and beyond the call of duty," he has also offered his personal services to the program.

Sources: "Senator Henderson Honored with 'The Human Kindness Award,'" *Navajo Times*, Vol. 30, No. 38 (September 20, 1990), p. A-5.

1991 Franklin "Chaskae" McCabe III, (Assiniboin/Navajo), an enrolled member of the Colorado River Indian Tribes (CRIT), which includes the Mohave, Hopi, and Navajo, was the first of his tribe to receive the Arizona 12-Who Care/Hon Kachina Award. He achieved this honor at the age of sixteen. An activist throughout his school career, Chaskae has received numerous awards, honors, and citations, including membership in the National Honor Society (1989), president of the Parker High School student body, representative to Arizona Boys' State (1991), Ambassador for the United Indian Tribal Youth poster (1992), and member of the Governor's Youth Commission Against Drugs (1991). As a recipient of the prestigious Arizona 12 Who Care/Hon Kachina Award, he was noted for the range of his volunteer work, length of his services, and how his deeds made a difference within the community. Graduating with a degree in psychology in 1997, Chaskae plans to attend law school.

Sources: Flores, Amelia (director, Library/Archives Colorado River Indian Tribes), Personal communication to AnCita Benally, December 1996; Tiffen, J. "Parker Student to Be Honored in '12 Who Care' program," *Parker Pioneer,* September 11, 1991, p. 1.

1991 Wilson Hunter (Navajo) was the first American Indian to receive the Freeman Tilden Award, given by the National Park Service and the National Parks and Conservation Association. Hunter was one of ten regional winners and the first southwest regional winner to be chosen as a national winner. (Freeman Tilden, after whom the award was named, was a journalist and writer who devoted much time to conservation.) The award is given to a Park Service employee who has made significant and lasting contributions to the field of interpretation. In addition to earning this award, Hunter co-founded the Council for American Indian Interpretation to bring American Indian perspectives in informing the

Tribal leaders Peterson Zah (president of the Navajo Nation), Josiah Moore (chairman of the Tribal Council of the Tohono O'odham Nation), and Vernon Masayesva (chairman of the Tribal Council of the Hopi Nation) were honored during halftime ceremonies at the Arizona State University homecoming game, November 14, 1992.

public, now an official section of the National Association of Interpretation.

Sources: "Canyon De Chelly Park Employee First Indian to Earn National Honor," *Navajo Times*, Vol. 31, No. 52 (December 24, 1991), p. 5.

1991 Tina Descheenie (Navajo) was awarded the 1991 *Working Mother Magazine* Del Monte Dream Achiever Award. The award was given to working mothers who had overcome great obstacles to achieve their dreams. Descheenie was able to earn her bachelor's degree despite the difficulties of family illness and financial shortages to fulfill her lifelong dream, completing her degree years after she began her college career. Her motto was "dream and then do it."

Sources: "Hard Work Pays Off," *Navajo Times*, Vol. 31, No. 21 (May 23, 1991), p. A-8.

1992 The Arizona State University Alumni Association presented Community Leadership Awards to three American Indian alumni, all of whom were serving as heads of their tribal governments: Peterson Zah, president of the Navajo Nation; Josiah N. Moore, chairman of the Tohono O'odham Tribal Council; and Vernon Masayesva, chairman of the Hopi Tribal Council. The awards were given during halftime festivities of the homecoming football game on November 14, 1992.

Sources: *Insight,* Winter 1993, p. 27.

CULTURAL HISTORY

292 C.E. Tikal, a Mayan city in Guatemala, had a stela carved with the earliest known date from the Mayan lowlands. The date July 6, 292, (or roughly what it transfers to in the Western lunar calendar) was carved into the bas-relief of a pillar. (Other cities are known to have existed before this date, but this monument records the earliest date.)

Sources: Leitch, *Chronology of the American Indian,* p. 19.

573 C.E. The Maya from the city of Tulum carved a stela with the earliest known date in the Caribbean coastal area. The city was located on a cliff overlooking the coast. Eventually Tulum became a walled city with six-and-one-half foot thick walls on three sides and the sea on the fourth side. The settlement began in 1560. The residents carved the last date after a fifteen-hundred-year period of annually marking each year.

Sources: Leitch, *Chronology of the American Indian,* p. 24.

1150 The earliest known Hopi village, Oraibi, was established. Today it is the oldest continuously inhabited community in the United States.

Sources: Leitch, *Chronology of the American Indian,* p. 36.

1168 Aztec ancestors began their eighty-year migration to the Valley of Mexico. According to their chronicles, they were led by a wooden image of their war god, Huitzilopochtli, and established themselves in Chapultepec in 1248. In reality they were a small group with little military or political power, who sought permission from already established peoples living near the site of their future capital, Tenochtitlan, known today as Mexico City. Over the next eighty years they gradually gained military and political power through constant warfare and subjugation of smaller groups. They consolidated their power by entering into a triple alliance with the Texcoco and Tlacopan. The alliance remained intact until 1516.

Sources: Leitch, *Chronology of the American Indian,* p. 38.

1200 Mano Capac (Inca) began building the Inca empire, which was centered at Cuzco.

Sources: Leitch, *Chronology of the American Indian,* p. 38.

1492 The Taino of the Arawak Island were the first Native people to encounter Europeans when Christopher Columbus arrived at what are known today as the Watling Islands.

Sources: Francis, *Native Time,* p. 28.

1492 On December 24, 1492, Guacanagari (Taino) presented Christopher Columbus with the first American gold seen by Europeans when he gave a gift of a gold belt buckle. The sight of the gold ended the Europeans' speculation about the existence of riches. This was done after Columbus was invited to visit the Caciques village Marien in what is known today as Haiti.

Sources: Leitch, *Chronology of the American Indian.*

ca. 1500s Deganiwida (Huron) founded the Iroquois League with Hiawatha. They advocated peace and unity between the peoples who would comprise the League of Iroquois Nations. Deganiwida, who had a speech impediment, conceived of the plan and then depended on Hiawatha to be the spokesman and orator. According to tradition, his mother was told in a vision that her son would one day be called the "Master of Life" and would indirectly destroy his own people, the Huron. The Iroquois Confederacy did just that when its forces attacked and destroyed the Hurons in the Great Lakes region in 1649.

The league lasted into the nineteenth century and fulfilled many of the aspirations of its members, more so than other regimes. Based on democratic principles, the league gave women a powerful voice. Clan mothers nominated hereditary chiefs and openly voiced their opinions on political and military affairs. Sources calculate Deganiwida's lifetime to be during the late 1500s, but new evidence indicates that the Iroquois League was in existence long before 1500.

Sources: "Deganiwida,"*The American Indian;* Dockstader, *Great North American Indian,* pp. 71–72; Hirschfelder and Molin, *The Encyclopedia of Native American Religions,* p. 66; Waldman, *Who Was Who in Native American History,* p 96.

1523 Chicora (tribal affiliation unknown) was the first American Indian informant. He was captured by the Spanish and taken to Spain, where he provided historian Peter Matyr with information about indigenous peoples of the Americas. It was the first time that information on American Indian cultures, customs, and history from an American Indian perspective was recounted to Europeans.

Sources: Champagne, ed., *Chronology of Native North American History,* p. 38.

1524 Chontal Maya traders gave Hernan Cortes the first Native-made map ever seen by Europeans, of the inland trading routes along the gulf coast of the modern state of Tabasco, Mexico. Painted on cotton cloth, the map was a highly accurate depiction of four hundred miles of roads. The Chontal Maya traded extensively along the coast from Xicalanco (Tabasco, Mexico) to Nito (Honduras).

Sources: Leitch, *Chronology of the American Indian,* p. 67.

1524 Leonor (Tlaxcala), daughter of Dona Luisa Xicotencatl (Tlaxcala), also known as Techquilvasin, was the first reported child of mixed European and Native American ancestry. She was born March 22, 1524. Her mother was of noble birth, being from the royal family of the Tlaxcala kingdom of Mexico. Her father

was Pedro de Alvarado, a Spanish captain. The descendants of two of Leonor's brothers aligned with the Spanish duchy of Albuquerque.

Sources: *Biographical Dictionary of Indians of the Americas,* Vol. 2, p. 848.

1528 The first record of Indians capturing Europeans as slaves in the Southwest was that of Texas Indians capturing Alvar Núñez Cabeza de Vaca and his shipwrecked crew.

Sources: Schroeder, Albert H., and Omer C. Stewart, "Indian Servitude in the Southwest," in *Handbook of North American Indians,* Vol. 10: *History of Indian-White Relations,* edited by Alfonso Ortiz, p. 410.

1541 Aztec artist/recorders collaborated with Spanish priests to produce the Codex Mendoza. It was the first attempt by the Spanish to record Aztec history after having earlier ordered the burning of the extensive Aztec library, which housed not only religious texts, but the social and political history of the Aztec empire. The codex was commissioned by Viceroy Antonio de Mendoza for Charles V. The method of recording was based on the Aztec codices, or picture writing.

Sources: Leitch, *Chronology of the American Indian,* p. 77.

1542 The first mounted Indian warriors appeared in Mexico. The Spanish were forced to allow Indian conscripts to ride on horseback in order to suppress a serious rebellion. In 1659 a report by the governor of Santa Fe documenting the first Indians (Navajo warriors) mounted on horses in the American West was sent to Mexico City.

Sources: Champagne, ed., *Chronology of Native North American History,* p. 44; Hirschfelder and Kreipe de Montaño, *The Native American Almanac,* p. 302.

1550 The Quiche Maya of Guatemala, the most powerful of the Maya, entered the last recordings of their history in a text called the "Popul Vuh" (Community Book). A post-conquest collection of oral traditions that included religious text as well as political and social history, the "Popul Vuh" consisted of four sections, the first three of Quiche mythology and the last a narrative of their history.

Sources: Leitch, *Chronology of the American Indian,* p. 79.

1554 The Paulista (of mixed Indian and Portuguese ancestry) dominated the Sao Paolo region of Brazil, where they captured Native Americans, selling them as slaves to the sugar plantations. At the same time they were pursued by Portuguese authorities for harassing plantation slaves and for offering a life of freedom for them. Authorities feared that their freedom would encourage escapes or rebellion by the slaves. They travelled as far as Paraguay, eventually becoming a nuisance to authorities there.

Sources: Leitch, *Chronology of the American Indian,* p. 80.

1562 An order signed by Roman Catholic priests demanded that all Maya books be brought to Mani where they were burned. Only three books survived, the "Dresden Codex," a 78-page astronomical manual; the "Codex Peresianus," a guide to rituals; and the "Codex Tro-Cortesianus," a 112-page book on astrology. Religious objects and other artifacts were included in the order. In addition,

Opposite Page:
Depiction of Hiawatha,
one of the founders
of the Iroquois
Confederacy, addressing
his companions.

more than four thousand individuals were tortured and 158 were executed during interrogation.

Sources: Leitch, *Chronology of the American Indian,* p. 80; Wearne, *Return of the Indian, Conquest and Revival in the Americas,* p. 195.

1595 Pocahontas (Powhatan; ca. 1595–1617) was the only Indian woman to be received by English royalty as royalty herself; she was introduced as the daughter of an emperor. Pocahontas was the favored daughter of one of the most powerful sachems in New England history, Wahunsonacock. He headed the thirty-two-member Powhatan Confederacy in the Virginia tidewater area. Her fame arose from the alleged rescue of John Smith, the leader of the Jamestown settlement in 1608. The incident has been questioned and there is no substantial proof that the events happened as Smith claimed they did. In 1612 she was abducted and imprisoned in Jamestown. The colonists then used her as a pawn to obtain the release of Englishmen taken captive by the Powhatan. During her imprisonment she was converted to Christianity and rechristened, Rebecca. In 1613 she married John Rolfe, with the consent of her father, and the marriage brought several years of peaceful relations between the Powhatan and the colonists. In 1616 Pocahontas accompanied her husband to England, where she was received by King James I and Queen Anne. She was hailed as New World royalty and addressed as Lady Rebecca. The next year, as the entourage waited to sail back to Virginia, she died and was buried in St. George's Parish Church at Gravesend. She had one son, Thomas Rolfe, through whose lineage some prominent Virginia families trace their ancestry to Pocahontas and Wahunsanacock. The events of Pocahontas' life are colorful and much has been mythologized about her. In 1995, Walt Disney Studios released an animated movie based on the legend of Pocahontas.

Sources: Hodge, ed., *Handbook of American Indians North of Mexico,* Vol. 2, p. 269; Johansen and Grinde, *The Encyclopedia of Native American Biography,* pp. 294–95.

1621 Massasoit (Wampanoag), ninety of his warriors, and the pilgrims of Plymouth celebrated the first Thanksgiving feast in October 1621. Massasoit negotiated a treaty of friendship and peace earlier in March. The Pilgrims invited the Wampanoag to feast with them in recognition of the friendship and to validate the treaty. (The treaty was never broken.) The feast lasted three days and was the first of the annual American Thanksgiving Day celebrations. Many Native peoples had generations-old traditions of thanksgiving celebrations as well.

Sources: Waldman, *Who Was Who in Native American History,* p. 222.

1637 French Jesuits established an agricultural community of Montagnais people at a place they named Sillery in July 1637. This reserve, the first in Canada, had limited success mainly because the Jesuits insisted on impractical changes in the lifestyle, behavior, and attitudes of the Indian residents. Jesuits were convinced that Indians must be settled in order to be evangelized. In later years, this

Opposite page:
Nineteenth-century
engraving of Massasoit.

site became an important trading center and a crossroads for Indians and European traders and trappers.

Sources: Champagne, *Chronology of Native North American History,* p. 58.

1651 Rather than capitulate to the French, who were pursuing them, the last forty Carib inhabitants of Grenada, threw themselves over a cliff into Sauteurs Bay, committing mass suicide.

Sources: Leitch, *Chronology of the American Indian,* p. 97.

1672 American Indians served as mail couriers between New York City and Albany. The severe winter weather was thought to be too harsh for non-Indians.

Sources: Champagne, ed., *Chronology of Native North American History,* p. 69; Leitch, *Chronology of the American Indian,* p. 100.

1701 Zambo Indians, who were half Indian and half African, began raiding from their stronghold in Cabo Gracias a Dios in Nicaragua. Better armed than their targets, Spanish settlers, they attacked and enslaved any survivors.

Sources: Leitch, *Chronology of the American Indian,* p. 106.

1706 Assacombuit (Abenaki), also known as Charlevoix, is believed to be the only American Indian knighted by a European monarch. He supported the French, assisting them in ridding Newfoundland of a British presence. Assacombuit was rewarded with a trip through France in 1706 and 1707, where he was introduced to King Louis XIV, who knighted him.

Sources: *Biographical Dictionary of Indians of the Americas,* Vol. 1, p. 27; Johansen and Grinde, *The Encyclopedia of Native American Biography,* p. 17.

ca. 1796 The horseback culture of the High Plains began about this time.

Sources: Dennis, *The American Indian, 1492–1976,* pp. 21, 23.

1804 Sacajawea (Shoshoni; ca. 1784–ca. 1812), who at age fifteen, was the only woman to accompany the Lewis and Clark expedition as the American explorers traversed the newly acquired Louisiana territory. Her presence virtually guaranteed safe passage for the expedition. Potentially hostile tribes were persuaded that the exploring party was peaceful because a woman with a newborn child would not be accompanying a war party. In addition, Sacajawea provided knowledge of the land, vegetation, animal life, the people, and several languages through which Lewis and Clark were able to acquire additional information from the various tribes they met. With her French husband Toussaint Charbonneau, she guided the expedition throughout the Rocky Mountains and the Plateau region toward the Pacific Ocean. Several years earlier she had been captured by the Hidatsa with whom she resided until she was acquired by Charbonneau. During the expedition she was reunited with a brother who had become chief of their band. The reunion provided Lewis and Clark with much needed supplies and assistance. During another part of the trip, Sacajawea saved not only provisions, but the carefully kept notes of Lewis and Clark from being swept away in a river after a boat overturned. Had she not saved the papers, much of the meticulous notes would have been lost. On the return journey she guided Clark through the Montana mountains. Of her history after the expedition, little is known. According to Clark's papers, she died soon after an 1811 visit she made with her husband, at which time she entrusted her son Jean Baptiste to Clark. Others say she lived to be almost one hundred years old and died among her

people, the Shoshoni. She has been memorialized by several major statues and many books and articles about her.

Drawing of Sacajawea, the only woman on Lewis and Clark's Expedition.

Sources: Hodge, *Handbook of American Indians North of Mexico*, Vol. 2, p. 401; Johansen and Grinde, eds., *The Encyclopedia of Native American Biography*, pp. 330–31.

1836 A partially translated version of the Wallam Olum, sacred tribal chronology of the Lenni Lenape, was first published by a Frenchman, Constantine Samuel Rafinesque, as *The American Nations*. It was a pictographic record of the history of the world from creation on. The record had been kept by the Delaware and parts of it had been revealed to a Dr. Ward. Rafinesque supplemented the pictographic record with additional information he received from other Delaware. In 1885, anthropologist Daniel Brinton, who had initially doubted the authenticity of the record, published the entire pictography as *The Lenape and Their Legends with the Complete Text and Symbols of the Walam Olum*. Similar bark records were found among other Indian tribes.

Sources: *The American Indian;* Champagne, ed., *Chronology of Native North American History*, pp. 149, 160; Francis, *Native Time*, p. 10.

1847 The first monument to honor an Indian by whites was erected at "Sachem Plains" by the people of Norwich, Connecticut, in memory of Uncas, founder of the Mohegans, a dissident group of Pequot. The cornerstone was laid by President Andrew Jackson in 1833. Another memorial, a bronze statue, was erected by Mrs. Edward Clark on the site of the home of James Fenimore Cooper; Cooper used Uncas' name in his book, *Last of the Mohicans*. Although Uncas was lauded by New Englanders for his steadfast friendship with them, Uncas' allies and neighbors and his mentor, Sassacus, found him unscrupulous, dishonest, deceitful, self-serving, and despicable. Though he married a daughter of Sassacus and became a minor leader in the Pequot Confederacy, he rebelled against Sassacus and allied himself with the English colonists. He subverted the efforts of the Pequot, using intrigue and lies to cast suspicion on them. In 1642 he alleged that Miantinomo, a Narraganset chief was plotting to kill him. The accused was jailed and when he was released, led an attack in revenge on Uncas' village. The chief was recaptured and sentenced to execution, which was given to Uncas who arranged for it. During King Philip's War he supported the colonists, supplying them with warriors. However, in his late years he openly opposed the Christianization of his people and lost some of his popular support from the English. He died an alcoholic, but at the end of his life, he had probably ceded more lands of neighboring tribes, for which he had no authority, than anybody else did.

Sources: Dennis, *The American Indian, 1492–1976*, p. 29; Johansen and Grinde, *The Encyclopedia of Native American Biography*, pp. 401–402; Hodge, *Handbook of American Indians North of Mexico*, pp. 868–69.

1850 The Province of Canada initiated the first legal definition of "Indian" on August 10, 1850, defining who was Indian and who was not. It distinguished for the first time between "status" and "non-status" Indians, and it recognized those protected by treaties and eligible for rights and privileges guaranteed by treaties.

Sources: Champagne, ed., *Chronology of Native North American History*, p. 176.

1865 Jesse Chisholm (Cherokee) is attributed with blazing the Chisholm Trail from Texas to Kansas. The original Chisholm Trail was a cattle trail used by cattlemen to take cattle to railroad terminals in Kansas. Today a part of it is U.S. Highway 81. Besides blazing new trails, Chisholm was a renowned interpreter, mediator, diplomat and a businessman. He acted as an intermediary for the U.S. Army and Indian tribes and the U.S. government and Indian tribes. In addition he often settled or negotiated disputes between different Indian tribes. He built and maintained three trading posts in Indian Territory and often carried wagon loads of goods to Indian communities. In addition he held contracts with the U.S. Army outposts. He assisted in the negotiations that led to the largest Indian gathering at the Little Arkansas in 1865 and at Medicine Lodge in 1868. He was respected and trusted by all parties he represented and negotiated with.

Sources: *Biographical Dictionary of Indians of the Americas*, Vol. 1, pp. 129–30; Dennis, *The American Indian, 1492–1976*, p. 120; Dockstader, *Great North American Indians*, pp. 50–51; Waldman, *Who Was Who in Native American History*, pp. 65–66.

1869 In its first official census the Argentinean government calculated that there were 93,138 Indians in 1869. However, "Indians" were defined as those who were of pure Indian ancestry. Mixed-bloods were not counted as Indian.

Sources: Leitch, *Chronology of the American Indian*, p. 165.

1870s Although the campaign was not official, white sport hunters and amateurs began a campaign of wanton destruction of the American bison. U.S. Congressman James Garrison quoted the secretary of Interior as saying that when the buffalo are gone, Indians would be a worry of the past. The building of the Union Pacific Railroad cut through the middle of bison country creating a northern and a southern herd. In a two month period 260 thousand buffalo were killed, flooding the market with pelts and bringing their cost to $1 per skin. The southern herd was virtually wiped out by 1878. By 1889 the last four were killed in Texas. The northern herd was similarly destroyed, but a small herd escaped total demise. Some Indians who depended on the bison for food, clothing and shelter, attempted to prevent the destruction. In the battle of Adobe Wall Trading Post, seven hundred Comanche, Cheyenne, and Kiowa-Apache, under the command of Quannah Parker vainly attacked twenty whites staying at the post. The deadly accuracy of the long range buffalo guns was overwhelming; more than one hundred Indians died, but no whites. The bison herds were brought to the brink of total extinction. And, the Indians dependent on the buffalo herds were brought to the brink of destruction as well.

Sources: Dennis, *The American Indian, 1492–1976,* p. 38.

1889 Iron Tail (Oglala Sioux, 1850–1916), who later became one of three models James Earle Fraser used to design the "Indian head/buffalo nickel," was a respected leader among his people, became part of Buffalo Bill Cody's Wild West Show in 1889 and was treated like a celebrity in France and England during the show's European tour.

Sources: *Biographical Dictionary of Indians of the Americas,* Vol. 1, p. 308.

ca. 1902 The last Sadlermiut (or Sadliq) Inuit died. The Inuit of Southampton Island were gradually ravaged by foreign diseases.

Sources: Champagne, ed., *Chronology of Native North American History,* p. 254; Leitch, *A Concise Dictionary of Indian Tribes of North America,* p. 443.

1907 Members from several tribes symbolically buried old resentments and animosities and staged a goodwill show. The resulting outcome was the annual celebration of the All American Indian Days.

Sources: Dennis, *The American Indian, 1492–1976,* p. 48.

1913 John Big Tree (Onondaga), Iron Tail (Sioux), and Two Moons (Cheyenne) served as the models for the "Indian head/buffalo nickel" that was issued. Designed by James Earl Fraser, it was a composite of an idealized image of an Indian man on one side and a buffalo on the other.

Sources: *Biographical Dictionary of Indians of the Americas,* Vol. 1, pp. 308–309; Vol. 2, p. 772; Dennis, *The American Indian, 1492–1976,* p. 50; Waldman, *Who Was Who in Native American History,* p. 219.

1913 The site of what would have been the largest public memorial to the American Indians was dedicated on February 22, George Washington's birthday. The National Memorial to the Indian was to be larger than the Statue of Liberty and was to overlook New York Harbor. It was to stand with its right hand raised in a gesture of peace. A congressional act authorized it and the dedication ceremonies were attended by President Howard Taft, members of his cabinet, high-ranking army and navy officers and thirty-two notable Indian leaders from various tribes. Each of the Indian leaders signed a declaration of allegiance to the United States and then hoisted an American flag. The forts in New York Harbor provided a twenty-one gun salute. The memorial, however, was not completed.

Sources: Leitch, *Chronology of the American Indian,* p. 190.

1916 The Society of American Indians designated May 13 as "Indian Day," encouraging the recognition of the cultures and achievements of American Indian peoples, as well as bringing attention to their needs. It was not, however, made an American national holiday.

Sources: Dennis, *The American Indian, 1492–1976,* p. 50.

1916 Ishi (Yahi Yana, 1860–1916) was the last member of his tribe. The Yahi lived in what is known today as Northern California, near Mount Lassen. Ishi spent the last five years of his life at the Museum of Anthropology at the University of California in San Francisco. During this time he taught the staff about his traditions, religious ways, and language.

Sources: *Biographical Dictionary of Indians of the Americas,* Vol. 1, p. 311; Malinowski, ed., *Notable Native Americans,* pp. 206–209.

1917 For the first time in fifty years the birthrate among American Indians exceeded the death rate. From this point on, the Indian population has continuously increased.

Sources: Dennis, *The American Indian, 1492–1976,* p. 50; Francis, *Native Time,* p. 270.

1921 Bessie Coleman (tribal affiliation unknown), a mixed African and American Indian of the Oklahoma Territory, was the first Native American woman to receive an international pilot's license.

Sources: Patterson and Snodgrass, *Indian Terms of the Americas,* p. 24.

1922 The first annual Gallup Inter-Tribal Indian Ceremonials was launched in Gallup, New Mexico. The four day event features dancing, art displays, feasting, trading, and celebration by Native Americans from the United States and Canada. Eventually becoming one of the major Native American gatherings in the Southwest and in the nation, at times it has been controversial as opponents have accused non-Indian organizers of exploiting Indians and not supporting them in more serious issues.

Sources: Dennis, *The American Indian, 1492–1976,* p. 51; Francis, *Native Time,* p. 272.

1922 Hollow Horn Bear (Brulé Dakota Sioux) had the distinct honor of having his image placed on a fourteen-cent U.S. postage stamp and on a $5 silver certificate. The stamp was part of a regular postal series representing Native Americans. Hollow Horn Bear was a noted leader renowned for his oratorical skills. This skill made him an important asset in treaty negotiations and he was a member of several negotiating parties. In his early days he fought against white expansion, participated in attacks on forts along the Bozeman Trail, and led raids on Union Pacific Railroad workers' camps. He is best known as the chief who defeated Lt. William Fetterman. In 1873, tired of the deaths of so many of his people, he reconciled himself to life on a reservation and followed Spotted Tail there. He was appointed head of the Indian police at the Rosebud Agency in South Dakota. While he favored maintaining peace with whites, he did not cease protesting the injustices perpetuated against his people and the disregard of their basic human rights. He unsuccessfully opposed General George Crook's plan to take advantage of the internal friction among the Brulé and break up the Great Sioux Reservation. During his tenure with the tribal police, he was involved in the arrest of Crow Dog for the murder of Spotted Tail. He participated in two inaugural parades; in 1905 he took part in President Theodore Roosevelt's inauguration and in 1913 he was part of President Woodrow Wilson's inauguration. He died while participating in the latter event.

Sources: *Biographical Dictionary of Indians of the Americas,* Vol. 1, p. 286; Dockstader, *Great North American Indians,* pp. 111–13; Johansen and Grinde, *The Encyclopedia of Native American Biography,* pp. 172–73.

1928 Hosteen Tsosi (Navajo) performed in the *Navajo Mountain Chant,* marking the first time a Navajo ceremony was filmed. The film was done by Laura Adams Armer.

Sources: Dennis, *The American Indian, 1492–1976,* p. 53.

1959 The Lumbee were perhaps the first group of American Indians to be directly challenged by the Ku Klux Klan. The Lumbee chased the Klan off of their land with shotguns after the Klan tried to intimidate them into ceasing their efforts to have a public school established closer to their community.

Sources: Davis, ed., *Native America in the Twentieth Century,* pp. 61, 322; Dennis, *The American Indian, 1492–1976,* p. 61.

1964 The American Indian Historical Society was founded by Rupert Costo and Jeannette Henry Costo. The organization dedicates itself to historical research and education about American Indians and their history. The society publishes *The Indian Historian,* a journal devoted to historical research from an Indian perspective.

Sources: Champagne, ed., *Chronology of Native North American History,* p. 344.

1968 The first commemorative stamp recognizing a Native American leader was issued by the U.S. Post Office honoring Chief Joseph (Nez Percé). Striving to bring the Nez Percé people out from the domination of the United States, Joseph led them on a seventeen-hundred-mile trek, endeavoring to reach the safety of Sitting Bull's camp in Canada. Just before reaching the Canadian border, however, the Nez Percé were blocked by U.S. troops and forced back. In his surrender speech Chief Joseph uttered his famous oratory, beginning with, "From where the sun now stands, I will fight no more forever." He kept his word. Although he has been credited by historians as possessing expertise as a military strategist, he was more influential as a diplomat and known as a man of peace.

Sources: Hirschfelder and Kreipe de Montaño, *The Native American Almanac,* p. 306; Malinowski, ed., *Notable Native Americans,* pp. 218–19.

1986 The first national memorial honoring Native American veterans was dedicated at Arlington National Cemetery in Washington, D.C., by the Vietnam Era Veterans on November 11, 1986. Its inscription reads, "We are honored to remember you, the indigenous people of the Americas."

Sources: Hirschfelder and Kreipe de Montaño, *The Native American Almanac,* p. 231.

1989 The first permanent monument honoring the Navajo Code Talkers was dedicated in Phoenix, Arizona, on March 2, 1989.

Sources: Hirschfelder and Kreipe de Montaño, *The Native American Almanac,* p. 312.

1992 In January 1992 the Canadian government announced that it would build the first Native minimum-security prison on the Samson Cree Reserve.

Sources: Champagne, ed., *Chronology of Native North American History,* p. 479.

1992 The Indian Boys and Girls Club was established on the Pine Ridge Indian Reservation in South Dakota. It was the first boys and girls club to be established on an Indian reservation specifically to serve Indian youth. It was the culmination of a dream expressed by Sioux athlete SuAnne Big Crow, who died unexpectedly at the height of her athletic career. The club was funded by ACTION Drug Alliance and the SuAnne Big Crow Memorial Fund established by the tribe. Serving six to eighteen year old children, it aimed to provide youth with productive activities in a drug-free environment.

Sources: "First Indian Boys, Girls Club Starting Up," *Indian Country Today,* Vol. 12, No. 19 (November 5, 1992), p. B-1.

Opposite page:
Chief Joseph, the last independent Nez Percé leader.

Navajo Code Talkers were used as messengers during World War II. Here former Code Talker Dan Akee receives a medal in a 1989 ceremony in Phoenix, Arizona.

EDUCATION

1536 The College of Santa Cruz de Tlatelolco was the first European-established college in America.

Sources: Greenleaf, Richard E., "Persistence of Native Values: The Inquisition and the Indians of Colonial America," *Journal of the Americas,* Vol. 50, No. 3 (January 1994), pp. 351–76.

1568 The Jesuit Order of the Catholic church organized the first school for Indian children in Havana, Cuba. The children were those who had been brought from Florida.

Sources: Champagne, ed., *Chronology of Native North American History,* p. 48.

1618 Plans were initiated to build a college for the "children of the infidels." The directors of the Virginia Company gave orders to the governor to set a site to build a college. Although ten thousand acres were set aside and a sizeable amount of money was raised, hostilities with Indians in 1622 terminated any further plans.

Sources: Dennis, *The American Indian, 1492–1976,* p. 5.

1635 The first residential schools for American Indian children were established by the Jesuits.

Sources: Champagne, ed., *The Native North American Almanac,* p. 29.

1665 Caleb Cheeshateaumuck (Wampanoag; d. 1666) was the first American Indian to receive a degree from Harvard University. He graduated in 1665. A text he wrote in Latin, *Honoratissimi Benefactores,* published in 1663, is the earliest known publication by a North American Indian. Though he had great promise, he died soon after completing his studies.

Sources: *Biographical Dictionary of Indians of the Americas,* Vol. 1, p. 124; Hodge, ed., *Handbook of American Indans North of Mexico,* p. 240; Wiget, ed., *Dictionary of Native American Literature,* p. 145.

1720 The first permanent Indian school was established in Williamsburg, Virginia.

Sources: Champagne, ed., *Chronology of Native North American History,* p. 82; Dennis, *The American Indian, 1492–1976,* p. 13.

1723 Indian students attended the College of William and Mary in such large numbers that Brafferton Building was built especially for their use as a gathering place. It was the first Indian student center. The building still stands.

Sources: Dennis, *The American Indian, 1492–1976,* p. 13.

1754 Dartmouth College was established from a school for American Indian and white youth. Samson Occom (Mohegan; 1723–1792), a preacher, went on a lecture tour in England to raise money for the Indian Charity School. The school closed so that Dartmouth College could be established in 1761.

Sources: Szasz, *Indian Education in the American Colonies, 1607–1783*, pp. 200, 218.

1784 The first school in Alaska for Alaska Natives was established by the Russians at Three Saints Bay, Kodiak Island.

Sources: Dennis, *The American Indian, 1492–1976*, p. 17.

1794 For the first time, education was mentioned as a specific condition in a treaty between the United States and the Oneida, Tuscarora, and Stockbridge. Timothy Pickering, the U.S. commissioner, negotiated the Treaty of Canandaigua on December 2, 1794.

Sources: Dennis, *The American Indian, 1492–1976*, p. 21; Prucha, *American Indian Treaties*, pp. 94–96.

1842 The Choctaw Academy, one of the first Indian schools established by an Indian tribe was founded. It was an achievement the Choctaw had nurtured for the purpose of providing their children with training in the knowledge and skills of white civilization.

Sources: Dennis, *The American Indian, 1492–1976*, p. 25.

1843 The first mission school for the Inuit was established in Nushagak, Alaska, by Russian-Greek Orthodox missionaries.

Sources: Dennis, *The American Indian, 1492–1976*, p. 29.

1860 The first Indian boarding school was opened at the Yakima Indian Agency in Washington state. It opened in November with twenty-five students in residence. The boarding school was a result of the treaty agreement between the United States and the Yakima Nation concluded in 1855.

Sources: Dennis, *The American Indian, 1492–1976*, p. 32.

1870 The first appropriations specifically for Indian education were made by Congress when it appropriated $100,000 for the operation of federal industrial schools for Indians.

Sources: Dennis, *The American Indian, 1492–1976*, p. 36.

1878 Indian students began attending Hampton Normal School, an agricultural institute in Virginia established to educate blacks. In the twelve years that it was open to Indians, 460 were trained there. Hampton kept an extensive record of students while they attended and then kept track of them after they left. Out of 460, only fifty-two were graded as poor or bad. Although Hampton was successfully training Indian youth, many whites felt that black students were a bad influence on Indians, and further frowned on mixing Indians with blacks. As a result Carlisle Indian School was established exclusively for Indians.

Sources: Dennis, *The American Indian, 1492–1976*, p. 41.

1879 Carlisle Indian School was founded by Captain Richard H. Pratt in Pennsylvania. Pratt, a retired general who had fought the Indians, turned his

Carlisle Indian School, established in 1879, was the first off-reservation industrial boarding school.

attention to educating and civilizing them. He thought old unused military forts should be turned over to the civilizing of Indians. Carlisle had been one of the most successful Indian schools. By 1900 more than twelve hundred students from seventy-nine tribes were enrolled. Some of the most influential political leaders, sports figures, and Indian activists were trained at Carlisle Indian School. Pratt firmly believed that to civilize the Indian, it was imperative that they be removed from their societies, placed among whites, be required to live and work among whites, and be kept there. The outing program he initiated at Carlisle gave students opportunities to live with white families, work for them, earn money, and thus become better adapted to civilization. In essence, Pratt advocated total assimilation. In 1882 Congress passed laws to convert unused army forts into Indian schools.

Sources: Dennis, *The American Indian, 1492–1976*, p. 41.

1883 The Canadian government began establishing residential schools for Native Americans in the West. Most parents desired an education for their children, but they resisted the assimilationist aims of schools.

Sources: Champagne, ed., *The Native North American Almanac*, p. 1.

1884 Haskell Institute in Lawrence, Kansas, and Chilocco Indian School in Oklahoma opened beginning vocational education programs for Indians by the government. On September 17, twenty-two Pawnee children entered Haskell and three days later eighty Arapaho and Cheyenne students were enrolled by their leaders. Haskell developed from a vocational school to a junior college and finally into a four year university, Haskell Indian Nations University. Chilocco on the other hand has diminished in its function.

Sources: Dennis, *The American Indian, 1492–1976*, p. 43.

1884 For the first time, Congress specifically allocated funds for education in Alaska. The funds were to be distributed among mission schools. Dr. Sheldon Jackson was appointed general agent for education in Alaska.

Sources: Dennis, *The American Indian, 1492–1976,* p. 43.

1895 Rachel Caroline Eaton (Cherokee; 1869–1938) was the first American Indian woman to achieve prominence as both an educator and historian. She graduated from the Cherokee Female Seminary when she was eighteen and cum laude in 1895 from Drury College in Missouri. She went on to receive her M.A. and Ph.D. from Chicago University. In 1920 she was elected superintendent of schools in Rogers County, Oklahoma. After retirement she spent time conducting research and published it in two acclaimed studies—*John Ross and the Cherokee Indians* and *The History of the Cherokee Indians.* The Oklahoma Memorial Association named Eaton one of Oklahoma's outstanding citizens in 1938.

Sources: *Biographical Dictionary of Indians of the Americas,* Vol. 1, p. 207.

1899 Students at Bureau of Indian Affairs (BIA) boarding schools were required to have Christian religious instruction at least three hours a week. This was the result of pressure from religious groups anxious to Christianize Indians. The practice continued into the 1970s.

Sources: Dennis, *The American Indian, 1492–1976,* p. 46.

1902 The first local school board was established in Nome, Alaska. It was an attempt to involve parents and community in education to make school more relevant to Native Americans of Nome—Aleut and Eskimo.

Sources: Champagne, ed., *Chronology of Native North American History,* p. 251; Dennis, *The American Indian, 1492–1976,* p. 47.

1915 Henry Roe Cloud (Winnebago; ca.1884–1950) established the first college preparatory school for American Indians. He was also the only American Indian member of the Institute for Government Research, now known as the Brookings Institute. Further, in 1931, he became the first American Indian superintendent of Haskell Institute. He co-authored the "Meriam Report," which detailed the destitution caused by the Dawes (General Allotment) Act of 1887. In 1935, Cloud received the third Indian Achievement Medal of the Indian Council Fire. In 1936, he was appointed supervisor of Indian education by the Bureau of Indian Affairs (BIA).

Sources: *Biographical Dictionary of Indians of the Americas,* Vol. 1, p. 133; Crum, Steven, "Henry Roe Cloud, a Winnebago Indian Reformer: His Quest for American Higher Education," *Kansas History,* 11 (Autumn 1988): pp. 171–84; Dockstader, *Great North American Indians,* pp. 51–52; Hirschfelder and Kreipe de Montaño, *The Native American Almanac,* p. 97.

Henry Roe Cloud.

ca. 1920 John Joseph Mathews (Osage; 1894–1979) was the first American Indian to be offered a Rhodes scholarship. He declined the scholarship and instead used his personal funds to study at Oxford University in England, where he earned a B.A. in 1923. Mathews traveled extensively throughout Europe and Africa before returning to the United States. He went on to a distinguished career as a writer. Among his best known works are *Wahkontah, Talking to the Moon,* and *The Osages.*

See also: Literature, 1932.

Sources: Bailey, Garrick, "John Joseph Mathews, Osage, 1894– ," in *American Indian Intellectuals,* edited by Margo Liberty, pp. 205–14; *Biographical Dictionary of Indians of the Americas,* Vol. 1, p. 400; Dennis, *The American Indian, 1492-1976,* p. 140; Malinowski, ed., *Notable Native Americans,* pp. 266–67; Wiget, ed., *Dictionary of Native American Literature,* pp. 245–49; Witalec, ed., *Native North American Literature,* pp. 409–16.

Archie Phinney.

1926 Archie Phinney (Nez Percé; 1903–1949) was the first Native American to graduate from the University of Kansas. After earning a B.A. he continued his education at George Washington University and New York University studying anthropology. At Columbia University he specialized in the study of life on Native American reservations. With his background in anthropology, Phinney made one of the most significant contributions to the preservation and understanding of his tribal culture. During his youth he spent much time listening to his mother recite tribal stories. As an anthropologist, he took an active interest in recording these stories and interpreting them. As a tribal member thoroughly acquainted with the language and the subtle nuances of Nez Percé stories, he was able to contribute a deeper and more genuine interpretation of them. In 1934, he collaborated with his mother to publish *Nez Percé Texts.* He not only presented an accurate account of the stories, but was able to address his fellow tribesmen and show them how the stories were taken out of context and misunderstood. Further, he was able to demonstrate their purpose in the overall Nez Percé culture.

An activist concerned with American Indian issues, Phinney was a member of the National Congress of American Indians (NCAI). In 1946, he was awarded the prestigious Indian Achievement Medal from the Indian Council Fire. In addition, he was a recipient of an honorary degree from the Academy of Science in Leningrad, the Soviet Union, now St. Petersburg, Russia. He died at age forty-six in 1949.

Sources: Champagne, ed., *The Native North American Almanac,* pp. 1131–32; Gridley, ed., *Indians of Today,* pp. 72–73; Malinowski, ed., *Notable Native Americans,* pp. 329–30.

1934 The Johnson-O'Malley Act was passed by Congress authorizing the secretary of the Department of the Interior to contract with states for the education of Indian children, and to allow the use of federal property to be used by local schools.

Sources: Dennis, *The American Indian, 1492–1976,* p. 53.

ca. 1954 Joe Dan Osceola (Seminole) was the first Seminole to graduate from a public high school. His parents stressed the importance of education to him and his siblings; so despite objections from the community, they attended public school. Osceola later attended Georgetown College. When he returned, he became the youngest member to become chairman of the Seminole Tribal Council.

Sources: *Biographical Dictionary of Indians of the Americas,* Vol. 2, p. 354; Gridley, ed., *Indians of Today,* p. 431; Osceola, Jolin, Personal communication to AnCita Benally, April 21, 1997.

1957 Ada Deer (Menominee; 1935–) was the first Menominee to graduate from the University of Wisconsin-Madison. In 1961, she also became the first Native American to earn a master's degree in social work from Columbia University. She has been an activist for American Indian concerns, particularly those of her own tribe. She was one of the key participants in the successful efforts to overturn the termination of Menominee reservation status.

Sources: Bataille, ed., *Native American Women,* pp. 76–78; Champagne, ed., *The Native North American Almanac,* p. 1041; Malinowski, ed., *Notable Native Americans,* pp. 111–13.

1960s Andrew Acoya (Laguna Pueblo; 1943–) was the first American Indian from a Southwest tribe to attend Massachusetts Institute of Technology (MIT). His area of specialty was low-income housing and planning for underdeveloped areas. In 1969, Acoya became a project director for squatter-housing in Bogota, Colombia. He was also a member of a research project to study self-help housing programs in the United States.

Sources: *Biographical Dictionary of Indians of the Americas,* Vol. 1, p. 3; Champagne, ed., *The Native North American Almanac,* p. 997; Gridley, ed., *Indians of Today,* p. 6.

1963 George A. Gill (Omaha; 1925–) was the first American Indian to receive a M.A. in Indian education from Arizona State University, the first institution of higher learning in the nation to institute an Indian Education degree. Gill served in the U.S. Navy for twenty-five years on active and inactive duty. He served in Europe from 1943 to 1945 during World War II, the Mediterranean, and the Pacific. He was recalled to the front during the Korean Conflict and served from 1951 to 1955. Among the many medals he has received are the Navy Good Conduct Medal and the Victory Medal. Following his retirement from the navy, he taught in public schools and at the Phoenix Indian School in Phoenix, Arizona. From 1966 to 1970, he was director of the Center for Indian Education and edited the *Journal of American Indian Education,* the only professional journal to focus exclusively on Indian education. In 1960 he was appointed Arizona delegate to the White House Conference on Children and Youth. After earning his M.A., he taught at Arizona State Universtiy (ASU) as an assistant professor. He retired in 1983, but continued to work at ASU until 1991.

Sources: *Biographical Dictionary of Indians of the Americas,* Vol. 1, p. 245; Gridley, ed., *Indians of Today,* p. 86; Gill, George A., Personal communication to AnCita Benally, April 15, 1997; Gridley, ed., *Indians of Today,* p. 86.

1966 Rough Rock Demonstration School was established on the Navajo Indian Reservation. It was the first school to be completely controlled and administered by an American Indian community. Its curriculum was uniquely designed to include Navajo language, culture, and history as its core. The Navajo community was involved in the planning and implementation of the school and its curriculum.

Sources: Champagne, ed., *Chronology of Native North American History,* p. 347.

1969 The Navajo Community College, established in Many Farms, Arizona, was the first tribally chartered and controlled community college.

Sources: Szasz, *Education and the American Indian,* p. 155.

1969 The National Indian Education Association (NIEA) was organized in Minneapolis, Minnesota, in November 1969. Its aim was to improve the quality of education for American Indian children. In later years it brought together educators of Indian children from across the country to discuss issues and concerns related to educational improvement, methods, and strategies, and to advocate for greater attention to issues specific to educating American Indian children.

Sources: Champagne, ed., *Chronology of Native North American History,* p. 365.

1969 Pulitzer Prize-winner N. Scott Momaday (Kiowa/Cherokee; 1934–) established an American Indian literature program at the University of California at Berkeley, endeavoring to create a program that would aid in preserving American Indian legends and folklore.

See also: Literature, 1969.

Sources: *Biographical Dictionary of Indians of the Americas,* Vol. 1, p. 432.

1969 Henry Gatewood (Navajo; 1929–) was the first Navajo to become a superintendent of a public school district. He became superintendent of the Chinle public school district, the largest school district in the lower forty-eight states. Gatewood earned a B.S. and a M.A. from Northern Arizona State University. Active in many community organizations, Gatewood has sought to provide activities for youth. Among his many community service accomplishments was bringing in the first television to the western portion of the Navajo reservation. During the Korean Conflict, he served with the U.S. Army paratroopers for two years and received several medals.

Sources: *Biographical Dictionary of Indians of the Americas,* Vol. 1, p. 237; Gridley, ed., *Indians of Today,* pp. 168–69.

1969 The first Native studies program in Canada was established at Trent University in Peterborough, Ontario, in September of 1969.

Sources: Champagne, ed., *The Native North American Almanac,* p. 116; Champagne, ed., *Chronology of Native North American History,* p. 362.

1969 Will Antell (Ojibwa; 1935–) was the first president of the National Indian Education Association (NIEA). Born on the White Earth Reservation in Minnesota, Antell received his Ph.D. in educational administration from the University of Minnesota. In 1969, he became the state director of Indian Education in Minnesota. Antell taught at Harvard under the Bush Foundation fellowship from 1973 to 1974, when he became assistant commissioner of Education. This position entailed directing the department's special and compensatory education division.

Sources: *Biographical Dictionary of Indians of the Americas,*Vol. 1, p. 24.

1970 William G. Demmert Jr., (Tlingit/Dakota Sioux; 1934–), who was born in Klawock, Alaska, and was one of the founders and original directors of the National Indian Education Association (NIEA), attended the First Convocation of American Indian Scholars at Princeton University in 1970. Demmert received his doctorate in education from Harvard University. While at Harvard he became a consultant for the U.S. Senate. In this capacity, Demmert worked on the Indian Education Act (Title IV, PL 92-138) in 1973.

Sources: *Biographical Dictionary of Indians of the Americas,* Vol. 1, p. 188.

1970 The Northwestern Alberta Cree Band was the first Indian band to take control of its own school when it acquired the Blue Quill School from the Canadian government on September 1, 1970.

Sources: Champagne, ed., *Chronology of Native North American History,* p. 378; Champagne, ed., *The Native North American Almanac,* p. 118.

ca. 1970 Bahe Billy (Navajo) was the first member of his tribe to receive a Ph.D. in agriculture. He studied at the University of Arizona, where he earned M.S. and Ph.D. degrees. His interest in soil science began in his early youth, when he lived with his uncle on a farm. His dissertation discussed the principles of coordinating and combining fertilization methods and climatic conditions with vegetation and soil types to maximize range forage to increase the land's economic potential. He also studied the relationship between water quality and plant production. Billy has worked extensively with the Navajo Irrigation Project to turn non-arable land into commercially productive areas. In 1970 he was awarded the Lamanite Leadership Award from the Church of Jesus Christ of Latter-Day Saints (Mormons).

Sources: Gridley, ed., *Indians of Today,* p. 177.

ca. 1970s Samuel Billison (Navajo; 1925–) was the first American Indian to receive a Ph.D. in education from the University of Arizona. Billison was born in Ganado, Arizona. During his career, Billison worked as a high school principal in Oklahoma and Texas and a coordinator for the Neighborhood Youth Corps on the Navajo Reservation. Billison also functioned as an elected member of the Navajo Tribal Council. During World War II, he served in the U.S. Marines, participating in the landing on Iwo Jima.

Sources: Champagne, ed., *The Native North American Almanac,* pp. 1012–13; Gridley, ed., *Indians of Today,* p. 57.

1971 Deganawida-Quetzalcoatl University (DQU) was formally given 647 acres to establish an American Indian-Chicano university on April 2, 1971.

Sources: Champagne, ed., *Chronology of Native North American History,* p. 385.

1974 The American Indian Higher Education Consortium (AIHEC) was organized to provide tribal colleges with technical assistance.

Sources: Champagne, ed., *Chronology of Native North American History,* p. 397.

1976 Charlotte Anne Wilson Heth (Cherokee; 1937–) founded and became the director of the first American Indian studies master's degree program. A musician by training, Heth earned a Ph.D. in ethnomusicology from the University of California-Los Angeles. Her dissertation analyzed Cherokee stomp dance music. While continuing her work in American Indian music, she taught music to high school and college students and devoted two years to the Peace Corps, serving in Ethiopia. Her research has led her to the study of Cherokee hymns and music of the Iroquois condolence ceremony. Heth has been active in promoting quality educational opportunities for American Indian students; most importantly, she has been instrumental in educating Native and non-Native students about Native American musical forms.

Sources: Bataille, ed., *Native American Women,* pp. 109–110; Champagne, ed., *The Native North American Almanac,* p. 1071; Malinowski, ed., *Notable Native Americans,* pp. 189–90.

1976 Veronica Velarde Tiller (Jicarilla Apache) was the first Jicarilla Apache woman to earn a Ph.D. She studied history at the University of New Mexico, where she received her degree. In 1983, she published *The Jicarilla Apache Tribe: A History 1846–1970.*

Sources: Riley, Rhonda (Office of Higher Education, Jicarilla Apache Tribe, Dulce, New Mexico), Personal communication to AnCita Benally, March 1997.

1976 In May 1976, Saskatchewan Indian Federated College became the first college to come under Native control. An independent college integrated with the University of Regina, as an institution it aimed to further socio-economic development in Native communities. Enrollment was open to Native and non-Native students.

Sources: Champagne, ed., *The Native North American Almanac,* p. 121.

1982 The National Native American Honor Society was founded by Frank Dukepoo (Hopi; 1943–). The purpose of the Society was to encourage Indian students to achieve and to reward them for their efforts and accomplishments. To become a member, students must have attained a 4.0 grade-point average for at least one semester. Dukepoo has strictly enforced this requirement. In his view, if excellence is required, students will strive for it and there is no reason why Indian students cannot achieve this. The Society also sponsors a leadership course titled "Eagle Force," which is designed to build confidence and self-esteem.

Sources: Coutere, Cheryl, "Frank Dukepoo and the National Native American Honor Society," *Winds of Change,* Vol. 6, No. 4 (Autumn 1991), pp. 172–75.

1984 Elizabeth Anne Parent (Athabascan; 1941–) was the first Alaska Native woman to earn a Ph.D. She received her degree in education from Stanford University and wrote her dissertation on the relationships of Moravian missionaries with the Yupik people of the Bethel area. Parent was honored with a postdoctoral fellowship from the University of California-Los Angeles American Studies Center, a Ford Foundation fellowship in 1975, and a Danforth fellowship from 1975 to 1980.

Sources: "AISES News," *Winds of Change,* Vol. 5, No. 1 (Winter 1990), p. 73; Anderson, ed., *Ohoyo One Thousand,* p. 88; Champagne, ed., *The Native North American Almanac,* p. 1125; Johnson, Trebbe, "Betty Parent: Woman with a Mission," *Winds of Change,* Vol. 5, No. 4 (Autumn 1990), pp. 17–20.

1988 Karen Gayton Swisher (Standing Rock Sioux) became the first woman to direct the Center for Indian Education at Arizona State University and the first woman to serve as editor of the *Journal of American Indian Education* (JAIE). The Center for Indian Education, established in 1959, is the only center of its kind at a major university devoted to the study of Indian education. The JAIE, established in 1961, is the only international publication devoted exclusively to Indian education. Dr. Swisher was the sixth center director in its thirty-seven-year history.

Sources: Archives, Center for Indian Education, College of Education, Arizona State University.

1991 L. A. Napier (Cherokee) was the first Native American female director of Pennsylvania State University's Native American Indian leadership program. She was a 1989 graduate of the program, receiving her D.Ed. degree. In 1994 Napier received a W. K. Kellogg national fellowship, which she used to study indigenous leaders throughout the world and to develop a documentary from her interviews.

Sources: Napier, L. A. (Colorado), Personal communication to AnCita Benally, April 14, 1997; Tippeconnic, John W., III (Pennsylvania State University), Personal communication to AnCita Benally, April 14, 1997.

1991 Weber State University graduated seven Navajo women with teaching degrees, the largest number of graduates from one tribe graduating at the same time with teaching degrees from the same Utah college or university.

Sources: "Ambition to Succeed Pays Off for WSU Grads," *Navajo Times,* Vol. 31, No. 27 (July 3, 1991), p. A-6.

1991 Velma Kee (Navajo) was the first Navajo to win the Arizona State Spelling Bee contest, after correctly spelling "oxylophyte." A student at Tse Ho Tso Middle School in Fort Defiance, Arizona, she went on to represent Arizona in the National Spelling Bee, where she advanced to the sixth round. Kee became interested in the spelling contest in the fifth grade and trained by studying the dictionary for an hour each day.

Sources: Donovan, Bill, "Hot Speller Pupil First Navajo to Win State, Go to National Bee," *Arizona Republic,* May 28, 1991, p. B-1; Garcia, Patricia, "Victory by State Bee Spells Lots of Pride for Native Americans," *Arizona Republic,* April 7, 1991, p. B-6; "Kee Is State Champion," *Navajo Times,* Vol. 31, No. 15 (April 11, 1991), p. 6.

1996 The Josiah N. Moore Memorial Scholarship became the first scholarship offered at Arizona State University (ASU) to honor Native American alumni of ASU who have become leaders. It was also the first to be offered by the ASU Native American Alumni Association. (Josiah N. Moore was chairman of the Tohono O'odham Tribe.)

Sources: Darr, Deanna, *State Press,* Vol. 81, No. 39 (October 21, 1996), p. 9.

1996 Charles Cuny (Lakota Sioux) was the first person of Lakota descent and first non-Jesuit to serve as chairman of the board of directors for Red Cloud Indian School. As a youth he attended Red Cloud School and Holy Rosary School. As an adult he was principal at Red Cloud and served on its school board for four years.

Sources: *Indian Country Today,* Vol. 16, No. 20 (November 11–18, 1996).

GOVERNMENT

U.S. FEDERAL GOVERNMENT

1870 Hiram M. Revels (Lumbee) was the first person of American Indian ancestry to be elected a U.S. senator. He was of Lumbee and African American ancestry and was elected to represent the state of Mississippi.

Sources: *Indian Country Today,* November 26, 1992, p. A-2.

1870 With the support of the military, U.S. federal Indian policy initiated food and clothing rationing to American Indians placed on reservations, thereby beginning the government's responsibility to meet the social welfare needs of Indian people.

Sources: Dennis, *The American Indian, 1492–1976,* p. 37.

1878 For the first time physicians serving on Indian reservations were required, by a congressional act, to be graduates of medical colleges. At this time about half the Indian agencies had physicians on staff.

Sources: Leitch, *Chronology of the American Indian,* p. 173.

1887 Matthew Stanley Quay (Delaware) was the first individual of American Indian ancestry to be elected a U.S. senator from the state of Pennsylvania.

Sources: *Indian Country Today,* November 26, 1992, p. A-2.

1892 Charles D. Curtis (Kansa-Kaw/Osage; ca. 1870–1936) was the first person of American Indian ancestry to be elected to the U.S. House of Representatives, where he served longer than anyone else in Congress—forty years. He was later elected to the U.S. Senate, and to the office of vice president of the United States.

See also: Government: U.S. Federal, 1907, 1929.

Sources: *Biographical Dictionary of Indians of the Americas,* Vol. 1, pp. 174–75; *Indian Country Today,* November 26, 1992, p. A-1.

1907 Charles D. Curtis (Kansa-Kaw/Osage; ca. 1870–1936) was the first person of American Indian ancestry to be elected to the U.S. Senate, where he served until 1913, and again from 1915 until 1929, when he resigned his position to become vice president of the United States under Herbert Hoover.

See also: Government: U.S. Federal, 1892, 1929.

Sources: *Biographical Dictionary of Indians of the Americas,* Vol. 1, pp. 174–75; Champagne, ed., *Chronology of Native North American History,* p. 260.

1907 Robert L. Owen (Cherokee) was the first Cherokee and the first American Indian elected to represent Oklahoma in the U.S. Senate.

Sources: *Indian Country Today,* November 26, 1992, p. A-2.

1914 Houston Benge Tehee (Cherokee) was appointed by President Woodrow Wilson as the registrar of the U.S. Treasury, becoming the only American Indian to hold this government position. His signature was printed on all U.S. currency during his appointment. Tehee served in public office several times. He also served the Cherokee Tribe of Oklahoma as U.S. probate attorney. In 1908, he was elected mayor of Tahlequah, Oklahoma, the same year he established a private law practice. In 1911 he became a member of the Oklahoma House of Representatives but resigned to finish an unexpired term as county attorney. In 1926, he became attorney general for the state of Oklahoma and then became a member of the Supreme Court Commission. Tehee graduated from the Cherokee Male Seminary at Tahlequah and then attended Fort Worth University briefly. In his early twenties he worked as a bank cashier while studying law in the evenings. In addition to public service, he was active in business as well.

Sources: *Biographical Dictionary of Indians of the Americas,* Vol. 2, p. 741; Gridley, ed., *Indians of Today,* p. 116.

CHARLES D. CURTIS (CA. 1870–1936)

1929 Charles D. Curtis (Kansa-Kaw/Osage; ca. 1870–1936) was the first and only person of Native American ancestry to hold the office of vice president of the United States. Born in 1870, Curtis spent his early childhood attending Indian boarding schools in Oklahoma. He was a strong and active advocate of American Indian assimilation into white society.

In 1892, he was elected to the U.S. House of Representatives, where he served until 1906. Later, he was elected to the U.S. Senate, serving from 1907 to 1913 and 1915 to 1929. During that time he sponsored the Curtis Act (1898), calling for the dissolution of tribal governments and the institution of civil government in Indian Territory. The Curtis Act authorized the extinguishment of tribal title to Indian lands and paved the way for Oklahoma statehood by ending efforts to organize a state of Sequoyah, which would have been an exclusively American Indian state.

Charles Curtis.

In 1929 Curtis ran as Herbert Hoover's running mate in his campaign for the U.S. presidency. He became vice president of the United States from 1929 to 1933. Opponents attempted to use his American Indian ancestry against him; however, Curtis was able to gain political advantage from his Indian background and served in Washington, D.C., longer than any active politician of his time—forty years.

See also: Government: U.S. Federal, 1892, 1907.

Sources: *Biographical Dictionary of Indians of the Americas,* Vol. 1, pp. 174–75; Malinowski, ed., *Notable Native Americans,* pp. 105–107; Waldman, *Who Was Who in Native American History,* p. 89.

1943 Will Rogers Jr. (Cherokee) was elected as California's first American Indian representative to the U.S. Senate.

Sources: *Indian Country Today,* November 26, 1992, p. A-2.

1944 William Stigler (Choctaw) was the first member of his tribe to be elected to the U.S. House of Representatives. He was elected by the state of Oklahoma.

Sources: *Indian Country Today,* November 1992.

BENJAMIN REIFEL (1906–1990)

1961 Benjamin Reifel (Brulé Lakota Sioux; 1906–1990) was the first Native American to win a seat in the U.S. Congress from the state of South Dakota. A member of the Republican Party, he was the only American Indian in Congress at that time. He served for ten years, completing four consecutive terms. He studied chemistry and dairy farming, earning a B.S. and M.S. from South Dakota State College, and a M.A. and Ph.D. from Harvard University in 1952, where he studied public administration. After graduation from South Dakota State College, he worked in the Indian Service in 1933 as a U.S. farm extension agent at the Pine Ridge Reservation; and in 1935, he worked as an organizational field agent for the upper Great Plains states. During World War II, he served in the U.S. Army, primarily with the military police. When he left the service in 1946, he had attained the rank of major. That same year he became the first district tribal relations officer for the northern Great Plains states under the newly reorganized Bureau of Indian Affairs (BIA). In 1954, twenty-one years after his first job appointment with the Indian Service, Reifel returned to his home on the Pine Ridge Reservation as the first Indian superintendent of the BIA. After his retirement from Congress, Reifel served as the last commissioner of Indian Affairs in 1976. During his tenure with the Indian Service, the BIA, and Congress, he sought to bridge the gap between American Indian and white communities; and he sought to serve each with integrity and a strong sense of public responsibility.

Benjamin Reifel.

Sources: *Biographical Dictionary of Indians of the Americas,* Vol. 1, pp. 403–406; Botone, Barnie (Albuquerque Indian Center), Personal communication to AnCita Benally, October 5, 1996; Champagne, ed., *The Native North American Almanac,* pp. 1142–43; Gridley, ed., *Indians of Today,* p. 1; Malinowski, ed., *Notable Native Americans,* pp. 357–58.

1969 Brantley Blue (Lumbee) was the first American Indian to serve as Indian commissioner on the Indian Claims Commission. He was also the first Lumbee lawyer. He practiced law in Tennessee from 1955 to 1959 and became president of the Kingsport Bar Association in 1956. In 1969, Blue was awarded the Distinguished Alumnus Award by Pembrook College.

Sources: *Biographical Dictionary of Indians of the Americas,* Vol. 1, p. 79; Gridley, ed., *Indians of Today,* p. 88; *Wassaja,* Vol. 7, No. 5 (September 1979) p. 20.

1978 Claudeen Bates Arthur (Navajo) became the first Native American woman to attain the rank of field solicitor for the U.S. Department of the Interior. She served for four years. She also became the first and only Navajo woman to func-

Opposite page:
Vice President Charles Curtis standing at the Senate rostrum with the gavel he used to call the Senate to order.

tion as attorney general for the Navajo Nation, serving under the administration of Peterson Zah.

See also: Law and the Judiciary, 1983.

Sources: Anderson, ed., *Ohoyo One Thousand*, p. 11; Arthur, Claudeen Bates (St. Michaels, Arizona), Personal communication to AnCita Benally, March 1997; Bataille, ed., *Native American Women*, p. 14; Calvin, Barbara (administrative assistant, Office of the Attorney General, The Navajo Nation, Window Rock, Arizona), Personal communication to AnCita Benally, March 1997; Wood, Beth, and Tom Barry, "The Story of Three Navajo Women," *Integrateducation*, 16 (March/April 1978), pp. 33–35.

1987 Benjamin Nighthorse Campbell (Northern Cheyenne; 1933–) was the first American Indian from the state of Colorado to be elected to the U.S. House of Representatives.

See also: Government: U.S. Federal, 1992; and U.S. State, 1982; Sports: Judo, 1964.

Sources: *Indian Country Today*, November 1992.

1990 Virginia Robicheau's (Santa Clara Pueblo) appointment as Southwest regional curator marked the first time a person of Native American descent was offered that position. In this capacity, she was responsible for providing professional and technical guidance in the acquisition, storage, preservation, and administration of National Park Service museums in the six-state Southwest region that includes New Mexico, Texas, Oklahoma, Arkansas, Louisiana, Nebraska, and Arizona. In 1982 she was named museum curator at Bandelier. She earned a B.A. from New Mexico State University.

Sources: "National Park Service Hires First Indian Curator," *Navajo Times*, March 8, 1990, p. 15.

1991 Barbara Booher (Uintah-Ouray Ute) was the first American Indian woman to be appointed superintendent in the National Park Service. In 1991, she was named to supervise the Custer Battlefield National Monument. Booher was raised in Ft. Duchesne, Utah; her mother is Ute and her father is Cherokee.

Sources: Stapleton, Rob, and Susan Braine, "Booher Draws Strength from Wisdom of Elders," *Lakota Times*, Vol. 10, No. 27 (January 1, 1991), p. B-1.

1992 Benjamin Nighthorse Campbell (Northern Cheyenne; 1933–) was the first American Indian elected to the U.S. Senate since Charles D. Curtis in 1907. The second American Indian to serve in the Colorado legislature, Campbell was elected to the U.S. House of Representatives in 1987. An accomplished politician, Campbell also won a gold medal in judo at the 1963 Pan-American Games. He was a member of the 1964 U.S. Olympic Judo team. Moreover, as an artist, Campbell has won numerous awards for his innovative jewelry designs.

See also: Government: U.S. Federal, 1987; and U.S. State, 1982; Sports: Judo, 1964.

Opposite page:
Benjamin Nighthorse Campbell, first American Indian since Charles D. Curtis to be elected to the U.S. Senate.

Sources: Champagne, ed., *The Native North American Almanac*, p. 1024; Johansen and Grinde, eds., *The Encyclopedia of Native American Biography*, p. 59; Malinowski, ed., *Notable Native Americans*, pp. 64–65.

1994 Robert D. Ecoffey (Oglala Lakota Sioux) became the first Native American to hold the office of U.S. marshal in the Justice Department when he was appointed marshal for South Dakota. He was sworn into office at the Pine Ridge High School, the same school where he graduated. In addition to his appoint-

ment, he was presented with an eagle feather, symbolizing high accomplishment in battle.

Sources: Johansen and Grinde, eds., *The Encyclopedia of Native American Biography*, p. 122; McElwain, Judy, "Ecoffey Sworn In As Federal Marshall," *Indian Country Today*, March 23, 1994, p. B-1.

U.S. STATE GOVERNMENT

1926 Jessie Elizabeth Randolph Moore (Chickasaw; 1871–1956) was the first Indian woman, and the second woman in Oklahoma history, elected to a state office. In 1926, Moore was elected clerk of the Oklahoma Supreme Court. She passed the Oklahoma bar in 1923. When the Great Depression began, Moore organized a statewide emergency relief program as head of the Women's Division of Emergency Relief. By 1933, the federal government had adopted her relief plan and had implemented it on a national scale.

Sources: *Biographical Dictionary of Indians of the Americas*, Vol. 1, p. 440.

1932 Dolly Smith Akers (Assiniboin) was the first American Indian woman elected to the Montana state legislature. She also served as chair of the Federal Relations Committee. In addition, she functioned as a personal representative of the governor on two occasions. In 1934, Akers went to Washington, D.C., to request that American Indians be involved in all phases of the new public welfare act. In 1960, she became the governor of Montana's delegate to the White House Congress on Children and Youth. Holding the distinction of being the first woman ever elected to her tribal council, in 1960, she also became the first woman elected to chair her tribal council.

Sources: *Biographical Dictionary of Indians of the Americas*, Vol. 1, p. 16; Champagne, ed., *The Native North American Almanac*, p. 998; Dennis, ed., *The American Indian 1492–1970*, p. 97; Malinowski, ed., *Notable Native Americans*, p. 998.

Joseph R. Garry.

1957 Joseph R. Garry (Coeur d'Alene; 1910–) was the first American Indian elected to the Idaho state legislature. He served first as a representative, then as a senator. Eventually, he became the only Indian to serve in local, state, regional, and national offices simultaneously. Garry, who spoke only his Native language until the age of ten, also served as chairman of his tribal council and president of the Affiliated Tribes of Northwest Indians and the National Congress of American Indians (NCAI). Garry opposed federal termination policy, which attempted to disband tribal governments; and he chose to remain with his tribe to serve at a time when many other American Indians with similar educational and professional backgrounds were leaving American Indian society and joining mainstream American society. Garry is a descendant of Chief Spokane Garry, for whom the city of Spokane, Washington, was named. This ancestor also founded the first school in Washington state. Garry has won numerous honors for his service to his tribe, the state of Idaho, and national Indian organizations. Among his awards are the Outstanding American Indian Citizen from the American Indian Exposition in 1957, the Boy Scouts of America Award in 1957; the Golden Deeds Award for outstanding public service in 1961; and the Award of Merit from the Coeur d'Alene Tribe in 1963.

Sources: *Biographical Dictionary of Indians of the Americas*, Vol. 1, p. 236; Gridley, ed., *Indians of Today*, p. 104; Hoxie, ed., *Encyclopedia of North American Indians*, pp. 215–16.

1957 Constance Harper Paddock (Athabascan) was the first Alaska Native to hold the position of chief clerk of the Alaska House of Representatives. She first began working for the legislature as an assistant chief clerk and later became secretary to the secretary of state. She was born in Nenana, Alaska. Her paternal grandfather led the way for exploration into the Yukon and became the first person to raise the American flag on Mt. McKinley—the highest point in North America. Paddock has been actively involved in Alaska Native issues and concerns.

Sources: *Biographical Dictionary of Indians of the Americas,* Vol. 2, p. 507; Gridley, ed., *Indians of Today,* p. 385.

1959 William E. Beltz (Inuit; 1912–1960) was president of Alaska's first state Senate. Known as an advocate of Native rights, he also supported policies to help the working class, including minimum wage and workmen's compensation. He was elected to Alaska's House of Representatives territorial legislature in 1948 and the territorial senate in 1950. Beltz was the first Inuit to head either house.

Sources: *Biographical Dictionary of Indians of the Americas,* Vol. 1, p. 46.

1964 James D. Atcitty (Navajo; 1933–) from Shiprock, New Mexico, and Monroe Jymm (Navajo), from Tohatchi, New Mexico, were the first two American Indians elected to the New Mexico House of Representatives. Atcitty served from 1964 to 1966, Monroe from 1965 to 1967.

Sources: *Biographical Dictionary of Indians of the Americas,* Vol. 1, pp. 31, 327; Gridley, ed., *Indians of Today,* p. 63.

1966 Tom Lee (Navajo) became the first American Indian to be elected a state senator in New Mexico. Lee served in the military during World War II and was captured by Japanese soldiers. He participated in the Bataan March.

Sources: *Biographical Dictionary of Indians of the Americas,* Vol. 1, p. 354.

1966 Lloyd Lynn House (Navajo/Oneida; 1931–) was the first American Indian elected to the Arizona House of Representatives, serving from 1966 to 1968. House worked toward ensuring social security benefits for self-employed Navajos. This benefit also recognized medicine men as self-employed doctors. After serving in the state House, he went on to graduate from Arizona State University with a doctorate in education in 1973. House enlisted in the U.S. Marines and served in Korea. He is proficient in four languages: Navajo, Apache, English, and Spanish.

Sources: *Biographical Dictionary of Indians of the Americas,* Vol. 1, p. 291; Gridley, ed., *Indians of Today,* p. 360.

1970s Vivien Hailstone (Yurok/Karok; 1916–) was the first Native American to serve on the California Department of Parks and Recreation Commission. Concerned about pride and self-esteem among American Indian youth, and hoping to foster understanding and sensitivity about American Indians, Hailstone worked to promote Indian names for parks, develop a reburial policy for Indian remains and funerary objects, create an acquisition policy and procedure for gathering traditional materials, and eradicate stereotyping of American Indians.

Sources: Bataille, ed., *Native American Women,* pp. 100, 101.

1971 Arthur Raymond (Dakota Sioux/Oglala Lakota Sioux) was the first journalist and the first Sioux Indian to be elected to the North Dakota state legislature. He was born in Winner, South Dakota. He began his newspaper career at the *Mitchell Daily Republic*. In 1958, an article he wrote won the Associated Press' national first prize and was also chosen by the Pulitzer awards committee for award consideration. In 1971, Arthur became director of Indian studies at the University of North Dakota.

Sources: *Biographical Dictionary of Indians of the Americas,* Vol. 2, pp. 589–90; Gridley, *Contemporary American Indian Leaders,* pp. 156–61.

1982 Benjamin Nighthorse Campbell (Northern Cheyenne; 1933–) became the first American Indian to be elected to the Colorado House of Representatives. In addition to being a political leader, Campbell has also been an Olympic athlete, an educator, jewelry designer, artist, rancher, and author.

See also: Government: U.S. Federal, 1987, 1992; Sports: Judo, 1964.

Sources: Hirschfelder, *Artists and Craftspeople,* p. 101; Hirschfelder and Kreipe de Montaño, *The Native American Almanac,* p. 311; Malinowski, ed., *Notable Native Americans,* pp. 64–65.

1982 Maryetta Patch (Mohave) was the first Mohave tribal member elected as La Paz County supervisor of District 1 in Arizona. The district included the Colorado River Indian Reservation, where Patch was born and raised. She received a B.S. from Northern Arizona University in 1968 and a M.A. in 1977. Expertise in judicial matters enabled her to serve two terms as chief judge for the Colorado River Indian Tribes (CRIT). In 1984, she was elected to a four-year term as a council member of the CRIT. Patch was not only active as a leader within the CRIT community, she was involved at the state and national levels as well. As a leader she sought to improve educational and judicial policies and to bridge understanding among county, state, and tribal governments.

Sources: Colorado River Indian Tribes Enrollment Department *(for further information)*; Flores, Amelia, "Maryetta Patch Tsosie to Run for District 1 Supervisor," *Parker Pioneer,* September 30, 1982, p. 6; "Maryetta Patch Tsosie to Run for Supervisor of District 1," *Colorado River Indian Tribes Newsletter,* September 1982, p. 7.

1991 Larry Echohawk (Pawnee) became the first Native American elected as a state attorney general in the United States. In 1992, he was the first American Indian to head a state delegation to the Democratic National Convention, in which he participated as a speaker. In 1994, he ran unsuccessfully for the office of governor of Idaho. Echohawk attended Brigham Young University, where he played football and earned an undergraduate degree. In 1973, he received a J.D. from the University of Utah. He also served as general counsel for the Shoshoni/Bannock tribes at Fort Hall, Idaho. He was elected to the Idaho House of Representatives in 1982 and 1984.

Sources: Johansen and Grinde, *The Encyclopedia of Native American Biography,* pp. 121–22.

1992 Donald E. Loudner (Crow/Creek/Sioux) was the first Native American appointed to sit on South Dakota's Veterans Affairs Commission. His term runs through 1998. Loudner served in the U.S. Infantry during the Korean Conflict and

Larry Echohawk.

remained active in the National Guard and the Army Reserve. He retired with the rank of chief warrant officer after thirty-five years of service.

Sources: "Loudner Appointed to Vets Panel," *Indian Country Today*, November 5, 1992, p. B-3.

1996 Lynda Morgan Lovejoy (Navajo) was the first American Indian woman elected to the House of Representatives in the state of New Mexico. She was elected from District 69. In June 1991 she received the New Mexico Governor's Award for Outstanding New Mexico Women.

Sources: Albuquerque Indian Center, Fax to AnCita Benally, October 5, 1996; "Morgan, Coho Receive Governor's Award for 'Outstanding Women,'" *Navajo Times*, Vol. 31, No. 27 (July 3, 1991), p. A-5.

1997 Sally Ann Gonzales (Yaqui) and Debora Norris (Navajo) became the first Native American women to be elected to the Arizona House of Representatives. Gonzales, who is a Democrat, received her M.A. in multicultural education from the University of Arizona; she has been active in bilingual education and in education programs of the Pascua Yaqui Tribe. She is also a past member of the Yaqui Tribal Council in Tucson. She was elected by Legislative District 10. Norris grew up on the Tohono O'odham Reservation.

Sources: Office of Representative Sally Ann Gonzales (Arizona State Congressional Office, Phoenix, Arizona), Personal communication to AnCita Benally, March 1997; Office of Representative Debora Norris (Arizona Commission of Indian Affairs, The State of Arizona, Phoenix, Arizona), Personal communication to AnCita Benally, March 1997.

Debora Norris.

U.S. LOCAL GOVERNMENT

1974 Eben Hopson (Inuit; 1912–) was the first mayor of the North Slope Borough, Alaska. Hopson also became a state senator for Alaska. Before a career in politics, he served in World War II, earning a good conduct medal and a presidential unit citation.

Sources: *Biographical Dictionary of Indians of the Americas*, Vol. 1, p. 288.

ca. 1990 Mark Maryboy (Navajo) was the first elected Navajo commissioner for San Juan County, Utah. He was also the youngest person ever elected to a commission seat in Utah, taking office at the age of thirty. Known for his outspokenness and his forthright and knowledgeable leadership, he has gained national recognition. He earned a B.A. from the University of Utah. Maryboy is also a member of the Navajo Tribal Council, representing his constituents from the Aneth Chapter.

Sally Gonzales.

Sources: *Navajo Times*, June 14, 1990, p. 7.

1991 The community of Kayenta, Arizona, was the first town on the Navajo Reservation to apply for full-fledged township status.

Sources: "Kayenta Gets Support in Bid for Township," *Navajo Times*, Vol. 31, No. 22 (May 30, 1991), p. A-2.

CANADIAN GOVERNMENT

1870 John Norquay (Métis) was elected by acclamation to Manitoba's first legislature. He was first minister of public works and later minister of agriculture. In 1878, upon the resignation of the premier of Manitoba, he became premier of the province. During his tenure he was faced with the complex issue of French representation in government. He served until 1887, when his proposal to extend a railroad line to the United States instead of Manitoba backfired and he was forced to resign.

Sources: Champagne, ed., *Chronology of Native North American History,* p. 166; Champagne, ed., *The Native North American Almanac,* p. 1116.

1949 Frank Arthur Calder (Nishga) became the first American Indian elected as a provincial legislator in Canada. In that same year, he was also elected representative of the Cooperative Commonwealth Federation. In 1955, he became the first president of the Nishga Tribal Council, the first tribal council ever formed by that tribe. He was an outspoken advocate of enfranchisement for people of the First Nations. As a legislator he introduced the first court case pertaining to Native land claims in Canada—the Nishga land claim. The court ruled in *Calder v. The Queen* (1973) that aboriginal peoples of British Columbia possessed special rights to their ancestral lands that survived the establishment of the province. It was a landmark decision. Calder served as a member of the National Assembly of British Columbia for twenty-six years and as a provincial cabinet minister for a short time during the 1970s.

Sources: Champagne, ed., *Chronology of Native North American History,* pp. 272–73, 319; Champagne, ed., *The Native North American Almanac,* p. 1024; Gridley, ed., *Indians of Today,* p. 79.

James Gladstone, who bears the tribal name Akay-Na-Muka, which means "Many Guns," was the first Native member of the Canadian Senate.

1950 For the first time the Canadian government extended the right to vote in federal elections to the Inuit people on June 30, 1950; however, Indians were not given the same right. The government justified the discrepancy in treatment of Native peoples by the fact that Inuits were not exempt from taxation. Status Indians would be permitted to vote if they signed a waiver agreeing to relinquish their tax-exempt status.

Sources: Champagne, ed., *Chronology of Native North American History,* p. 321.

1958 James Gladstone (Blood) was appointed as Canada's first Native senator on February 1, 1958. He was also the president of the Indian Association of Alberta.

Sources: Champagne, ed., *Chronology of Native North American History,* p. 333.

1963 The provincial franchise (right to vote) was extended to Indians living on reserves in New Brunswick and Prince Edward Island.

Sources: Champagne, ed., *Chronology of Native North American History,* p. 342.

1967 The first in-depth study of Native treatment within the law was completed in August 1967. The study, entitled "Indians and the Law," was commissioned by the Department of Indian Affairs. It found police protection and legal services inadequate in serving Native individuals. It also reported that Indians comprised one-third of Canada's prison population.

Sources: Champagne, ed., *Chronology of Native North American History,* p. 350.

1968 Leonard Marchand (Interior Salish/Okanagon) was the first Native elected to the House of Commons on June 25, 1968. A member of the Liberal Party, he was re-elected in 1972 and 1974. He later became a member of the Cabinet. In 1965, he was the first Indian appointed as special assistant to a cabinet minister. In addition, Marchand was the first Indian to graduate from his hometown's high school. In 1979, when the Liberal government was defeated, he returned to British Columbia and worked as an administrator for the Nicola Valley Indian Bands. Holding a B.S. in agriculture and a M.S. in forestry, he returned to a career in agriculture. In 1984, Marchand was appointed to the Canadian Senate. Active in advancing Native causes, he was named Honorary Chief by the Okanagon.

Sources: Champagne, ed., *The Native North American Almanac,* pp. 116, 1100-1101; Gridley, ed., *Indians of Today,* p. 7.

1970s Frank Calder (Nishga) was the first treaty Indian elected to a Canadian provincial legislative assembly. A member of the National Assembly of British Columbia for twenty-six years, Calder earned a reputation of fighting for Indian rights. He was particularly active in land claims issues involving Indians. He initiated and won a landmark court case, *Calder v. The Queen,* in which the court declared that aboriginal peoples possessed special rights to their ancestral lands. He believed that the Indian reserve system created inferiority and dependency among Indians and worked to eliminate it. Calder also founded and became the first president of the Nishga Tribal Council, which united four clans from diverse communities.

Sources: *Biographical Dictionary of Indians of the Americas,* Vol. 1, p. 108; Champagne, ed., *The Native North American Almanac,* p. 1024.

1974 Ralph Steinhauer (Saddle Lake Cree) became the first Native in Canadian history to be sworn in as lieutenant governor of a Canadian province on July 2, 1974. He served as lieutenant governor of Alberta from 1974 to 1979. For his public service he was named a Companion of the Order of Canada. He also received two honorary doctoral degrees from the University of Alberta. In addition to serving the Province of Alberta, Steinhauer was formerly chief of the Saddle Lake Cree band and the founder of the Indian Association of Alberta.

Sources: Champagne, ed., *Chronology of Native North American History,* p. 399; Champagne, ed., *The Native North American Almanac,* p. 1170.

1977 The era of elected government was initiated by the Supreme Court of Canada when it upheld a federal order to establish an elected system of government at the Six Nations Reserve. Since the 1920s there had been strong opposition from traditional leaders to having elected councils.

Sources: Champagne, ed., *Chronology of Native North American History,* p. 411.

1979 Peter Freuchen Ittinuar (Inuit) was elected as a member of Parliament, becoming the first Inuit member.

Sources: Champagne, ed., *The Native North American Almanac,* p. 124.

1982 In March 1982 the Penticton Okanagon Band became the first Native band in British Columbia to settle a claim for compensation for land "cutoff" its reserve following the McKenna-McBride Commission Report in 1916. Of the thirty-four reserves who had lands removed from their control, twenty-one sued for compensation.

Sources: Champagne, ed., *Chronology of Native North American History,* p. 436.

1982 The Wagnatcook Micmac Band became the first Atlantic Canadian Native group to settle specific land claims disputes on March 27, 1982. They were compensated $1.2 million for lands improperly taken from them.

Sources: Champagne, ed., *Chronology of Native North American History,* p. 436.

1984 The Micmac of Newfoundland became the only recognized Indian band on the island of Newfoundland on June 12, 1984. They were recognized under the provisions of the Indian Act. In 1949, when Newfoundland joined Canada as its tenth province, both the provincial and federal governments specifically excluded Indians from the provincial franchise. Previously, the government of Newfoundland had not recognized the existence of Indians on the island. Consequently, they negotiated provincialhood with the federal government of Canada without regard to Natives on the island and any land surrendered by them.

Sources: Champagne, ed., *Chronology of Native North American History,* pp. 319, 445.

1988 Ethel Blondin (Dene) became the first Native woman elected to Parliament in November 1988. Running against two male opponents, she won by a landslide. She represented the Liberal Party. Born and raised in the Northwest Territories, Blondin began her leadership training at age fourteen when she was sent to Grandin College for leadership training. She received a bachelor of education degree from the University of Alberta in 1974. She has served as acting director of the Public Service of Canada's indigenous development program in Ottawa and as assistant deputy minister in the Department of Culture and Communications. An outspoken cabinet minister, Blondin has brought Native issues to the forefront of Canadian politics.

Sources: Champagne, ed., *The Native North American Almanac,* p. 1; Malinowski, ed., *Notable Native Americans,* pp. 41–42.

1988 Wilton Littlechild (Alberta Cree) was the first treaty Indian elected to the Canadian House of Commons, on November 21, 1988. A member of the Progressive Conservative Party, he represented the western Arctic riding (electoral district).

Sources: Champagne, ed., *Chronology of Native North American History,* p. 458; Champagne, ed., *The Native North American Almanac,* p. 1092.

1992 On October 7, 1992, the Canadian Royal Commission on Aboriginal Peoples issued its first report and called for the establishment of aboriginal self-government. The commission considered the latter a crucial first step to ameliorating the Canadian federal government's relationship with Native peoples.

Sources: Champagne, ed., *Chronology of Native North American History,* p. 488.

1993 In January 1993, W. Yvon Dumont (Métis) was appointed by Prime Minister Brian Mulroney as lieutenant governor of Manitoba, becoming the first Native to attain such a distinction. He was likely the youngest Native American to enter into Native political leadership. At the age of sixteen he was elected secretary-treasurer of the St. Laurent local of the Manitoba Métis Federation. At twenty-one he became president of the Native Council of Canada, a national organization representing non-status Indians and Métis. In 1984, he was elected president of the Manitoba Métis Federation and hired Thomas Berger, a noted Indian rights activist, to pursue a Métis land claim. Under Dumont's leadership, the Métis Federation's financial affairs were stabilized and its political clout was strengthened.

Sources: Champagne, ed., *Chronology of Native North American History,* p. 323; Champagne, ed., *The Native North American Almanac,* p. 1050.

GOVERNMENT OF MEXICO

1835 Vacant land was set aside by the Mexican government for peaceful, "civilized" American Indians who may have been brought or introduced into Texas.

Sources: Dennis, *The American Indian, 1492–1976,* p. 27.

1861 Pablo Benito Juarez (Zapotec) was elected president of Mexico, becoming the first Native American to head a national government. He was also the first civilian in Mexico ever elected president. He was re-elected in 1864 and served until 1871. Previously, he had been appointed constitutional governor in 1857. Orphaned at age three, Juarez spoke no Spanish until he was twelve. He attended law school and was admitted to the bar in Oaxaca in 1834. By 1847 he was governor of the state of Oaxaca. He joined the Mexican revolutionaries and was appointed minister of justice by Juan Alvarez, and in that capacity he issued his famous "Ley Juarez," a set of reform measures that guaranteed civilians more power. After becoming chief justice of the Mexican Supreme Court, he was appointed constitutional governor, first in line to the presidency, in 1857. When the provisional president was forced from office, Juarez succeeded him to the presidency of Mexico. Although the United States recognized his government, political conservatives and the clergy opposed the Ley Juarez and led an opposition that triggered a civil war—the War of Reform. Passage of the Ley Juarez put a mandatory separation between the government and the Catholic church and increased civilian authority. Known as the "Mexican Washington," Juarez was a strong advocate on the side of the common masses, particularly Indians.

Sources: *Biographical Dictionary of Indians of the Americas,* Vol. 1, p. 324; Jimenez, *The Mexican American Heritage,* p. 115; Wearne, *The Return of the Indian,* p. 198.

1940 The first Interamerican Indian Congress was held in Patzcuaro, Michoacán, Mexico. It marked a major turning point for Indian affairs in Latin America. Each participating American state was to set up an Indian institute that would be devoted to Indian concerns. The Interamerican Indian Institute, the central institute, was to be a clearinghouse of information and communication for all of the states. The congress was sponsored by the Pan-American Union and the Organization of American States.

Sources: Leitch, *Chronology of the American Indian,* p. 214; Washburn, *Handbook of North American Indians,* p. 108.

CENTRAL AND SOUTH AMERICAN GOVERNMENT

1844 Rafael Carrera (mixed-blood) became the first president of independent Guatemala. Beginning in 1838, he led a revolt against the Spanish in a series of battles. As he was about to storm Guatemala City, the Spanish capital, a large ransom dissuaded him and he turned his attention instead to Mita, a smaller city. He and his followers established themselves there and declared themselves rulers.

Sources: Leitch, *Chronology of the American Indian,* p. 150.

1983 Mario Juruna (Xavante) became the first person of indigenous ancestry elected as a member of the Brazilian Congress.

Sources: Wearne, *Return of the Indian,* p. 200.

1993 Victor Hugo Cardenas (Aymara) became the first indigenous person to assume an executive-level leadership position of a country since Benito Juarez became president of Mexico. He was the first Native American elected vice president of Bolivia and served in this office during the administration of Gonzolo Sanchez de Lozada. At his inaugural he not only donned the vice-presidential sash, but wore a vicuna scarf as well, the traditional Aymara badge of authority. In his speech he used the country's three main indigenous languages—Aymara, Guarani, and Quechua—to declare that Bolivia had entered a new era, emphasizing that Bolivia was a nation of nations and that it was imperative that this multicultural, multiethnic, and pluricultural character be acknowledged. He further petitioned that Bolivians be united, abandoning centuries of exclusionary practices. Cardenas' thought reflected the new movement among indigenous peoples to reassert themselves and to take control of their future.

Sources: Wearne, *Return of the Indian,* pp. 1, 203.

TRIBAL GOVERNMENT

AMERICAN INDIAN

1715 The Iroquois Confederacy formed into the Indian League of Nations. The Tuscarora joined the Cayuga, Mohawk, Onondaga, Oneida, and Seneca, the five original members of the Iroquois Confederacy.

Sources: Dennis, *The American Indian, 1492–1976,* p. 12.

1778 White Eyes (Delaware), also known as Koquethagechton, appeared before the Congress of Philadelphia and proposed that the Delaware tribe constitute the fourteenth state in the original union of the thirteen colonies. The points were incorporated into the Treaty of Pittsburgh, September 17, 1778. He was killed, however, and the proposition was never implemented.

Sources: *Biographical Dictionary of Indians of the Americas,*Vol. 2, p. 817; Johansen and Grinde, *The Encyclopedia of Native American Biography,* p. 420.

1840 A four-nation alliance was established between the Cheyenne, Kiowa, Arapaho, and Comanche nations at a great council on the Arkansas River. Despite wars with other tribes and with the United States, the alliance has not been broken.

Sources: Leitch, *Chronology of the American Indian,* p. 122.

1851 The treaty of Fort Laramie was the first U.S. treaty drafted that defined the basis of future dealings with the United States in the northern Plains region. It was also the first treaty to include so many different tribes. The treaty of Fort Laramie was attended by about ten thousand members of the Sioux, Cheyenne, Arapaho, Crow, Arikara, Assiniboin, and several other western tribes. In the treaty, Plains tribes agreed to allow settlers to travel the Oregon Trail without attack and not to interfere with the building of roads and construction of forts in Indian country. It remained in effect for forty years.

Sources: Leitch, *Chronology of the American Indian,* p. 155.

1854 The confederation of the Five Civilized Tribes began when the Cherokee, Chickasaw, Choctaw, Creek, and Seminole tribes united to safeguard their rights and to support each other. In their eastern homelands they had fought and competed for the same lands and political power, but necessity brought them together. The federation was loosely organized in its beginnings, but it developed into a powerful confederacy. It succeeded in providing the crucial political clout to negotiate effectively with U.S. government officials and to counter their efforts to divest the Confederacy members of lands and sovereignty. It was officially disbanded in 1907 by the United States when it abolished tribal governments in Oklahoma and forbade members of the Five Tribes to elect their own leaders.

Sources: Leitch, *Chronology of the American Indian,* p. 155.

1854 Cloudman (Mdewakanton Dakota Sioux; ca. 1790–1862), along with his brother Paul Mazakutemani, founded Hazelwood Republic, a Christian Indian community with a constitutional government. Earlier he had established Lake Calhoun Village, the site of present-day Minneapolis.

Sources: Waldman, *Who Was Who in Native American History,* pp. 71, 226.

1854 Paul Mazakutemani (Mdewakanton Dakota Sioux; ca. 1806–1885) was elected the first president of Hazelwood Republic. He and his brother Cloudman founded the community, which had a constitutional government and was established especially for American Indian people who had converted to Christianity. Mazakutemani himself was a Christian convert and supported missionary work among his people. During the Minnesota Uprising, he worked for peace and helped organize the pro-white Friendly Soldier's Lodge with Cloudman, Akipa, Mazonmani, and Gabriel Renville.

Sources: Waldman, *Who Was Who in American Indian History,* pp. 71, 226.

1856 Cyrus Harris (Chickasaw; 1817–1888) was the first governor of the Chickasaw Nation after the tribe adopted the new constitution in 1856 in Indian Territory.

Sources: *Biographical Dictionary of Indians of the Americas,* Vol. 1, p. 267.

1860 Chief George Hudson (Choctaw; 1808–1865) was the first principal chief of the Choctaw Nation under the new Doaksville Constitution adopted in January 1860.

Sources: *Biographical Dictionary of Indians of the Americas,* Vol. 1, p. 298.

1868 Delgadito (Navajo) was the only leader to actually sign the 1868 treaty between the Navajo Nation and the U.S. government. He wanted future generations of youth to know that they had a leader who could do as well as the white man. The other leaders marked "X"s. Delgadito may also have been the first Navajo silversmith, having learned smithing from a fort smith and then employing the smithing techniques to silver jewelry.

Sources: *Biographical Dictionary of Indians of the Americas,* Vol. 1, p. 184; Waldman, *Who Was Who in Native American History,* p. 97.

1868 Red Cloud (Oglala Lakota Sioux; 1822–1909) was the only American Indian leader to force the United States to retreat from assuming tribal territory. In the Treaty of Fort Laramie, signed on November 6, 1868, the United States agreed to abandon the building of forts along the Bozeman Trail. Red Cloud refused to sign unless the United States agreed to carry out the terms of the treaty completely. Thereafter, Red Cloud kept his part of the agreement to the Treaty. He

visited Washington and New York as a delegate to plead for the cause of his people. During the 1870s and 1880s, he fought against the reservation system and the
U.S. military, but always counseled peace first. He met Othniel C. March, a Yale
professor who wanted to search for dinosaur bones on Lakota lands. Red Cloud
granted permission as March promised to investigate the allegations of gross mis-
management of the Pine Ridge Reservation. He kept his promise, which resulted
in a congressional investigation and newspaper exposes of the scandal. Red Cloud
and March remained friends thereafter. Red Cloud died on the Pine Ridge
Reservation, old and blind, on December 10, 1909. In his prime, he was a highly
acclaimed warrior, known for his skill and bravery. He assumed the chieftainship
when he was chosen over Young Man Afraid of His Horses (Oglala Lakota Sioux;
1830–1900), the hereditary claimant. As a leader, he was highly respected and
admired for his skills as a statesman and military man, and for his compassion.

Sources: Dockstader, *Great North American Indians,* pp. 231–34; Johansen and Grinde, *The
Encyclopedia of Native American Biography,* pp. 311–13.

1922 Alice Brown Davis (Seminole; 1852–1935) became the first woman chief of
the Seminole tribe when President Warren Harding appointed her to fill this position in 1922. She addressed the many Seminoles who protested her appointment
because she was a woman, asserting that ability and dedication were more crucial
characteristics in a leader than maleness. A very prominent member of her tribe
even before her role as chief, Davis had been superintendent of the Seminole girls'
school and active in resisting the takeover of Indian affairs by the state government after Oklahoma statehood in 1907. She was also an expert interpreter and
was often called upon to serve as a court interpreter. Her concern that the
Seminole people receive fair treatment from the government and by oil contrac-
tors led her to become involved in negotiations with the tribal government over
oil leases. Eventually this activity lead to her appointment as chief of the
Seminole, a position she held until her death in 1935.

Alice Brown Davis.

Sources: *Biographical Dictionary of Indians of the Americas,* Vol. 1, p. 178; Malinowski, ed., *Notable
Native Americans,* p. 1040; *Self Guiding Tour of the National Hall of Fame for Famous American
Indians and Anadarko Visitors' Center,* p. 5.

1923 Henry Chee Dodge (Navajo; 1860–1947) became the first chairman of the
Navajo Tribal Council on July 27, 1923. In his youth, Dodge was the first interpreter who could speak both Navajo and English. In 1884, he was appointed head
Navajo chief by commissioner of Indian Affairs Dennis M. Riordan. His appointment by a non-Navajo to such an elevated position marked the end of the traditional system of electing leaders and was an indication of how much autonomy
the Navajo had lost.

Dodge was also a successful businessman, investing in trading posts and
sheep ranching. He worked for Indian agents in resolving disputes between the
Navajo and government officials, encouraging education and convincing parents
to send their children to school, and urging the development of natural resources.
When oil, gas, and coal were discovered on the Navajo Reservation, Dodge began
urging the development of a centralized, modern Navajo government that could
deal with lease negotiations and agreements. Strong encouragement from the
Department of the Interior spurred the movement for the establishment of a trib-

Henry Chee Dodge.

al council among the Navajo. In 1922, a three-man business council was formed, which signed some leases for oil exploration. However, when outsiders petitioned for increased control over the leases, New Mexico territorial governor Herbert J. Hagerman was given authority to sign leases on behalf of the six Navajo jurisdictions. Finally, on July 7, 1923, the Navajo Tribal Council was formed and Dodge was elected the first Council chairman. He served until 1928 and was re-elected in 1942 and 1946. He died in office in 1947.

Sources: *Biographical Dictionary of Indians of the Americas,* Vol. 1, p. 191; Malinowski, ed., *Notable Native Americans,* pp. 127–29; Waldman, *Who Was Who in Native American History,* p.100.

1935 Sam Jimulla (Yavapai) was the first chief of the Prescott Yavapai Indian Tribal Council after settlement on a reservation. He was appointed chief by the commissioner of Indian Affairs and at the same time was elected by his own people. He died in 1940 and was succeeded by his wife Viola Pelhame Jimulla, who was then succeeded by her daughter Grace Mitchell.

Sources: Bataille, ed., *Native American Women,* p. 125.

1937 Jay Gould (Mohave; 1894–1992) was the first tribal chairman of the Fort Mohave Indian Tribes. Born on July 15, 1894, on the Fort Mohave Indian Reservation, Gould received his education from boarding schools at Ft. Mohave and Albuquerque, New Mexico. He attended Haskell Institutite in Lawrence Kansas, where he studied business. In 1924, he began his own farming business on the Colorado Indian Reservation. He became tribal chairman and remained involved in tribal government until his retirement in 1970, at which time he was recognized by President Richard Nixon for his outstanding commitment and service to the people of the Colorado River Indian Tribes (CRIT).

As a leader, Gould was dedicated to obtaining title for the 264 thousand acres of land that comprised the reservation, established in 1865. Consequently, one of the greatest accomplishments he lived to see was the 1966 bestowal by the U.S. Congress of legal title of reservation lands to CRIT. Until his death in October 1992, he remained active, particularly as a member of the first Mohave Elders group, a special group formed to advise the tribal council on traditional matters related to tribal affairs.

Sources: Bucci, G. "Long-time Leader Mourned by CRIT," *Parker Pioneer,* October 21, 1992, p. 21; Jay Gould, Personal Information Awards and Certificates, CRIT Library/Archive 970.2-MA-G-862; CRIT Tribal Enrollment Department *(for further information).*

1940 Viola Pelhame Jimulla (Yavapai) was elected as the first woman chief upon the death of her husband, Sam Jimulla. She handled the affairs of the tribal council until her death in 1966, after which her daughter Grace Mitchell succeeded her. In addition to public service in the political field, Jimulla was also a recognized spiritual leader. In 1922, she was named elder of the Yavapai Indian Mission (Presbyterian), and, in 1957, she helped found the Trinity Presbyterian Church in Prescott, Arizona. In addition, she was an accomplished basket weaver and teacher of the craft.

Sources: Bataille, ed., *Native American Women,* pp. 124–25; Khera, Sigrid, and Patricia S. Mariella, "Yavapai," in *Handbook of North American Indians,* Vol. 10: *History of Indian-White Relations,* edited by Alfonso Ortiz, pp. 44–45.

Opposite page:
Red Cloud, the only American Indian chief to force a U.S. government retreat from the Bozeman Trail.

1942 Mountain Chief (Blackfoot; ca. 1848–1942) was the last hereditary chief of the Blackfoot Nation.

Sources: *Biographical Dictionary of Indians of the Americas,* Vol. 1, p. 449.

1943 Agnes Wilson Savilla (Mohave; 1900–1983) was the first woman elected to serve in the Colorado River Tribal Council. She served until 1968. Born and raised on the Colorado River Indian Tribes (CRIT) reservation, Savilla was competent and knowledgeable in her tribal language and culture and served as an interpreter for two well-known anthropologists, Alfred Kroeber and George Devereux. Her determination and strength as a leader brought her recognition as a tribal leader within the state of Arizona and nationally. Her honors include: the Special Service Award, Outstanding Arizona Indians citation awarded by the Indian Basketball Association, 1960; Citation of Merit for Outstanding Contribution in Encouraging Employment of the Handicapped, Social Advisory Group to Governor of Arizona; the Arizona Fair Lady Award, 1964; U.S. Delegate to the Fifth Inter-American Indian Conference in Ecuador, 1964; U.S. Presidential Commendation, 1970; and selection as a delegate to the first White House Conference on Aging, 1971. In 1976, Savilla was presented with the Lady Georgette Award for community service by the Parker Area Chamber of Commerce. In 1979, she was recognized and honored by the Save the Children for Cultural Enhancement for Indian Reservation Youth at the first National Indian Child Conference. In 1980, CRIT dedicated the "Agnes Wilson Bridge." Savilla established a children's home and housing quarters for the elderly, and, as a tribal leader, she dedicated tireless service for the welfare and education of her tribal people.

Sources: *Biographical Dictionary of Indians of the Americas,* Vol. 2, p. 673; Colorado River Enrollment Department *(for further information)*; Flores, Amelia (librarian/archivist, Colorado River Indian Tribes Library/Archives), Personal communication to AnCita Benally, November 1996; Gridley, ed., *Indians of Today,* p. 441; Sharp, G. "Touch of a Guiding Hand," *Manitoba Messenger,* September 19, 1980, p. 5; Travis, J. "Agnes Wilson Savilla Succumbs," *Parker Pioneer,* June 23, 1983, pp. 1, 12.

1952 D'Arcy McNickle (Flathead; 1904–1977) created and served as first director of the American Indian Development Program in 1952. McNickle designed this project to focus on leadership training and group development within American Indian communities. Leading a varied professional life, McNickle was an Indian rights activist, scholar, novelist, and administrator. McNickle had worked for the Bureau of Indian Affairs (BIA) for seventeen years, co-founded the National Congress of American Indians (NCAI) in 1946, and served as a professor on the Regina campus of the University of Saskatchewan, where he was asked to organize an anthropology department. He attended Oxford University in England and lived in Paris, France, for a time. He became a Guggenheim fellow in 1963. In addition, McNickle wrote several novels in which he addressed the problems of ethnic identity and belonging that are often faced by mixed-bloods like himself. Finally, he functioned as the founding director of the Newberry Library's Center for the History of the American Indian, which was later named after him as the D'Arcy McNickle Center.

Sources: *Biographical Dictionary of Indians of the Americas,* Vol. 1, p. 414; Champagne, ed., *The Native North American Almanac,* p. 1105; Malinowski, ed., *Notable Native Americans,* pp. 267–69.

1959 The Navajo Tribal Council created the first Navajo Tribal Court with a complex and extensive organization. The large population and expansive reservation required a complex court system; and the Navajo Courts have innovated a unique court called "Peacemaker Court," which has been studied by other tribes and countries, including the United States. Based on the traditional justice system of the Navajo Nation, these courts are designed to settle disputes and avoid lengthy litigation.

Sources: Shebala, Mary, "And Then, There Were Two," *Navajo Times,* Vol. 32 No. 1 (December 31, 1991), p. 1.

1967 Betty Mae Tiger Jumper (Florida Seminole; 1923–) was the first woman elected to chair the Seminole Tribal Council. She began her public service career as a nurse in Oklahoma. When she returned to Florida she was assigned to serve the Seminoles on their three reservations, as well as the Miccosukee, who lived along the Tamiami Trail. In 1957, she was elected vice-chair of the newly formed Seminole Tribal Council. She then served as a member of the board of directors before she was asked to run for chair.

In addition to the distinction of being the first woman to serve as executive of the Seminole tribal government, Jumper and a cousin were the first Seminoles to graduate from high school. Against tribal law, they attended public school at a time when American Indians were not welcome in public white schools. Jumper's determination to attend school was a traumatic departure from the wishes of her family.

Sources: Bataille, ed., *Native American Women,* pp. 131–32; *Biographical Dictionary of Indians of the Americas,* Vol. 1, p. 326; Gridley, ed., *Indians of Today,* pp. 283–84; Malinowski, ed., *Notable Native Americans,* pp. 219–21.

1971 Overton James (Chickasaw; 1925–) was the first elected governor of the Chickasaw Nation since Oklahoma became a state. One of the provisions of Oklahoma statehood was the abolishment of Indian governments and the cessation of Indian people electing their own leaders. All leaders were federally appointed. James' first term in office was through a federal appointment in 1963. He was the twenty-seventh governor and the youngest one.

Sources: *Biographical Dictionary of Indians of the Americas,* Vol. 1, p. 316; Gridley, ed., *Indians of Today,* p. 222.

1971 W. W. Keeler (Cherokee) became the first principal chief elected by the Cherokee people since Oklahoma statehood. In 1949, he was federally appointed to serve in that office by President Harry S Truman, as decreed by the terms allowing Oklahoma to receive statehood. Indian tribal governments were abolished and Indians were denied the right to elect their own leaders. In 1954, Keeler was appointed as chief indefinitely; and during his tenure in office he was a controversial figure. Many traditional Cherokee opposed him and questioned his eligibility (he was only one-sixteenth Cherokee) to head the tribal government.

Moreover, his close affiliation with Phillips Petroleum Company caused concern. Keeler, who had begun working for the company in 1928, advanced through the ranks until he was named chief executive officer and chairman. He had a close association with many political leaders, especially those in a position to affect the treatment of Cherokee lands and natural resources. In 1973, he was convicted of making illegal contributions to Richard Nixon's 1972 presidential campaign. Further, he and other Phillips executives pleaded guilty to concealing corporate funds from the Internal Revenue Service. His manipulation of tribal monies and land came under question. Keeler retired in 1975 and endorsed Ross Swimmer for tribal executive leadership.

Although his time in office was wracked with scandal, he stabilized Cherokee finances and contributed to advancing Cherokee and American Indian issues to

Betty Mae Jumper, the first woman to lead the Seminole Tribal Council.

the forefront of national politics. In the years before his death, his reputation in Cherokee politics improved, and in 1987 a group of new buildings was named in his honor—the W. W. Keeler Complex. His other honors include the All-American Indian Award in 1957, Outstanding American Indian of the Year in 1961, and election to the Oklahoma Hall of Fame in 1966.

Sources: Champagne, ed., *The Native North American Almanac,* pp. 1081–82; Davis, ed., *Native America in the Twentieth Century,* p. 98; Malinowski, ed., *Notable Native Americans,* pp. 223–25.

1971 The National Tribal Chairmen's Association was formed in February 1971 in response to a meeting of tribal leaders from fifty reservations and twelve states who wished to raise awareness on how reservation people could affect national American Indian policy making. A concern of reservation leaders was that urban and militant American Indian activists were steering the course of recent American Indian policy and neglecting the needs and concerns of reservation people.

Sources: Champagne, ed., *Chronology of Native North American History,* p. 384.

1972 Teacher and American Indian activist Beatrice Gentry (Wampanoag; 1910–) helped establish the first Massachusetts Indian Commission in the twentieth century while she served on the Massachusetts Commission on Indian Affairs. She also functioned as president of the Wampanoag Tribal Council of Gay Head from 1972 to 1976. During this time Gentry helped create a more modern organization of tribal government.

Sources: *Biographical Dictionary of Indians of the Americas,* Vol. 1, p. 238.

1985 Wilma Mankiller (Cherokee; 1945–) became the first female principal chief of the Cherokee Nation in 1985, and the first woman to lead an American Indian tribe this large. Replacing Ross Swimmer, who resigned to take a position in Washington, D.C., Mankiller served as chief from 1985 to 1995. She had been deputy chief since 1983 and next in line to head the tribal government. In 1987, she was elected in her own right and again in 1991.

Before becoming a principal chief, Mankiller overcame several personal tragedies. As a child, she and her family were relocated to California as part of the government's relocation program. As a young adult, she took part in the Alcatraz takeover by Indian rights activists. The deaths of her brother and father, and her own brush with death, in an automobile accident, in addition to a serious illness, spurred her to use her time and talents to help others. She worked as community development director for the Cherokee Tribe, and in this role she led the Bell Community Project, which provided access to running water for the entire Cherokee community. In 1987, Mankiller was the first Native American honored as *Ms.* magazine's Woman of the Year. In 1994, she was entered into the Woman's Hall of Fame in New York City.

Sources: *Biographical Dictionary of Indians of the Americas,* Vol. 1, p. 391; Champagne, ed., *The Native North American Almanac,* pp. 1098–99; Malinowski, ed., *Notable Native Americans,* pp. 256–58.

1987 Elsie Gardner Ricklefs (Hoopa) was the first woman elected to chair the Hoopa Tribal Council. As chairwoman Ricklefs led her tribe to establish a new hospital after the Indian hospital was closed. A strong advocate of education and political involvement, and convinced that both are essential to the future of Native Americans, Ricklefs also served as regional vice president for the National Congress of American Indians (NCAI).

Sources: *Biographical Dictionary of Indians of the Americas,* Vol. 2, p. 611; Gridley, ed., *Indians of Today,* pp. 302–303.

Wilma Mankiller, the first woman to serve as Principal Chief of the Cherokee Nation of Oklahoma.

1987 Verna Olguin Williamson (Isleta Pueblo) became the first woman elected governor of the Isleta Pueblo.

Sources: Champagne, ed., *Chronology of Native North American History,* p. 453.

1992 Marge Anderson (Ojibwa) was the first and only woman elected as chief executive of the Mille Lacs Band Ojibwa within the six-band Chippewa Tribe in Minnesota. Under her leadership the band has utilized its casino revenues to build new schools on the reservation. In 1996, the Minnesota Education Association honored her as Outstanding American Indian Tribal Official.

Sources: "Anderson Re-elected as Chief Executive," *Mille Lacs Register,* June 19, 1996; "Mille Lacs Chief Executive Honored," *Indian Country Today,* Vol. 16 No. 22 (December 2, 1996), p. A-2.

1993 Octaviana V. Trujillo (Yaqui) was the first woman elected to chair the Pascua Yaqui Tribal Council.

Sources: Trujillo, Octaviana, Personal communication to AnCita Benally, November 1995.

Marge Anderson.

INDIAN AFFAIRS

1824 The Bureau of Indian Affairs (BIA) was created by John C. Calhoun, the Secretary of the Department of War. Thomas L. McKenney was appointed to oversee the office.

Sources: Leitch, *Chronology of the American Indian,* p. 142.

1832 The office of U.S. commissioner of Indian Affairs was created by Congress in the Department of War. In 1834 the office was reorganized and the U.S. Department of Indian Affairs was created by Congress. The new office was given authority over all issues concerning U.S. relations with indigenous peoples in the United States.

Sources: Leitch, *Chronology of the American Indian,* pp. 146, 148.

1849 Regulation of Indian affairs was transferred out of the War Department of the Interior despite objections from reformers advocating the creation of a separate department devoted exclusively to Indian affairs.

Sources: Champagne, ed., *Native America,* p. 173; Dennis, *The American Indian, 1492–1976,* pp. 29, 30; Leitch, *Chronology of the American Indian,* p. 154.

1854 American Indian preference in hiring was enacted for the first time by the Indian Office. When two qualified persons were under consideration, persons of one-fourth or more Indian blood were to be given preference. Today most employees of the Bureau of Indian Affairs (BIA) are of American Indian descent.

Sources: Dennis, *The American Indian, 1492–1976,* p. 32.

1868 Ely S. Parker (Seneca; 1828–1895) was appointed by President Ulysses S. Grant as the first American Indian commissioner of Indian Affairs. Born in 1828 at Indian Falls near New York, Parker studied law, however, he was denied entry to the bar; his American Indian heritage made him ineligible to be an American citizen. In 1851, he published with Lewis H. Morgan a scientific study of North American Indian tribes entitled *League of the Iroquois.* He then studied civil engineering and worked on a number of contracts, including the Genesee Valley Canal and the Erie Canal, until he enlisted in the Union Army during the Civil War.

Again, he was denied a commission by the governor of New York and the U.S. secretary of war because of his non-citizen status. Parker served with the Seventh Corps of the Army Corps of Engineers instead, and was eventually commissioned captain of engineers. He became Grant's staff officer and in 1864, he became lieutenant-colonel and military secretary to General Grant. On April 8, 1865, Parker transcribed the final copy of the surrender by General Robert E. Lee and his Confederate Army. At the end of the war he was promoted to brigadier general, the highest military rank ever held by an Indian in the U.S. Army.

In 1868, when Grant was elected U.S. President, he appointed Parker as commissioner of Indian Affairs. During his tenure as commissioner, he worked to rectify past injustices against American Indians, but political opposition prevented his success and he resigned in 1871. He died August 31, 1895.

Sources: *Biographical Dictionary of Indians of the Americas,* Vol. 2, pp. 514–15; Champagne, ed., *The Native North American Almanac,* p. 1126; Dockstader, *Great North American Indians,* pp. 204–206; Malinowski, ed., *Notable Native Americans,* pp. 317–19.

1924 The Indian Health Division was created within the Bureau of Indian Affairs (BIA).

Sources: Dennis, *The American Indian, 1492–1976,* p. 52.

1934 Robert Yellowtail (Crow) was the first American Indian to be elected superintendent of the Crow Agency in Montana. He was elected by his tribe.

Sources: "Indian Superintendents," *Indian Truth II, October 1934,* pp. 3-4; Crum, Steve, "Crow Warrior," *Tribal College,* Vol. F1, No. 4 (Spring 1990), pp. 19–23.

1934 John Collier (tribal affiliation unknown) was appointed commissioner of Indian Affairs. Under his directorship the Bureau of Indian Affairs (BIA) revamped its Indian policy. Many were critical of Collier's policies as they feared the Indians' "return to the blanket." Although, his policies were sympathetic to Indians, not all Indian tribes embraced them. Some of them were perceived as detrimental rather than beneficial.

Sources: Dennis, *The American Indian, 1492–1976,* p. 52.

ca. 1936 Fred H. Massey (Choctaw) was the first American Indian appointed assistant commissioner of Indian Affairs for the Bureau of Indian Affairs (BIA). He began his career with the BIA after graduating from college and worked for more than thirty years. In 1956, he was named Outstanding American Indian at the Annual American Indian Exposition. He served in the U.S. Army from 1945 to 1956.

Sources: *Biographical Dictionary of Indians of the Americas,* Vol. 1, p. 401; Gridley, ed. *Indians of Today,* p. 275.

1966 Robert LaFollette Bennett (Oneida; 1912–) was the second American Indian to hold the office of commissioner of the Bureau of Indian Affairs (BIA) in one hundred years. During his service as commissioner from 1966 to 1969 he supported many innovative changes. For example, he developed the first presidential message on Indian affairs to be sent to Congress. His other "first" achievements include: the first commissioner to rise through the ranks of the BIA, the first commissioner to travel and visit with all tribes, and the organizer of the first agreements with a state employment agency (South Dakota) for special services to Indians. Bennett wanted tribes to become responsible for their own "BIA-type" services.

Sources: *Biographical Dictionary of Indians of the Americas*, Vol. 1, p. 49; Gridley, ed., *Indians of Today*, pp. 212–13; "Originator of 'Bennett Freeze Area' Receives Award for Lifetime Work," *Navajo Times*, Vol. 30, No. 39 (September 27, 1990), p. 1.

1970 Helen White Peterson (Oglala Sioux; 1915–) became the first woman to be appointed assistant to the commissioner of Indian Affairs. She also established the first Bureau of Indian Affairs (BIA) intergovernmental office in Denver in 1972. She

Robert L. Bennett rose through the ranks to become an innovative comminssioner of the Bureau of Indian Affairs.

was born on August 3, 1915, on the Pine Ridge Reservation. Throughout her professional life she worked to improve race relations and resolve minority issues. She has been active both in Native American and Hispanic affairs. She founded the Colorado Field Service Program, which was incorporated into an extension division of the University of Colorado, and, in 1948, she created and directed the Mayor's Committee on Human Relations, which was renamed the Denver Commission on Community Relations. In 1949, she became a member of the second Inter-American Indian Conference in Cuzco, Peru, where she authored a resolution on Indian education. From 1953 to 1961, she was executive director of the National Congress of American Indians (NCAI). She assisted the NCAI in writing a comprehensive document outlining Indian concerns. She has received numerous accolades and awards for her work, including an honorary doctorate from her alma mater Chadron State College in Nebraska. She retired from the BIA in 1985.

Sources: *Biographical Dictionary of Indians of the Americas*, Vol. 2, p. 538; Champagne, ed., *The Native North American Almanac*, p. 1131; Gridley, ed., *Indians of Today*, pp. 199-200; Malinowski, ed., *Notable Native Americans*, pp. 328–29.

1971 Anthony Lincoln (Navajo) became the first Navajo to hold an administrative post in the Bureau of Indian Affairs (BIA). He was appointed deputy associate commissioner for Indian Education and Programs. He had been the director of the Navajo Tribe's industrial and economic development program and deputy director of the Office of Navajo Economic Opportunity.

Sources: Gridley, ed., *Indians of Today*, p. 470.

1971 Wilma L. Victor (Choctaw) became the first American Indian woman to be appointed special assistant for Indian Affairs in the Interior Department. She also became the first Indian woman to hold such a high level position. She was formerly a principal and first academic director of the Institute of American Indian Arts in Santa Fe, New Mexico, and principal of the Intermountain School in Utah. In 1967, she was one of six women chosen for the Federal Women's Award. Victor served in the U.S. Army, Women's Army Corps (WAC), from 1943 to 1946, rising to the rank of first lieutenant. She received the WAC Service Ribbon, American Theatre Campaign Medal, and the Victory Medal. She was recipient of the Indian Council Fire National Indian Achievement Award, the Anadarko Indian Exposition's Indian of the Year Award (1971), the University of Wisconsin's Distinguished Alumnus Award (1972), and the Distinguished Service Award from the Department of the Interior. She is well known for her contributions in the field of Indian education.

Sources: Champagne, ed., *The Native North American Almanac*, pp. 1181–82; Dennis, *The American Indian, 1492-1976*, p. 146. Gridley, ed., *Indians of Today*, pp. 351–52.

1973 Shirley Plume (Oglala Lakota Sioux) was the first American Indian woman appointed, on December 3, 1973, to serve as superintendent of a Bureau of Indian Affairs Indian Agency, supervising the Standing Rock Agency in North Dakota.

Sources: Dennis, *The American Indian, 1492–1976*, p. 105.

ca. late-1970s Forrest J. Gerard (Blackfoot) was appointed as the first assistant secretary of Indian Affairs by President Jimmy Carter. The position elevated the

Bureau of Indian Affairs (BIA) administration to an equitable level with other agencies within the Department of the Interior. The move was first proposed by President Richard M. Nixon.

Sources: *Biographical Dictionary of Indians of the Americas*, Vol. 1, p. 241; Champagne, ed., *The Native North American Almanac*, p. 1062; Davis, ed., *Native America In the Twentieth Century*, pp. 39, 76.

1983 Henrietta Mann Morton (Southern Cheyenne), also known as Henrietta Whiteman, was the first American Indian woman appointed to serve as the director of the Office of Indian Education in the Bureau of Indian Affairs (BIA). She

Wilma Victor, the Department of the Interior's first woman special assistant for Indian Affairs.

became the highest ranking woman in Indian Affairs. In 1986, she was accorded one of the highest honors in Cheyenne society when she became Sundance Woman, a ceremonial person and a medicine person.

Sources: Bataille, ed., *Native American Women,* p. 162; Morton, Henri Mann, and James Prier Morton, "Doctor- Doctor," *Winds of Change,* Vol. 5, No. 1 (Winter 1990), pp. 54–58.

Ada Deer.

1993 Ada Elizabeth Deer (Menominee) was the first American Indian woman to be confirmed by the U.S. Senate as assistant secretary of Indian Affairs in the U.S. Department of Interior. She was sworn into office on August 7, 1993, by a Menominee woman tribal judge, whom she appointed when she headed the tribal government.

She received her M.A. in social welfare from Columbia University in 1961. Deer was one of the leading influences that helped restore the Menominee people to tribal status. As a result of her work, Congress repealed the termination status of the Menominee tribe and the Menominee regained their federal status and their treaty rights. In 1966, Deer was chosen Outstanding Young Woman of America. She has worked to encourage dignity and self worth among Indian people.

See also: Education, 1957.

Sources: Bataille, ed., *Native American Women,* pp. 76–78; *Biographical Dictionary of Indians of the Americas,* Vol. 1, p. 181; Champagne, ed., *Chronology of Native American History,* p. 493; Champagne, ed., *The Native North American Almanac,* p. 1041.

NATIVE PEOPLES OF CANADA

1949 James Sewid (Kwakiutl; 1913–) was the first elected chief of his tribe following the elimination of hereditary chiefs. He was recognized throughout Canada as a tribal and national leader among people of the First Nations. A creative leader, Sewid instituted innovative community and governmental help programs. As a child, he had constructed a small automobile out of scrap material, bringing the first automobile to Alert Bay, British Columbia, his home. As a leader he introduced an electric light plant to Village Island, British Columbia, the first village in that area to have such a convenience. Sewid was instrumental in altering the band governmental structure from hereditary to elective leadership. In addition, he perceived the need for an inter-tribal council and created one. Further, he originated biracial organizations to tackle the problem of juvenile delinquency. He pursued a multicultural emphasis in the programs he initiated. In 1969, his autobiography, *Guests Never Leave Hungry,* was published by Yale University Press.

Sources: *Biographical Dictionary of Indians of the Americas,* Vol. 2, p. 675; Gridley, ed., *Indians of Today,* p. 9; Sewid, James, *Guests Never Leave Hungry: The Autobiography of James Sewid, a Kwakiutl Indian,* Yale University Press, 1969.

1955 The Nishga Tribal Council was formed, becoming the first tribal council established by Natives themselves. Frank Arthur Calder was elected to serve as the council's first president.

Sources: Champagne, ed., *Chronology of Native North American History,* pp. 272–73, 319; Champagne, ed., *The Native North American Almanac,* p. 1024.

1967 Noted statesman Omer B. Peters (Delaware; 1908–1978) formed the Union of Ontario Indians and served as its first president. Born in Moravian of the Thames, Ontario, Peters became a band councilor, chief, and band administrator for the Moravian Reserve. From 1970 to 1974, he served as vice president of the National Indian Brotherhood (NIB). In 1977, he functioned as chairman of the Council of Elders of the National Indian Brotherhood. On May 13, 1988, he was inducted into the Indian Hall of Fame.

Sources: *Biographical Dictionary of Indians of the Americas,* Vol. 2, p. 537.

1968 Walter Deiter (tribal affiliation unknown), from Saskatchewan, became the first president of the National Indian Brotherhood (NIB) in February 1968. The organization was founded to work toward protecting the rights of status Indians.

Sources: Champagne, ed., *Chronology of Native North American History,* p. 352; Champagne, ed., *The Native North American Almanac,* p. 116.

1974 Billy Diamond (Cree) was elected the founding president of the Grand Council of the Cree of Quebec and held the position until 1984. In his lifelong career as a public servant, Diamond has been involved in the fight against the James Bay Hydroelectric Project, participating in the negotiations that resulted in the continuation of the project with the Cree maintaining significant control over their autonomy. Diamond also served as chairman of the Cree Regional Authority, chairman of the James Bay School Board (which was one of the first Native-controlled school boards), and president of the Air Creebec, a Cree-owned regional airline.

Sources: Champagne, ed., *Chronology of Native North American History,* p. 319; Champagne, ed., *The Native North American Almanac,* p. 1045.

1988 Omer B. Peters (Delaware), noted statesman, was inducted into the Indian Hall of Fame on May 13, 1988. Born in 1908 in Moravian of the Thames, in Ontario, Canada, he became band councilor, chief, and band administrator for the Moravian Reserve. In 1967, he organized the Union of Ontario Indians and served as its president. From 1970 to 1974, he served as vice-president of the National Indian Brotherhood (NIB). In 1977 he served as chairman of the Council of Elders of the NIB.

Sources: *Biographical Dictionary of Indians of the Americas,* Vol. 2, p. 537.

NATIVE PEOPLES OF MEXICO

968 C.E. Topiltzin (Toltec), also known as Quetzalcoatl, was the ruler and founder of the Toltec empire, a precursor to the Aztec empire, which was subdued by the Spanish.

Sources: Champagne, ed., *Chronology of Native North American History,* p. 24.

ca. 1000 Mixtec peoples of southern Mexico developed one of the most efficient systems of centralized government, with succeeding smaller communities answering to larger centers. Urban communities and their outlying communities were ruled by *caciques* (chiefs). The system was so practical that Spanish conquerors later adopted the system with only minor changes and allowed the Mixtec much latitude in administering the governance of their own communities. Today both the political system and the language of the Mixtec remain a vital part of Native culture in Mexico.

Sources: Leitch, *Chronology of the American Indian,* p. 35.

1396 Acamapichtli (Aztec) was the first Aztec *huey tlatoani,* or chief speaker. He was selected after the Aztec received permission from the ruling Culhuacan family for the privilege of selecting their own chief speaker. Such a speaker was the equivalent of a king or emperor. During Acamapichtli's reign, the Aztec continued to pay tribute to the Tepanec of Atzcapotzalco. The next chief speaker was also elected, but afterward chief speakers became hereditary positions.

Sources: *Biographical Dictionary of Indians of the Americas,* Vol. 1, p. 3; Leitch, *Chronology of the American Indian,* p. 44.

1427 Serving as the last ruler of the Tepanec Empire, Maxtla (Tepanec) ruled from 1427 to 1429. The Tepanec Empire was defeated by a combined force of Tenochtitlan, Texoco, and Tlacopan. The Aztec took advantage of this defeat by expanding their influence.

Sources: *Biographical Dictionary of Indians of the Americas,* Vol. 1, p. 404.

1440 Moctezuma Ilhuicamina (Aztec), commonly known simply as Montezuma, turned a city-state into an empire. From 1440 to 1458 he served as chief speaker of the Aztec at Tenochtitlan (Mexico City). He was the first Aztec ruler to conquer territory outside the immediate vicinity of the Valley of Mexico.

Sources: *Biographical Dictionary of Indians of the Americas,* Vol. 1, p. 428.

1473 Moquihuix (Aztec), also known as Xoquiuix and Moquiuixtli, was the last independent ruler of Tlatelolco. Moquihuix ruled Tlatelolco (known as the commercial center of the Valley of Mexico) from around 1460 to 1473.

Sources: *Biographical Dictionary of Indians of the Americas,* Vol. 1, p. 443.

NATIVE PEOPLES OF CENTRAL AND SOUTH AMERICA

1925 Nele De Cantule (Cuna), also known as San Blas, won Cuna independence from the Panamanian government in February 1925. The Cuna people gained control over their islands, located just off the Atlantic coast of Panama. After armed conflict with the territorial government in Panama, Cantule declared the San Blas Republic of Tule independent. Although Tule received aid from Panama, their lands remained free from white management.

Sources: *Biographical Dictionary of Indians of the Americas,* Vol. 1, p. 111.

1992 Rigoberta Menchu (K'iche' Maya) was the first Indian to receive a Nobel Peace Prize for her work on behalf of the indigenous peoples of Guatemala. At 33 years of age, she was the youngest person to be honored with this prize. She accepted the award stating that it was a tribute, not just to herself, but to all indigenous women of Guatemala, as well as the world. She received the award as a refugee living in Mexico, where she had been a tireless campaigner for the rights of indigenous peoples, particularly those from Guatemala.

In her 1984 biography, *I, Rigoberta Menchu,* she explained the process of land lost and the exploitation of her family and others of her indigenous Guatemalan community. She escaped from persecution inflicted by both the Guatemalan army and the rebel forces. Her parents and a brother were killed in brutal battles between the two forces. Only as a refugee, has she been able to bring attention to the abuse of basic human rights imposed on thousands of Mayan victims in her homeland. She has continued to speak on their behalf.

Sources: Wearne, *Return of the Indian,* pp. 1, 187–88.

LANGUAGE

1534 For the first time, an Iroquoian language was translated and put into print by Europeans when a Jesuit priest compiled and translated a list of Iroquoian words. It was the oldest recorded list of Iroquoian words.

Sources: Lee, *Native Time*, p. 34.

1593 The two oldest surviving studies of the Mixtec language were undertaken in 1593. The Reyes grammar study was produced in Mexico City, and the Alvarad study was done by a Dominican friar in Tamazulapan. The Mixtec language, based in Mexico, is still in use today.

Sources: Leitch, *Chronology of the American Indian*, p. 84.

1642 An Indian-English dictionary, *A Key into the Language of America*, was published by Roger Williams. The book includes brief descriptions of the customs and practices of American Indians in New England. An Indian rights advocate, Williams urged English colonists to employ humane and just treatment in their dealings with Indians. This dictionary was an attempt to provide some information about Indians to facilitate improved treatment of them by colonists.

Sources: Champagne, ed., *Chronology of Native North American History*, p. 56; Dennis, *The American Indian, 1492–1976*, p. 7.

1650 Job Nesutan (Natick) and Cockenoe (Montauk) offered valuable assistance in the translation of the Bible into the Massachusetts language, the first Bible to be printed in America. They were hired by John Eliot to serve as translators and interpreters after learning to read and write in English and Natick. Although Eliot is credited with the translation of the Bible, it is likely that these American Indian assistants performed the majority of the translation work. Cockenoe was captured by the British during the Pequot War; while serving in Richard Collicot's household, Eliot, upon becoming aware of his proficiency in English, arranged for Cockenoe to tutor him in Algonquian languages. During the war between the English and Metacom; also known as King Philip (King Philip's War), Nesutan aided the English and was killed in July 1675.

Sources: *Biographical Dictionary of Indians of the Americas*, Vol. 2; "Nesutan," in *The American Indian;* Waldman, *Who Was Who in Native American History*, p. 248.

1653 The first book published in an American Indian language in New England was *Catechism in the Indian Language,* written in an Algonquian language by John

Eliot. Eliot earlier had committed himself to learning dialects of the Algonquian languages, since he was convinced that Native people would be able to accept Christianity if they could be taught in their own languages. Although Eliot initiated the translation of several texts, the Bible, hymns, and this tract, he likely received assistance from Indian converts he was teaching.

Sources: Leitch, *Chronology of the American Indian*, p. 97.

1661 The first Bible text to be printed in America was an Algonquian-language Bible translated by John Eliot and his Indian assistants. Entitled *The Testament of Our Lord and Savior Jesus Christ*, it was not only the first Bible printed in an Indian language, it was the first published in the New World.

Sources: Dennis, *The American Indian, 1492–1976*, p. 8.

1663 Wowanus (Nipmuc; ca. 1643–1728), also known as James the Printer, helped John Eliot translate and print the Bible into his Nipmuc language. The first edition of the translated St. James English Bible was printed in 1663.

Sources: *Biographical Dictionary of Indians of the Americas*, Vol. 1, p. 316.

1820s Sequoyah (Cherokee; 1770–1843) has been credited for inventing the Cherokee syllabary; however, the Cherokee had been using a written form of language for many generations. One of the last remaining scribes to know their ancient form of written communication, Sequoyah developed and introduced a modified version of the traditional syllabary. Sequoyah was afraid that this writing tradition would be lost in favor of written English and designed the syllabary for use by the general Cherokee public. Before this, most Cherokee were not taught the traditional form of writing. After Sequoyah developed the syllabary, large numbers of Cherokee became literate in their Native language.

Sources: Bird, *Tell Them They Lie*.

1837 Joseph Renville (1779–1846), the son of a Dakota woman and a French fur trader, translated the entire Bible into Dakota. He was born in 1779 at what is now St. Paul, Minnesota. By the age of ten, he had learned French. At age twenty-six, he acted as guide for Zebulon M. Pike as he explored the Rocky Mountains. During the War of 1812, he acted as interpreter for the British and achieved the rank of captain. In 1834, he met Dr. T. S. Williamson and arranged to accompany him to Lac Qui Parle to establish a mission, where, in 1841, he was chosen and ordained as a ruling elder. He maintained that position until his death in 1846.

Sources: *Biographical Dictionary of Indians of the Americas*, Vol. 2, p. 607; "Renville," in *The American Indian*; Waldman, *Who Was Who in Native American History*, p. 297.

1838 Pierre Paul Osunkhirhine (Abenaki) translated a large body of religious works into the Penobscot dialect of the Abenaki language. He attended Moore's Charity School in Hanover, New Hampshire, then returned to Quebec to work as a Protestant missionary. In this capacity he did his translations.

Sources: *Biographical Dictionary of Indians of the Americas*, Vol. 2, p. 503.

1891 *Indian Linguistic Families of America North of Mexico*, probably the first extensive assessment of North American Indian languages, was published by J. W.

Powell. He grouped the languages into fifty-one families. They were regrouped into six major language families in 1929 by Edward Sapir.

Sources: Leitch, *Chronology of the American Indian,* p. 182.

Cherokee syllabary in phonetic transcription and translation.

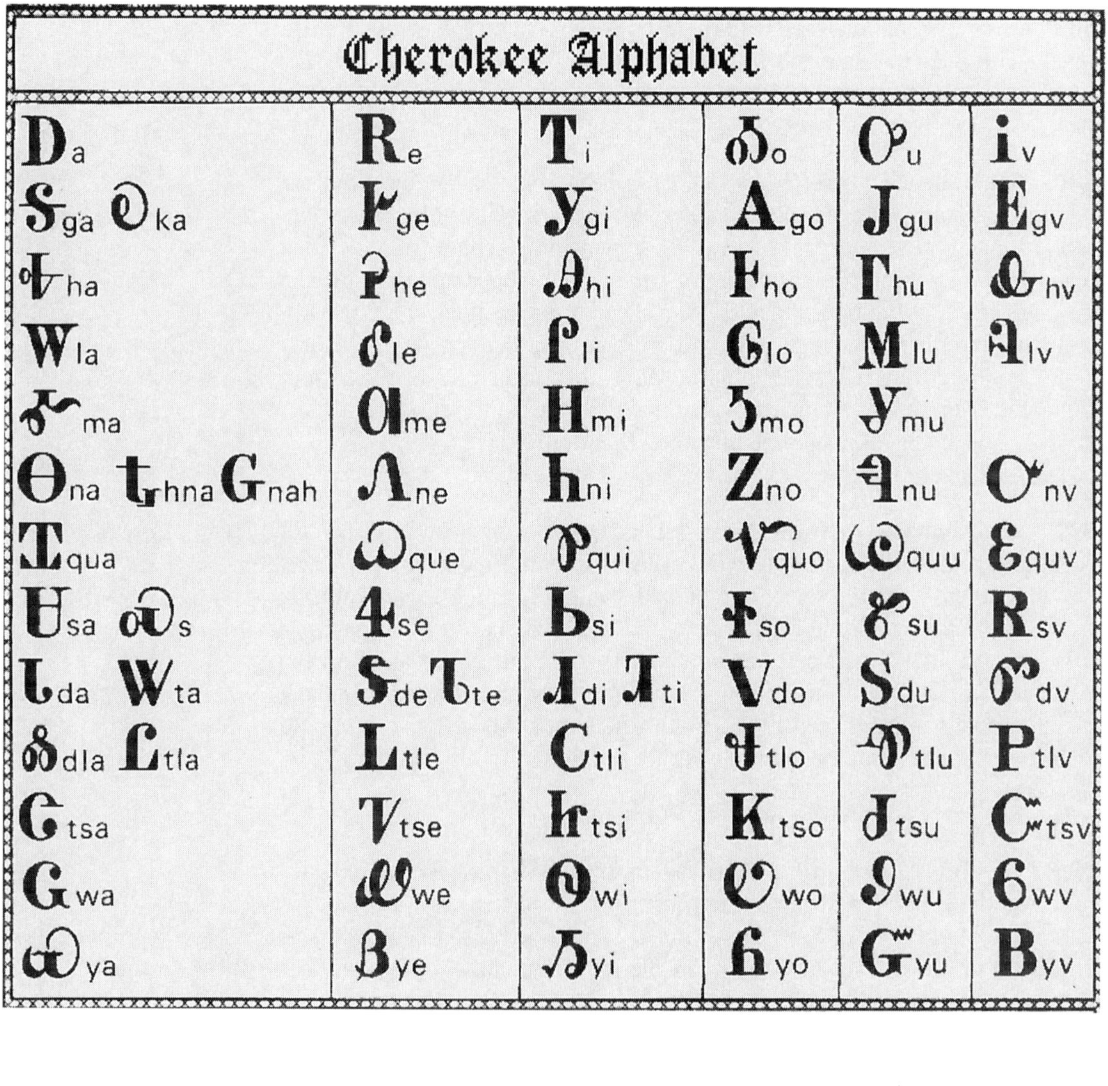

1917 Mohawk became the first American Indian language to be used as a wartime communication network.

See also: Military, 1917.

Sources: Champagne, ed., *Chronology of Native North American History,* pp. 243–44.

Cherokee Alphabet

D a	R e	T i	� o	O u	i v
S ga Ꮖ ka	Ꮅ ge	Ꮿ gi	A go	J gu	E gv
Ꮡ ha	Ꭹ he	Ꭿ hi	F ho	Ꮁ hu	Ꮣ hv
W la	Ꮉ le	P li	G lo	M lu	Ꮑ lv
Ꮎ ma	Ꮵ me	H mi	Ꮖ mo	Ꮩ mu	
Ꮎ na Ꮏ hna G nah	Ꮮ ne	Ꮒ ni	Z no	Ꮔ nu	Ꮕ nv
Ꮖ qua	Ꮺ que	Ꮖ qui	Ꮖ quo	Ꮖ quu	Ꮖ quv
Ꮖ sa Ꮝ s	4 se	Ꮥ si	Ꮖ so	Ꮖ su	R sv
Ꮖ da W ta	Ꮥ de Ꮦ te	Ꮧ di Ꮨ ti	V do	S du	Ꮬ dv
Ꮝ dla Ꮮ tla	L tle	C tli	Ꮙ tlo	Ꮖ tlu	P tlv
Ꮳ tsa	Ꮴ tse	Ꮵ tsi	K tso	Ꮶ tsu	Ꮷ tsv
G wa	Ꮺ we	Ꮻ wi	Ꮼ wo	Ꮽ wu	6 wv
Ꮿ ya	Ꮰ ye	Ꮖ yi	Ꮖ yo	Ꮖ yu	B yv

1918 The Choctaw language was the first American Indian language to be used as part the U.S. military communications system.

See also: Military, 1918.

Sources: Anderson, Jerry (EEO Manager, OASD [FM&P]-ADASD, The Pentagon), Personal communication to AnCita Benally, January 13, 1996; Hirschfelder and Kreipe de Montaño, *The Native American Almanac,* pp. 30, 232.

1942 The Navajo language was the first Native American language in the United States to be used as a codified military means of communication. As with other American Indian languages used—Choctaw, Comanche, Hopi, and Cherokee—this code was never deciphered by the enemy.

See also: Military, 1942.

Sources: Anderson, Jerry (EEO Manager, OASD [FM&P]-ADASD, The Pentagon), Personal communication to AnCita Benally, January 13, 1996; Hirschfelder and Kreipe de Montaño, *The Native American Almanac,* pp. 90, 233–34.

1944 Ella Cara Deloria (Standing Rock Sioux; 1888–1971) was the only woman and only American Indian to serve on the Navajo Enquiry Party that was sponsored by the Phelps-Stokes Fund. An anthropologist, Deloria worked with Franz Boas as a research specialist appointed by Columbia University in 1929. Her area of specialization was Lakota ethnology and linguistics. In 1932 she published *Dakota Texts,* beginning a serious effort to preserve the Dakota language. She co-authored two books on Dakota language with Boas. In 1943 she was honored by the Indian Council Fire with its prestigious Indian Achievement Medal. The University of South Dakota houses many of her papers in the Ella C. Deloria Project.

Sources: Bataille, ed., *Native American Women,* pp. 78–79; *Biographical Dictionary of Indians of the Americas,* Vol. 1, p. 184; Dockstader, *Great North American Indians,* pp. 74–75; Gridley, ed., *Indians of Today,* p. 348.

1984 Ofelia Zepeda (Tohono O'odham; 1954–) was the first member of her tribe to receive a doctorate in linguistics. She received a B.A., M.A., and Ph.D. from the University of Arizona, where she was hired to teach linguistics. Zepeda was actively involved in the passage of the Native American Languages Act. Pursuing the development of bilingual literacy among her tribe, in 1983, Zepeda created *A Papago Grammar,* the first Tohono O'odham language text book. She has been instrumental in the development of the Tohono O'odham Language Policy, which seeks to encourage Native language retention.

Sources: Bataille, ed., *Native American Women,* p. 289; Trujillo, Octaviana (assistant professor, Multicultural Education, Arizona State University-Tempe), Personal communication to AnCita Benally, December 1886; Zepeda, Ofelia (assistant professor, Department of Reading and Language, University of Arizona-Tucson), Personal communication to AnCita Benally, March 1997.

ca. 1990 Edna Cloud (Ojibwa/Cree) published the first Ojibwa-Cree dictionary.

Sources: Sorensen, Carole G., "Pattern for Performance," *Winds of Change,* Vol. 7, No. 2 (Spring 1992), p. 41.

1992 Kenneth Maryboy (Navajo) and L. A. Williams (Navajo) broadcast the first professional basketball game in an American Indian language at the invitation of the Phoenix Suns announcer, Al McCoy. The invitation came after officials of the Phoenix Suns observed Maryboy and Williams broadcasting high school basketball championship games in Navajo. KTNN has broadcast National Football League games and National Basketball Association games in addition to Suns games. Other broadcasts have included Phoenix Cardinals games, professional boxing matches, and the 1996 Super Bowl football game. Women's professional basketball games will be broadcast in Navajo as well. Williams described sportscasting in Navajo as painting pictures with words for listeners. The announcers worked hard to polish the language of sports and have essentially developed a new sports jargon. Williams was the first American Indian woman to do live broadcasts of professional sports.

Sources: Norrell, Brenda, "Super Bowl Sunday: A Touchdown for Navajo," *Indian Country Today,* February 1, 1996, p. C-2; Williams, L. A. (KTNN Navajo Radio Station, Window Rock, Arizona), Personal communication to AnCita Benally, June 6, 1997.

LAW AND THE JUDICIARY

1885 The Court of Indian Offenses was established on American Indian reservations. The secretary of the Department of Interior was authorized to form laws that would guide these courts. Seven major crimes were listed for which American Indians could be tried. This was in reaction to the 1883 Supreme Court decision (*Ex Parte Crow Dog*) that overturned Crow Dog's murder conviction for killing Spotted Elk. Although tribal customary law had been used by the Sioux to punish Crow Dog, federal authorities in the Dakota Territory tried, convicted, and sentenced him to death. The court ruled that while the Sioux had agreed to be governed by the laws of the United States, Congress had not clearly expressed how criminal laws would be imposed. The seven crimes were eventually increased to fourteen. American Indians committing crimes on reservations are subject to federal courts today.

Sources: Champagne, ed., *Native America,* p. 229; Dennis, *The American Indian, 1492–1976,* p. 42; Washburn, *Handbook of North American Indians,* pp. 229, 233.

1885 Through a law signed by President Ulysses S. Grant federal troops guarding Indian Territory were withdrawn. This opened the way for white settlers called "Boomers" and "Sooners" to squat on American Indian land.

Sources: Dennis, *The American Indian, 1492–1976,* p. 43.

1886 Quannah Parker (Comanche; ca. 1852–1911), the last of the Comanche hereditary chiefs, was appointed judge and served in the Court of Indian Affairs, the first of his tribe to hold such a position. He was, however, relieved of his duties for having too many wives, as polygamy was in violation of white law and the codes of the Court of Indian Offenses.

Sources: Champagne, ed., *Chronology of Native North American History,* p. 169; Dennis, *The American Indian, 1492–1976,* p. 45.

1924 Thomas Henry Dodge (Navajo), son of Henry Chee Dodge, is believed to be the first Navajo to receive a law degree. He graduated from St. Louis University School of Law and practiced law in Chicago before returning to the reservation. He was admitted to the bar in Missouri (1924) and in New Mexico (1926). He was elected chairman of the Navajo Tribal Council and served from 1933 to 1937. In 1946 he was appointed to the Truxton Canyon Agency and became the first Navajo appointed as reservation superintendent.

Sources: Davis, ed., *Native America in the Twentieth Century,* p. 380; Gridley, ed., *Indians of Today,* p. 102; Shepardson, Mary, "Development of Navajo Tribal Government," in *Handbook of North American Indians,* Vol. 10: *History of Indian-White Relations,* edited by Alfonso Ortiz, pp. 624–35; Thomas Dodge papers, Arizona Collection, University Libraries, Arizona State University, Tempe.

Quannah Parker, a Comanche tribal leader and successful businessman.

1967 Nora Guinn (Yup'ik) was the first woman and the first Alaska Native to be appointed a district judge in the state of Alaska. Proficient in several dialects of Yup'ik, Judge Guinn frequently conducted court in Yup'ik. Her district covered nearly one hundred thousand square miles, and she often traveled to small

remote villages to preside over cases. In addition to being a successful wife and mother (she raised ten children and has been married for more than fifty-five years), Guinn has also dedicated her life to preserving the rights and interests of all Alaskans. Especially interested in working with youth, Guinn has spent much time speaking to youth groups and has made significant strides in improving the welfare of youth in Alaska.

Guinn began her career of public service in the village of Tununak, on the Bering Sea, as a midwife and nurse. She later served as a Bureau of Indian Affairs (BIA) teacher, member of the Bethel City Council, deputy magistrate, and acting U.S. commissioner in Alaska prior to statehood. She has been awarded numerous honors and is a member of several distinguished organizations, including the Alaska Judges, the Juvenile Judges Association, and the Alaska Bar Association (an honorary member). In May 1978, the University of Alaska-Anchorage conferred an honorary doctor of law degree in recognition of her outstanding contributions to the legal profession in Alaska.

Sources: Gridley, ed., *Indians of Today*, p. 307; Proclamation of the Nineteenth Alaska State Legislature, April 1996; Pavil, Mary, Personal correspondence to Karen Gayton Swisher, August 21, 1996.

1969 Brantley Blue (Lumbee), the first American Indian to serve as Indian commissioner on the Indian Claims Commission, also became the first Lumbee lawyer. He practiced law in Tennessee from 1955 to 1959 and became president of the Kingsport Bar Association in 1956. In 1969, Blue was awarded the Distinguished Alumnus Award by Pembrook College.

Sources: *Biographical Dictionary of Indians of the Americas*, Vol. 1, p. 79; Gridley, ed., *Indians of Today*, p. 88; *Wassaja*, Vol. 7, No. 5 (September 1979) p. 20.

1970 John E. Echohawk (Pawnee; 1945–) was the first American Indian to graduate from the University of New Mexico Law School, 1970, after successfully completing a unique pre-law course, the first program of its kind. He was hired immediately by the Native American Rights Fund (NARF), a publicly supported legal service organization. In 1972, Echohawk became the deputy director of NARF, then director in 1973.

One of the most influential Indian lawyers and Indian rights activists in the country, he has successfully litigated major court cases regarding Indian rights. In 1991, he took part in forcing the Nebraska State Historical Society to return Pawnee remains to the tribe. He was also instrumental in securing an amendment to the Native American Religious Freedom Act. Echohawk served on President Bill Clinton's transition team for the Department of the Interior. He received the President's Service Award from the National Congress of American Indians (NCAI) and a Distinguished Service Award from the Americans for Indian Opportunity. In 1994, he was named one of the one hundred most influential lawyers by the *National Law Journal*.

Sources: *Biographical Dictionary of Indians of the Americas*, Vol. 1, p. 208; Champagne, ed., *Native North American Almanac*, p. 1052; Malinowski, ed., *Notable Native Americans*, pp. 139–40.

1971 Yvonne Knight (Ponca/Creek) was the first American Indian woman to receive a Juris Doctor degree, graduating from the University of New Mexico

Indian law program, which was established in 1967 to increase the number of American Indian lawyers. Soon after receiving her law degree, Knight became one of the first Native American attorneys hired by the Native American Rights Fund (NARF).

Sources: Anderson, *Ohoyo One Thousand*, p. 376; Champagne, ed., *The Native North American Almanac*, p. 66.

1974 On June 17, 1974, the U.S. Supreme Court refused to review the decision of a lower court to uphold the election of a Navajo Indian as a county supervisor. Voters had challenged the election on the grounds that, as a reservation Indian, the Navajo county supervisor-elect was immune from state taxes and thus the "normal" legal processes.

Sources: Champagne, ed., *Chronology of Native North American History*, p. 398.

1983 Claudeen Bates Arthur (Navajo), who was the first Native American woman to attain the rank of field solicitor for the U.S. Department of the Interior, was also the first attorney general for the Navajo Nation, serving under the administration of Peterson Zah. Previously the Navajo Nation employed legal counsel to take care of legal matters. The office of attorney general was initiated by Zah.

Arthur was born on the Navajo Reservation and attended Navajo Methodist Mission School in Farmington, New Mexico. After receiving a B.S. in biology from New Mexico State University, she taught science courses to high school students. Aware of the need for Navajos with expertise in the legal field due to her relationship with the Navajo community, she enrolled in the College of Law program at Arizona State University, where she received her J.D. in 1974. During her tenure as attorney general of the Navajo Nation she argued one of the most significant cases in the history of Indian law, *Kerr-McGee v. Navajo*. In April 1985, the Supreme

John Echohawk, the first American Indian to graduate from the University of New Mexico Law School, stands before the building that houses the Native America Rights Fund in Boulder, Colorado.

Opposite page: Nora Guinn, the first woman and first Alaska Native to be appointed district judge in the state of Alaska.

Court rendered a decision in favor of the Navajo Tribe's right to tax businesses on its land. Although Arthur has enjoyed many successes in her legal career, she considers being a mother and grandmother her most important roles.

Sources: Anderson, ed., *Ohoyo One Thousand*, p. 11; Arthur, Claudeen Bates (St. Michaels, Arizona), Personal communication to AnCita Benally, March 1997; Bataille, ed., *Native American Women*, p. 14; Calvin, Barbara (administrative assistant, Office of the Attorney General, The Navajo Nation. Window Rock, Arizona), Personal communication to AnCita Benally, March 1997; Wood, Beth, and Tom Barry, "The Story of Three Navajo Women," *Integrateducation*, 16 (March/April 1978), pp. 33–35.

1983 Arlinda Faye Locklear (Lumbee; 1951–) was the first American Indian woman to successfully argue a case before the U.S. Supreme Court. Locklear received her J.D. from Duke University School of Law in 1976 and a doctor of humane letters from New York State University in 1990. In 1983, she successfully argued *Solem v. Bartlett,* and in 1985, *Oneida Indian Nation v. County of Onieda,* both before the Supreme Court. Locklear is considered a leading authority on Indian land claims.

Sources: Champagne, ed., *The Native North American Almanac,* p. 1093; Medicine, Beatrice, "North American Indigenous Women and Cultural Domination," *American Indian Culture and Research Journal,* Vol. 17, No. 3 (March 1993), p. 129.

1985 Raymond Austin (Navajo) was the first Navajo attorney appointed as Navajo Nation judge. In 1991 he was the first Navajo law school graduate considered for the position of Navajo Nation Supreme Court chief justice. Past chief justices were trained in special programs but were not university-trained in law and were not licensed attorneys. In addition, in 1994 he became the first Navajo and possibly the first Native American to serve as judge *pro tempore* on the Arizona Court of Appeals, Division 1, in Phoenix, Arizona. In 1995 he became the first Native American to serve as the Herman Phleger Distinguished Visiting Professor of Law at the Stanford Law School in California, a position extended to persons of distinction in the field of law.

Austin received a bachelor's degree from Arizona University in 1979 and in 1983 earned a J.D. from the University of New Mexico Law School. He became a member of the bar in Arizona, Utah, and the Navajo Nation. He remains a leading advocate of using Indian tribal common law in tribal court decision making. He believes that the use of existing customary values, mores, and cultural ethics strengthens and expands the sovereignty of Indian nations. His theories encourage a return to basic tribal concepts and values.

Sources: Shebala, Mary, "And Then, There Were Two," *Navajo Times,* Vol. 32, No. 1 (December 31, 1991), p. 1; Austin, Ray (associate justice, Navajo Nation Supreme Court), Personal communication to Ancita Benally, April 7, 1997.

1991 Robert Yazzie (Navajo), together with Ray Austin (Navajo), were the first law school graduates considered for the position of Navajo Nation Supreme Court chief justice. Past chief justices were trained in special programs, but were not university trained in law. Robert Yazzie was chosen, becoming the first law school graduate to hold the position.

Sources: Shebala, Mary, "And Then, There Were Two," *Navajo Times,* Vol. 32, No. 1 (December 31, 1991) p. 1.

1991 The Navajo Nation Courts initiated "Peacemaker Courts," a unique form of dispute resolution based on Navajo common law and Navajo concepts of kinship and social harmony. The Peacemaker Courts are not adversarial and are conducted without the presence of a judge. The ultimate goal is to settle disputes without litigation and restore *K'e* (kinship). Peacemakers are selected from the local community in which there is a dispute. Chapter leaders (the most basic local community organization) select individuals to serve on the courts and listen to both sides to resolve a dispute. Opposing sides are encouraged to make a resolution themselves. The Peacemaker Courts have been successful because they are forms of dispute resolution that already exist in Navajo society. The success of these unique courts has brought not only other Indian tribes, but non-Indians from around the world to study them.

Sources: Austin, Ray (associate justice, Navajo Nation Supreme Court), Telephone conversation with AnCita Benally, April 7, 1997; Bluehouse, Philmer (director, Peacemaker Courts, Navajo Nation Judicial Administration, The Navajo Nation, Window Rock, Arizona), Personal communication to AnCita Benally, April 1997; Miller, Freddie (Navajo Law and Research Project, Navajo Nation Judicial Administration, The Navajo Nation, Window Rock, Arizona), Personal communication to AnCita Benally, April 1997.

LITERATURE

1609 El Inca, Garcilaso de la Vega (Inca), called the "Pliny of the New World," was the first person of Indian ancestry to write extensively on the history and culture of North American Indians. His work is especially unique in that he portrayed Native peoples not as curious objects of interest but as full human beings. His mother was Chimpa Ocllo, niece of Inca emperor Huayna Capac; his father, Don Sebastian Garcilaso de la Vega, was Spanish. Because of his royal status, he was educated in the history and culture of the Inca and learned to interpret the *quipas,* the knotted ropes that recorded history. He witnessed the decline and destruction of the Inca empire and he saw the executions and imprisonment of many of his relatives. Sent to Spain, he received a proper European education, learned Latin and Greek, and studied the classics. His first publication was a translation of the romantic poetry of the Portuguese Jewish physician, Judah Abarbanel, whose *nom de plume* was Leon Hebrero. Impressed with Abarbanel's determination to declare his Jewishness despite persecution, El Inca declared his own Indianness.

El Inca began his literary career with *General History of Peru,* published in two volumes; *Royal Commentaries* was published in Lisbon, Portugal, in 1609, and *General History of Peru* was published in Cordoba in 1616 after his death. His major work, *The Florida of the Inca,* was written during a thirty-two year period of research and writing. It is a study of the history and culture of the Indians from the Southeast, Southwest, the Plains, California, Mexico, and South America. He interviewed men returning from expeditions and campaigns, studied published accounts, and combined his own knowledge and experience of his people. He wrote at a time when Spain was grappling with the question, "What is an Indian?" His book reflects his advocacy that Indians were equal to Europeans in their intellect and humanity. He presented Indian cultures and histories as credible, complex, and viable. El Inca died in Spain in 1616 and was buried in Cordoba. In April 1782, 150 years after his death, his Florida book was banned because it incited Indians in Peru to rebel. In 1951, the University of Texas Press chose it as its first publication. Juan Carlos, king of Spain, returned El Inca's remains to Cuzco, Peru, and interred them at the site of the temple of the Inca Viracocha, now a cathedral, where his royal ancestors had also been buried.

Sources: Weatherford, *Native Roots,* pp. 324–51; *Biographical Dictionary of Indians of the Americas,* Vol. 2, p. 779.

1663 Caleb Cheeshateaumauk (Mohegan) published the earliest known piece of writing by a Native North American. Cheeshateaumauk wrote *Honoratissimi Benefactores* in Latin while he was attending Harvard's Indian College. In 1679 another Indian, referred to only as Eleazar, wrote "In obitum Viri vere Reverendi D. Thomae Thackeri." At the time Indians in white-run schools learned and wrote in Latin and Greek. Few were literate in their own languages.

Sources: Wiget, ed., *Dictionary of Native American Literature*, p. 145.

1772 Samson Occom (Mohegan; 1723–1792) was the first Native American to publish a piece of literary work. He wrote *A Sermon Preached at the Execution of Moses Paul, an Indian,* which appealed to both American Indian and white audiences. He used the popular genre of the execution sermon to address the debilitating effects of alcoholism on Indian families. His publication was significant because of the manner in which he addressed an important issue while using a sophisticated literary style to engage the interest of his audience.

Sources: Wiget, *Dictionary of Native American Literature*, p. 145.

1794 Hendrick Aupaumut (Mahican) wrote *A Short Narration of My Last Journey to the Western Country,* in which he described his journey among American Indian tribes of the frontier West and his negotiations with them during his service as governmental liaison in the early 1790s. His publication was the first official report by a Native American person reporting on other Native American peoples. He recorded his journey in 1794 and published it in 1827.

Sources: Wiget, ed., *Dictionary of Native American Literature*, p. 148.

ca. 1826 Elias Boudinot (Cherokee; ca. 1803–1839) was one of the first American Indians to use protest writing to criticize and deplore American efforts to assimilate Indians. He wrote "An Address to the Whites," in which he declared that speculation and conjecture by whites about the feasibility of civilizing Indians must cease forever.

Sources: Dockstader, *Great North American Indians*, pp. 41–42; Waldman, *Who Was Who in Native American History*, p. 36; Wiget, ed., *Dictionary of Native American Literature*, pp. 146, 217–19.

1827 Pablo Tac (Luiseño; 1822–1841) published the first piece of literary writing produced by a California Native—an account of Luiseño life. Born in 1822 at Mission San Luis Rey de Francia, he was a Roman Catholic neophyte, who with another Luiseño youth, Agapito Amamix, was sent to Italy to complete his education and prepare for a religious life. The two boys registered at the Urban College in Rome on September 23, 1834. Agapito died in 1837. While at the college, Pablo met Giuseppe Caspar Mezzofanti, a well-known linguist who was interested in little-known languages. Mezzofanti began recording Pablo's native language. In addition, Pablo prepared a manuscript of Luiseño life and culture, which he also illustrated. The text was preserved in the Mezzofanti Collection of the Archiginnasio de Bologna library. Pablo wrote his tribal history between 1834 and his death on December 13, 1841.

Sources: Hewes, Minna and Gordon, "Indian Life and Customs at Mission San Luis Rey," *Americas*, Vol. 9, No. 1 (July 1952), pp. 87–106; Onis, José de, ed., *Las Misiones espanoles en los estados unidos. Tratado de Pablo Tac, neofito indio*, [Romaciza], ca. 1835; Traducción de Minna y Gordon Hewes, [New York], 1958.

ca. 1827 David Cusick (Tuscarora; d. ca. 1840) was the first person of his tribe to record tribal mythology; and he was one of the first Indians to attempt to preserve mythology and information about tribal social and cultural customs of Indian people. He was also the first Indian to interpret Iroquoian spirituality through Western pictorial art. Cusick's efforts included woodcuts on which he illustrated important stories relating to the founding of the Iroquois League. The publication of *David Cusick's Sketches of Ancient History of the Six Nations* met with much popularity and was reprinted several times. Although contemporary critics have dismissed the illustrations as primitive, confusing, imperfect, and rude, they remain an invaluable source for tribal members and non-Indians alike.

Sources: Brydon, Sherry, "Ingenuity in Art: The Early 19th Century Works of David and Dennis Cusick," *american indian art*, Vol. 20, No. 2 (Spring 1995), pp. 60–69; Champagne, ed., *The Native North American Almanac*, p. 756; Wiget, ed., *Dictionary of Native American Literature*, p. 147.

1829 William Apess (Pequot; 1798–1839), preacher, writer, and activist, authored the first full-length autobiography, *A Son of the Forest*. It merges the literary tradition of a Christian confession with sharp criticism of white mistreatment of Indians. Probably because its publication came at the height of the debate of Indian removal, it became popular and was reprinted several times. Apess later became involved in the Mashpee land dispute with the Commonwealth of Massachusetts. He was the most prolific of nineteenth-century Native American writers, intertwining sermons with the issue of Christian hypocrisy in matters concerning Indians. In addition to his autobiography, Apess authored several monographs and tracts. Most were devoted to Indian rights issues. In an essay entitled "An Indian's Looking-Glass for the White Man," he dared to point out to white readers that Jesus was not white.

Sources: Malinowski, ed., *Notable Native Americans*, pp. 14–16; Wiget, ed., *Dictionary of Native American Literature*, pp. 146, 179, 207–10; Witalec, ed., *Native North American Literature*, pp. 134–42.

1847 George Copway (Ojibwa; 1818–ca. 1863) published the first full-length travelogue by an Indian, *The Life, History, and Travels of Kah-ge-ga-gah-bowh*. In 1850 it was followed by publication of *The Traditional History and Characteristic Sketches of the Ojibway Nation*, the first tribal history in English by a Native American. Copway has been credited with being the first Indian to publish in English, but John Richardson's publication preceded his by fifteen years; nevertheless, he was Canada's first Native literary celebrity to gain prominence in the United States. He was twenty-nine when he published his travelogue and the public was intrigued to read a first-hand account written by an Indian; by 1848, it had been reprinted seven times. Copway became an international traveller and was acquainted with some of the leading literary giants of the time, including James Fennimore Cooper, Washington Irving, William Cullen Bryant, Henry Wadsworth Longfellow, and Francis Parkman.

Copway was born to full-blooded Ojibwa parents in 1818, and his parents converted to Methodism in 1828 when Ojibwa missionary Peter Jones arrived; Copway converted in 1830 after his mother's death. From the start, he was active in church work, first as an interpreter, translating part of the New Testament, and as a missionary. In exchange for his service, he was able to receive some schooling. In 1845 he was accused of taking funds without permission and was arrested and imprisoned; and he lost his standing in the Methodist church. He turned to writing for income and published his autobiography in 1847, gaining much prominence. His fame was short-lived, however, and he spent the rest of his life in relative obscurity. He is reported to have died around 1863.

Sources: Dockstader, *Great North American Indians*, p. 59; Malinowski, ed., *Notable Native Americans*, pp. 89–91; Wiget, ed., *Dictionary of Native American Literature*, pp. 354–55.

1848 Maungwudaus, also known as George Henry (Ojibwa), published a work of travel literature entitled *An Account of the Chippewa Indians, Who Have Been Travelling Among the Whites*. It was the first travelogue written by a Native American commenting about white people. Maungwudaus formed a dance troupe and during their tour through Europe he wrote his travelogue. Maungwudaus was a lapsed Methodist missionary who wrote of his impressions and provided amusing anecdotes of the people and customs he witnessed.

Sources: Wiget, ed., *Dictionary of Native American Literature*, pp. 148, 355–56.

1854 John Rollin Ridge (Cherokee; 1827–1867), also known as Cheesquatalawny (Yellow Bird), published the first novel by a Native American, *The Life and Adventures of Joaquin Murietta*. Ridge also authored several poems published posthumously in 1868. He was born in 1827 into the wealthy and prominent Ridge family that supported land cessions to the United States and Cherokee removal to Oklahoma. Although not authorized to represent the Cherokee government, several of the Ridge men signed a treaty ceding land. Resentment from political opponents forced the Ridge family to move to Arkansas where Ridge finished school. In 1850, John Ridge moved to California after becoming involved in a dispute in which he killed Judge D. Kell. It was in California that he wrote his novel and published poetry. In addition, he founded, edited, and wrote for several newspapers. He was the first editor of the *Sacramento Bee*, which was started in 1857; he edited the *California Express*, the *Daily National Democrat*, the *San Francisco Herald*, the *Trinity National*, and the *Grass Valley National*.

Sources: Bolton and Wilson, *American Indian Lives*, pp. 11–23; Champagne, ed., *Native America*, p. 676; *Dictionary of Native American Literature*, p. 149; Malinowski, ed., *Notable Native Americans*, pp. 361–63; Witalec, ed., *Native North American Literature*, p. 540.

1868 John Rollin Ridge (Cherokee; 1827–1867), also known as Cheesquatalawny (Yellow Bird), authored a group of poems that were published posthumously in 1868. The publication may be the first book-length collection of poetry by a Native American. Few of the poems have American Indian themes, however.

Sources: *Dictionary of Native American Literature*, p. 149.

ca. 1880s Susette La Flesche (Omaha; 1854–1903), writing under the name "Bright Eyes," published what is believed to be the first non-legend short story written by an American Indian. "Nedawi" was published in *St. Nicholas*, a children's magazine. In 1883 La Flesche published "Omaha Legends and Tent Stories" in the June issue of *Wide Awake*. She was the sister of Susan LaFlesche Picotte and Francis La Flesche.

Sources: Champagne, ed., *Chronology of Native North American History*, p. 227; Malinowski, *Notable Native Americans*, pp. 240–42.

1883 Sarah Winnemucca Hopkins (Paiute; ca. 1844–1891), one of the most prominent Indian leaders of the early reservation period, published the first autobiography written by an American Indian woman, *Life Among the Piutes: Their Wrongs and Claims*. The book is also a colorful narrative of tribal history with a central theme of Indian-white relations. An interpreter, lecturer, teacher, and writer, Winnemucca was also known for her courage, serving the U.S. Army as a scout, and for her skill in diplomacy. She had a talent for languages and spoke Paiute, English, Spanish, and several Indian languages. She was an Indian rights activist and educator, establishing in 1884 the first all-Indian school—the Peabody School for Indian children in Lovelock, Nevada. She envisioned a model school where both the student's native language and English would be taught. Lack of funding forced her to close the school after four years.

Sources: *Biographical Dictionary of Indians of the Americas,* Vol. 2, p. 830–34; Champagne, ed., *Native America,* p. 673; Fowler, Catherine S., "Sarah Winnemucca, Northern Paiute, 1844–1891," in *American Indian Intellectuals,* edited by Margo Liberty, pp. 33–42; Wiget, ed., *Dictionary of Native American Literature,* pp. 299–302; Witalec, ed., *Native North American Literature,* pp. 675–82.

1887 George Bushotter (Yankton-Miniconjou Sioux; 1864–1892) was the first Lakota ethnographer. He was born in 1864 in Dakota Territory and during his early life he participated in many of the traditional ceremonies. Many people thought he would become a medicine man because of the peculiar events in his early life. He was unafraid of dangerous and sacred animals and he often crossed the boundaries of propriety when he was around them. When he was still young his father was killed by white men and Bushotter gained a great fear of whites. Nevertheless, curiosity about white people led him east when he volunteered to attend Hampton in 1878. He studied there until 1881, returning to Lower Brulé as an assistant teacher before going to the East again for additional education. When dire financial circumstances threatened, James Owen Dorsey, a friend who was employed by the Smithsonian's Bureau of Ethnology, hired him to record information about tribal customs and stories. The job lasted less than one year, but what he wrote became the earliest recorded information about Lakota mythology, which also represented the first first-hand interpretation by a Lakota. Bushotter wrote 258 stories on 3,296 handwritten pages in about ten months. He had great enthusiasm for the project and his appreciation for his cultural background increased. Bushotter died on February 2, 1892, at the age of twenty-eight.

Sources: DeMallie, Raymond J., "George Bushotter: The First Lakota Ethnographer," in *American Indian Intellectuals,* edited by Margo Liberty, pp. 91–102; Champagne, ed., *The Native North American Almanac,* p. 1024; Waldman, *Who Was Who in Native American History,* p. 48.

1891 Sophia Alice Callahan (Creek; 1868–1894) wrote the first novel by an Indian woman. A fictional account of the murder of Sitting Bull and the Wounded Knee massacre, *Wynema: A Child of the Forest* was published in 1891 and was not well received; even today critics find many shortcomings. It is not especially well-written or well-plotted and uses the domestic romance plot common to women's literature of that period; however, Callahan incorporated Creek customs and values in her story.

Sources: Bataille, ed., *Native American Women,* p. 51; *Dictionary of Native American Literature,* p. 148; Foreman, Carolyn Thomas. "S. Alice Callahan, Author of Wynema: A Child of the Forest," *Chronicles of Oklahoma,* 33 (Autumn 1955), pp. 300–304.

Opposite page:
Sarah Winnemucca, a proficient interpreter during her time, was the first Indian woman to publish a book.

1899 Simon Pokagon (Potowatomie) has been credited with writing the first novel about Indian life by an Indian, *Queen of the Woods*. Using Potowatomie society as a background, the story tells of a man's return to his tribal culture after years of living among whites. The plot of the story recounts his reconciliation of his heritage with his experiences. Much of the story deals with alcohol abuse and its effects. True authorship of the book has been questioned, with critics suspecting that it was ghostwritten by Cyrus H. Engle, a publisher. The style of the story is melodramatic and some critics suggest that it imitates European literary conventions. Pokagon himself was controversial in his own tribal community because he dispensed tribal assets without approval. He was a strong advocate of Indian assimilation into white society and was lauded by the white community.

Sources: *Biographical Dictionary of Indians of the Americas,* Vol. 2, p. 542; Waldman, *Who Was Who in Native American History,* p. 278; Witalec, ed., *Native North American Literature,* p. 514.

1927 Mourning Dove (Colville Salish; 1888–1936), also known as Christine Quintasket, wrote a depiction of the great Montana cattle range, entitled *Cogewea the Half-blood,* which is considered the first novel published by an American Indian woman in the twentieth century. It is a depiction of the great Montana cattle range. (Sophia Alice Callahan published a novel in 1891, making that the first novel by an American Indian woman.) Mourning Dove spent fifteen years editing and rewriting before the publication of *Cogewea the Half-blood.* Critics have suggested that a close white friend and Indian rights activist, Lucullus Virgil McWhorter had written the book.

Sources: Witalec, ed. *Native North American Literature,* p. 463.

1930s Todd Downing (Choctaw) was probably the first Native American author of a series of detective/mystery novels. His stories, which are set in Mexico and the southwestern United States, contain minor Indian characters. Of Indian writers in the 1930s, Downing was the most prolific, writing nine novels. His books include *Murder on Tour* (1931) and *The Case of the Unconquered Sisters* (1934).

Sources: *Biographical Dictionary of Indians of the Americas,* Vol. 1, p. 195; Davis, *Native America in the Twentieth Century,* p. 317; Wiget, ed., *Dictionary of Native American Literature,* p. 152.

1932 John Joseph Mathews (Osage; 1895–1979) published the first book printed by the University of Oklahoma Press, *Wahkontah: The Osage and the White Man's Road,* which recounts the history of the Osage during the early reservation period. In 1931, Mathews was bequeathed the diary and notes of Laban J. Miles, a Quaker and federal agent assigned to the Osage reservation for fifteen years. From these notes and with the encouragement of Joseph Brandt, founder and director of the Oklahoma Press, he wrote *Wahkontah.* Hailed for its literary creativity and its frank presentation of the Osage struggle to adjust to the white world, the book was recommended by the Book-of-the-Month Club. Mathews went on to publish four more books. His last work, *The Osages: Children of the Middle Waters,* is a massive study based on meticulous archival research and oral history and is considered a nearly definitive history of the Osage and the most literary tribal history. The research was multidisciplinary in approach and critics consider it an outstanding example of the ethnohistorical mode. Mathews, a college athlete, also served on the Osage Tribal Council. He was offered a Rhodes scholarship to study at Oxford University but refused it.

See also: Education, ca. 1920.

Sources: Bailey, Garrick, "John Joseph Mathews," in *American Indian Intellectuals,* edited by Margo Liberty, pp. 205–14; *Biographical Dictionary of Indians of the Americas,* Vol. 1, p. 401; Malinowski, ed., *Notable Native Americans,* pp. 266–67; Wiget, ed., *Dictionary of Native American Literature,* pp. 245–49.

1936 D'Arcy McNickle (Cree; 1904–1977) published *The Surrounded,* a highly polished novel about life on the Flathead Indian reservation. It is considered the first novel of the Native American Renaissance in literature. McNickle himself was a Cree/French/Irish mixed-blood and not a member of the Flathead tribe, making his membership in the community tenuous. He did not legally belong to any Indian community until he and his sisters were adopted into the Salish Kootenai Confederated Tribes in 1905. *The Surrounded* reflects the conflicts and uncertainty connected with his lack of a sense of belonging and explores the interrelationships between Indians and whites, and between full-bloods and mixed-bloods, and ultimately self-discovery and self-acceptance. The novel also describes the disintegration of a tribe because of loss of land and the destruction of tribal religion and values.

McNickle also worked for the Bureau of Indian Affairs (BIA), where he was an ardent advocate of Indian rights. He resigned because he strongly disagreed with the termination policies of the BIA during the 1950s. He worked with the American Indian Development Corporation, which was devoted to Indian community development. From 1966 to 1971, he worked at the University of Saskatchewan, Regina campus, where he established a small anthropology department. Before his death he worked with the Center for the History of the American Indian at the Newberry Library, where he left his papers; the center now bears his name—The D'Arcy McNickle Center.

Sources: Champagne, ed., *The Native North American Almanac,* p. 1105; Malinowski, ed., *Notable Native Americans,* pp. 267–69; Wiget, ed., *Dictionary of Native American Literature,* pp. 251–58.

1942 Markoosie Patsang (Inuit) was the first Canadian Inuit to publish a book in English, *Harpoon of the Hunter.* Originally published in serial form by *Inuttituut* ("Eskimo Way"), an Inuit community magazine, and written in syllabics, it was then translated and published in book form by the author. A highly acclaimed novel, the story is of individual and community survival.

Sources: Wiget, ed., *Dictionary of Native American Literature,* p. 362; Witalec, ed., *Native North American Literature,* p. 404.

1961 Emily Pauline Johnson (Mohawk; 1861–1913) became the first Canadian author whose image appeared on a Canadian postage stamp. The issuance of the five-cent stamp marked the one-hundredth anniversary of her birth. A writer of poetry and short fiction, she also received a prize from *Dominion Magazine* for her short story "A Red Girl's Reasoning," published in her collection of short stories, *The Moccasin Maker,* in 1913. Her other published work includes *White Wampum, Canadian Born,* and *Flint and Feathers.*

Sources: *Biographical Dictionary of Indians of the Americas,* Vol. 1, p. 319; Champagne, ed., *Native America,* p. 690; Champagne, *The Native North American Almanac,* p. 1078; Malinowski, ed., *Notable Native Americans,* pp. 210–12; Wiget, ed., *Dictionary of Native American Literature,* pp. 239–43.

1969 On May 5, 1969, author N. Scott Momaday (Kiowa/Cherokee; 1934–) became the first American Indian to receive the Pulitzer Prize, for his novel *House Made of Dawn.* Momaday graduated with a B.A. from the University of New Mexico in 1958, a M.A. from Stanford in 1960, and a Ph.D. in 1963. Momaday is considered the first voice in the literary renaissance of the early 1970s. In 1989, he was the first literary artist to receive the Jay Silverheels Achievement Award from the National Center for American Indian Enterprise. The award is given annually to an outstanding individual of American Indian descent who has achieved personal and professional success while contributing to his/her community.

See also: Education, 1969; Literature, 1989.

Sources: *Biographical Dictionary of Indians of the Americas,* Vol. 1, p. 432; Champagne, ed., *Chronology of Native North American History,* p. 358; Champagne, ed., *The Native North American Almanac,* p.1109; Malinowski, ed., *Notable Native Americans,* pp. 273–75; "Momaday Selected to Receive Jay Silverheels Achievement Award," *Navajo Times,* September 20, 1990, p. A-5; Witalec, ed , *Native North American Literature,* p. 432.

1975 *Carriers of the Dream Wheel,* edited by Duane Niatum (Klallam; 1938–), was published; it was the first substantial collection of Native American poetry.

Sources: Champagne, ed., *Chronology of Native North American History,* p. 400.

1983 Joseph Bruchac (Abenaki; 1942–) published an anthology of new Native American writers that was the first of its kind. Through the Greenfield Press, which he and his wife founded, Bruchac has published the works of talented new Native writers, many of whom have later achieved critical success. He has also devoted his efforts to multicultural literature and has published the work of Asian Americans— *Breaking Silence: An Anthology of Asian American Poetry,* for which he won the American Book Award in 1984. Bruchac has also encouraged the writings of prison inmates, developing a writing program for them while teaching at Skidmore College. Bruchac is a prolific writer, having contributed more than four hundred poems and stories to publications. He has published several collections of short stories, including *Keepers of the Earth.* His Greenfield Review Press published *The Greenfield Review,* a literary journal devoted to multicultural publication.

Sources: Champagne, ed., *The Native North American Almanac,* p. 1021; Malinowski, ed., *Notable Native Americans,* pp. 58–60; Witalec, ed., *Native North American Literature,* pp. 184–94.

Opposite page: **Navarre Scott Momaday, one of the premier writers in the United States today, has immortalized his Kiowa heritage in numerous novels and poetry, one of which, *House Made of Dawn,* garnered a Pulitzer for fiction.**

1983 Beth Brant (Mohawk; 1941–) edited the first anthology of contemporary Indian women's art and literature, *A Gathering of Spirit: A Collection by North American Women.* The anthology includes the work of prominent authors as well as lesser known ones; and in preparing the work, Brant advertised in tribal newspapers and contacted writers in women's prisons. Because of its ground-breaking scope, this anthology has been reprinted several times. Brant is a published author in her own right; her books include *Mohawk Trail* and *Food and Spirits.* She has also provided creative workshops for women, including those in prison, and high school students.

Sources: Bataille, ed., *Native American Women*, p. 34; Malinowski, ed., *Notable Native Americans*, pp. 51–53; Witalec, ed., *Native North American Literature*, pp. 177–79.

1987 Leslie Marmon Silko (Laguna Pueblo; 1848–) became one of twenty-one recipients of a fellowship from the MacArthur Foundation. She is the only known American Indian to receive the coveted award. Silko is the author of such notable publications as *Ceremony* and *Almanac of the Dead*. In both novels she draws heavily on her roots as a Laguna woman and as an Indian woman. *Almanac of the Dead* has been called one of the most ambitions literary undertakings. She is one of the most prominent Indian writers.

Leslie Marmon Silko, a novelist and poet best known for *Ceremony*.

Sources: Bataille, ed., *Native American Women*, pp. 233–34; Champagne, ed. *Chronology of Native North American History*, p. 316; Wiget, ed., *Dictionary of Native American Literature*, p. 679; Witalec, ed., *Native North American Literature*, pp. 575–86.

1989 Rex Lee Jim (Navajo) published the first book of poetry in Navajo. A 1986 graduate of Princeton University, where he studied literature, Jim is a Ph.D. student at the University of Arizona studying computational linguistics. Upon his return to the reservation, he composed a libretto for a Navajo opera. Jim has taught Navajo literacy at Rock Point School. One of his purposes in publishing his poetry in Navajo was to provide literature printed in Navajo for the large population of adults and children who are literate in Navajo.

Sources: Dinéłtsoi, Mazii, *Saad;* Malinowski, ed., *Notable Native Americans,* p. 475; "Rock Point Author Publishes Poetry in Navajo," *Navajo Times,* Vol. 30, No. 1 (January 4, 1990), p.13.

1989 N. Scott Momaday (Kiowa/Cherokee; 1934–) was the first literary artist to receive the Jay Silverheels Achievement Award from the National Center for American Indian Enterprise. The award is bestowed annually to an outstanding individual of American Indian descent who has achieved personal and professional success while contributing significantly to his or her community. Momaday was the tenth recipient and the first artist so honored.

Sources: "Momaday Selected to Receive Jay Silverheels Achievement Award," *Navajo Times,* Vol. 30, No. 38 (September 20, 1990), p. A-5.

1989 Jeannette Armstrong (Okanagon; 1948–) established En'Owkin School of International Writing, the first credit-awarding, creating writing program designed for and operated by Native people in Canada. The school is affiliated with the University of Victoria. Armstrong has been the director since September 4, 1989. In 1990 En'Owkin published its first journal, *Gatherings.* One of the goals of the director is to educate young Native people about Indian culture and history. The two young adult novels Armstrong has written concern issues relevant to Indian youth as they struggle to reconcile their ethnic heritage with modern life among non-Indians.

Sources: Bataille, *Native American Women*, pp. 13–14.

1990 The letters of Tiana Bighorse (Navajo; 1917–) were edited by Noel Bennett and published as *Bighorse the Warrior.* This represents the first historical account of a Navajo warrior's personal military experiences during the 1860s and is the only book that addresses what life was like for the Navajo before and during the period of the Long Walk (1864–1868). Bighorse spent many childhood evenings hearing her father relate his experiences and retells the stories of her father's service under Manuelito's leadership before his final surrender. It reveals to outsiders information about military organization and what actually happened in the lives of Navajo fleeing before the advancing American military. The book is particularly unique in that it is the Navajo perspective told simply and straightforwardly.

Sources: Bataille, ed., *Native American Women*, p. 24.

MEDIA

PRINT

1826 *The Muzzinyegun of Literary Voyages,* a weekly magazine, was established by Henry Rowe Schoolcraft at Sault Ste. Marie, Michigan. It was the first magazine established to deal exclusively with issues and concerns of American Indians. Schoolcraft was not an Indian, but his wife and her brother and mother were, and they contributed heavily to the magazine and influenced its direction. The publication dealt with Ojibwa mythology, superstitions, history, current affairs, contemporary biographies, language, and information about other tribes, their leaders, western geography, scenery, Mexican civilization, and the fur trade. Poems and essays were also included. Schoolcraft's wife, and her mother and brother contributed the major portion of the articles printed. The publication was the first major effort to publish information about Indians on a regular basis, with Indians contributing a substantial part of the magazine.

Sources: Littlefield and Parins, eds., *American Indian and Alaska Native Newspapers and Periodicals, 1826–1924,* p. 44.

1828 *The Cherokee Phoenix* became the first American Indian newspaper in North America. It was also the first newspaper to be published in a Native language. Elias Boudinot, also known as Buck Watie (Cherokee; 1803–1839), was its first editor. It was established by the Cherokee Tribe as a response to attempts by the state of Georgia to extend its laws over the Cherokee Nation. Because of its opposition to land cessions and removal of Indian tribes from their lands, *The Cherokee Phoenix* was under constant attack by the state of Georgia. As a tribal paper, it was charged with presenting the tribal government's views. The issue of Georgia's efforts to extend jurisdiction over the Cherokee became a major issue. The Cherokee government under John Ross refused to give up tribal sovereignty and strongly opposed removal. Boudinot and his relatives saw no solution but to accept removal and so split with the Ross faction. Boudinot resigned as editor in 1832 but the paper continued until May 31, 1834, when the presses were confiscated by Georgia militia. Boudinot is known as a signatory of the Treaty of New Echota, December 29, 1835, also known as the Cherokee Removal Treaty. For this act, Boudinot was executed June 22, 1839, in Indian Territory.

Sources: *Biographical Dictionary of Indians of the Americas,* Vol. 1, p. 83; Danky and Hady, eds., *Native American Periodicals and Newspapers, 1828–1982,* pp. xvi, 102; Hodge, *Handbook of American Indians,* p. 232; Littlefield and Parins, eds., *American Indian and Alaska Native*

Newspapers and Periodicals, 1826–1924, pp. xii, 84–91; Waldman, *Who Was Who in Native American History,* p. 36.

1844 *The Cherokee Messenger* was the first periodical publication in Indian Territory. It preceded *The Cherokee Advocate,* a newspaper, by one month. Sponsored by the Baptist Mission, it was a religious magazine devoted to spreading Christianity among the Cherokee.

Sources: Littlefield and Parins, eds., *American Indian and Alaska Native Newspapers and Periodicals, 1826–1924,* p. 82.

1844 Edward Wilkerson Bushyhead (Cherokee) worked at the *Cherokee Messenger,* the first newspaper published in Arkansas. Bushyhead was only seven years old during the Trail of Tears, in which his people were removed from their homeland to Indian Territory, or present-day Oklahoma. He founded the *Union* newspaper in San Diego, the third paper printed in California. In 1889, Bushyhead became a partner in the Gould, Hutton and Company printing firm.

Sources: *Biographical Dictionary of Indians of the Americas,* Vol. 1, p. 104; Littlefield and Parins, eds., *American Indian and Alaska Native Newspapers and Periodicals, 1826–1924,* p. 82.

1844 William Potter Ross (Cherokee) was the first editor of the Cherokee newspaper, *The Cherokee Advocate,* the first Indian newspaper published in Indian Territory. Established by the Cherokee Tribal Nation as their official paper, the weekly newspaper was mandated by the Tribal Council as a bilingual (Cherokee and English) publication. It was published in Tahlequah. With the first printing, Ross announced his intent to uplift the moral and intellectual condition of the Cherokee people and to disseminate information about them that would demonstrate that. Consequently, articles dealt with tribal government news, agent's reports, laws, foreign news, fiction, prose, and general articles. Ross was particularly concerned about ignorance on the part of whites and sought to remedy that by publishing articles that demonstrated their "civilized" status. Ross and other Cherokee had just completed the removal from the eastern homelands and were convinced that ignorance had been the major cause of their removal. In October 1848, Ross was appointed a delegate to Washington and relinquished editorship of the publication. *The Cherokee Advocate* continued printing until 1911, when the federal government ordered the sale of the printing office and its equipment. The Cherokee type was sent to the Smithsonian Institute. This was following the abolishment of the tribal governments of the Five Civilized Tribes in Oklahoma.

Sources: *Biographical Dictionary of Indians of the Americas,* Vol. 2; Hodge, *Handbook of American Indians North of Mexico,* p. 232; Littlefield and Parins, eds., *American Indian and Alaska Native Newspapers and Periodicals, 1826–1924,* pp. 63–72.

1848 *The Choctaw Telegraph* was established in November 1848 "to advocate and disseminate morality, education, agriculture and general intelligence." It was printed in Choctaw and English and was edited by David Folsom (Choctaw) and published by D. G. Ball. Folsom attended the Choctaw Academy in Blue Springs, Kentucky, and in 1829 was one of six Choctaw boys selected by school founder and congressman Richard M. Johnson to return to Mississippi. The paper pledged to remain neutral in politics and religion and devote itself to news, foreign and domestic, and to provide regular information on agriculture. It also reported on the proceedings of the tribal government and printed new laws as they were passed. One of the most important elements was the paper's regular discourses against liquor and tobacco consumption. The paper folded in December 1849 for lack of funds.

Sources: Foreman, *Oklahoma Imprints, 1835–1907;* Littlefield and Parins, eds., *American Indian and Alaska Native Newspapers and Periodicals, 1826–1924,* pp. 106–107; Morrison, James D., "News for the Choctaws," *Chronicles of Oklahoma,* Vol. 17 (Summer 1949), p. 207–222.

1850 Publication of the *Dakota Tawaxitku Kin,* or the *Dakota Friend,* began. It was edited by Gideon Hollister Pond for the Dakota Mission. It attempted to provide non-Indians with information about the Dakota to promote improved understanding of American Indians. The publication also worked to raise interest among the Dakota in education.

Sources: Littlefield and Parins, eds., *American Indian and Alaska Native Newspapers and Periodicals, 1826–1924,* pp. 128–31.

1851 *Copway's American Indian* was the first newspaper to address intertribal concerns. It was established to encourage the development of an Indian territory on the Missouri River, which would become an Indian state in the Union. It would be populated by tribes from the Great Lakes region.

Sources: Littlefield and Parins, eds., *American Indian and Alaska Native Newspapers and Periodicals, 1826–1924,* pp. 112–16.

1854 *The Chickasaw Intelligencer* was the first newspaper of the Chickasaw Nation to be established by an association of private Chickasaw citizens rather than a tribal government. Its purpose was to provide information and advance science, literature, agriculture, education, the arts, and manufactures among the Chickasaw and other Indians. A perspectus was issued in 1852, and although no known copies survive, it was being published in 1854. Jackson Frazier served as president and B. S. Love was the secretary of the Chickasaw association that issued the paper.

Sources: Foreman, *Oklahoma Imprints, 1835–1907,* p. 115; Littlefield and Parins, eds., *American Indian and Alaska Native Newspapers and Periodicals, 1826–1924,* p. 414; Ray, *Early Oklahoma Newspapers.*

1854 *A Wreath of Cherokee Rose Buds* was the first American Indian student publication. Its editors were students of the Cherokee Female Seminary. It focused primarily on literary expressions of the students. Many of the students were receiving traditional education and were expected to be creative in their writings. The magazine gave them that opportunity. The publication remained active until 1857, when the school was closed for lack of funds. It was reopened several years after the end of the Civil War.

Sources: Littlefield and Parins, eds., *American Indian and Alaska Native Newspapers and Periodicals, 1826–1924,* pp. 407–408.

1857 John Rollin Ridge (Cherokee; 1827–1867), also known as Cheesquatalawny, (Yellow Bird), was the founding editor of the *Sacramento Daily Bee,* which was started in February of 1857. He was the first American Indian to edit a non-Indian newspaper. He later sold it to James McClatchy, and the paper became known as the *Sacramento Bee,* one of the nation's most prominent newspapers. From 1857 to 1867, Ridge also owned or edited at least ten other publications, including the *California Express* and the *Daily National Democrat.* He was a devoted supporter of the Union Democratic Party and was open about his political opinions. He was highly educated and well trained in the field of journalism.

See also: Literature, 1854.

Sources: Littlefield and Parins, eds., *American Indian and Alaska Native Newspapers and Periodicals, 1826–1924,* pp. xiv, 327–28; Malinowski, ed., *Notable Native Americans,* pp. 361–63; *Tribune Newspapers* (Mesa, Arizona), February 12, 1996, p. B-4.

1860 Founded by John C. Wheeler (Cherokee), the *Fort Smith Picayune* was a monthly publication dedicated to providing humorous articles, the first American Indian newspaper to focus on humor.

Sources: Littlefield and Parins, eds., *American Indian and Alaska Native Newspapers and Periodicals, 1826–1924.*

1868 *The San Diego Union* was begun by Edward Bushyhead (Cherokee) on October 10, 1868. It was the first newspaper privately owned by an Indian that did not focus exclusively on Indian issues. In 1870 Bushyhead became the principal owner when his partner sold his share to him. *The San Diego Union* was interested in promoting the economic development of California, particularly, San Diego. It was almost a booster paper in its tone and it reported regularly on railroad news, agriculture, silk culture, and local laws and elections. It reported and encouraged the development of natural resources. In this latter regard it published reports of difficulties with the Indians. It continues to be published today.

Sources: Littlefield and Parins, eds., *American Indian and Alaska Native Newspapers and Periodicals, 1826–1924,* pp. 330–33.

1872 William F. Wheeler and his son John C. Wheeler (Cherokee) began *The Wheeler's Independent,* the first non-tribally but Native-owned newspaper to address the concerns of the Native American community. The purpose of the Wheelers was to establish an affordable family newspaper; and farmers, mechanics, and business people were encouraged to subscribe. Eash issue included articles on agriculture, household hints, family medicine, and literary pieces.

Sources: Hudson, John A., and Robert L. Peterson, "Arkansas Newspapers in the University of Texas Collection," *Arkansas Historical Quarterly,* Vol. 14 (Autumn 1955), pp. 207–244; Littlefield and Parins, eds., *American Indian and Alaska Native Newspapers and Periodicals, 1826–1924,* pp. 401–402.

1872 *The Vindicator* began publication at Atoka, Indian Territory, on February 28, 1872. It was devoted to local, Choctaw national news and news of Indians in general. It was established by Elias Boudinot who used the paper to advocate for allotment of Indian lands and to allow for white settlers to move onto Indian lands of the Choctaw and Chickasaw.

Sources: Danky and Hady, eds., *Native American Periodicals and Newspapers, 1828–1982,* p. 437; Hodge, *Handbook of American Indians;* Littlefield and Parins, eds., *American Indian and Alaska Native Newspapers and Periodicals, 1826–1924,* pp. 371–73.

1873 *Our Monthly* was a community newsletter that was the first paper to focus on concerns common to two Indian Nations, the Creek and Choctaw. It was printed almost completely in Muskogee, a language common to both groups. It was issued from January 1873 through October 1875. Nearly 85–90 percent of it was published in Creek. The paper was published at Tallahassee, Creek Nation, with the Reverend W. S. and Miss A. A. Robertson as editors.

Sources: Danky and Hady, eds., *Native American Periodicals and Newspapers, 1828–1982,* p. 340; Hodge, *Handbook of American Indians,* p. 233.

1875 Elias C. Boudinot owned the first independent Cherokee-owned newspaper, *The Indian Progress.* It was established at Muskokgee, Creek Nation, Indian Territory, and was ordered by the Creek Council to close down after its first few publications. The purpose of the paper was to counter the official stance of the tribal leadership on political issues. It also aimed to advance the idea of removal and assimilation. Boudinot openly and steadfastly supported white settlement of Indian Territory. He was the first editor of the *Cherokee Phoenix,* the first Indian newspaper. During that time he opposed Indian removal and white settlement of Indian lands, however, when members of his family became convinced that removal was the best alternative for the Cherokee, he became a staunch supporter. He was removed as editor because of his political views. His involvement with *The Indian Progress* was to publicly oppose the Cherokee government's opposition to white settlement.

Boudinot was highly educated, having lived in New England during his years in school. He attended law school in Arkansas and was admitted to the Arkansas bar and the bar of the U.S. Court for the Western District of Arkansas. During the Civil War, he served in the regiment of Cherokee volunteers under Stand Watie. Following the war, Boudinot became immersed in the newspaper business. *The Indian Progress* was vehemently opposed to the John Ross Cherokee government and was openly critical of it. The unpopular opinions of *The Indian Progress* propelled the establishment of *The Indian Journal,* a paper chartered by the Creek Council, which would truly voice the opinions of Indians. *The Indian Progress* issued its last publication March 24, 1876.

Sources: Littlefield and Parins, eds., *American Indian and Alaska Native Newspapers and Periodicals, 1826–1924,* pp. 214–17.

1876 *The Indian Journal* was established in May 1876 to represent the interests of the Five Civilized Tribes. It was formed by representatives of the Cherokee, Choctaw, Chickasaw, Seminole, and Creek Nations, who were among the most influential citizens of the Indian Territory. It began as a joint-stock publishing company, chartered by an act of the Creek National Council and signed into law in 1875. In 1877 the Creek Council provided funds. William Ross became the first editor.

The Indian Journal began as a response to Elias Boudinot and E. Poe Harris establishing *The Indian Progress,* which the two used to advocate allotment and opening up Indian Territory for white settlement. Harris was ejected from the Cherokee Nation and Boudinot was ordered to move his press machines. Ross used his paper to oppose Boudinot and called his paper the "Terror-tionalizers." It promised to print news from the Creek and Cherokee and from the Sac and Fox Agency as well as the Wichita Agency. It also printed news of other Indian people. Although it soon lost its intertribal emphasis, it was the beginning of publications that addressed the common interests and concerns of Native Americans. The paper survived two burnings and several changes in editors and ownership. (At one time Alexander Posey was editor and owner.) In 1877 it passed from Indian ownership, but returned to its originators in 1887. The Journal Printing Company printed *The Indian Missionary, Our Brother in Red* while it was also printing *The Indian Journal*. It became the longest lasting Indian newspaper.

Sources: Danky and Hady, eds., *Native American Periodicals and Newspapers, 1828–1982*, pp. 183–84 ; Littlefield and Parins, eds., *American Indian and Alaska Native Newspapers and Periodicals, 1826–1924*, pp. 189–95.

1878 *The Choctaw News* was the first Choctaw tribal newspaper; and though it was short-lived, it became one of the first dailies published in the interest of an Indian tribe. Published at Chahta Tamaha in the Choctaw Nation, it reported daily on the deliberations of the Tribal Council's sessions and that of the Choctaw Supreme Court. Each day brought a report of Council deliberations, minutes of meetings that related to the Council sessions, committee agendas, local news, rumors of bills, the message of the principal chief in its entirety, local news, and news items that were broader in scope and more far-reaching. When it closed it promised to do its reporting again, but it was replaced by *The Indian Champion* in 1884. It was published between November and December 1878.

Sources: Danky and Hady, eds., *Native American Periodicals and Newspapers, 1828–1982*, p. 108; Littlefield and Parins, eds., *American Indian and Alaska Native Newspapers and Periodicals, 1826–1924*, pp. 105–106.

1879 *The Hallequah* was the first school monthly to be edited and published entirely by young women. Ida Johnson, Lulu Walker, and Arizona Jackson, students at the Seneca, Shawnee, and Wyandotte Industrial Boarding School at the Quapaw Agency in Indian Territory, produced the paper. It was published on behalf of the Hallequah Society, the school's literary club and included news about the school, the local mission, church announcements, letters from former students, and student writings, such as essays. The publication was the first attempt by the three young women and provided them with on-the-job training. Parts of the paper were translated into Shawnee and Wyandot. The school was in the care of Quakers and therefore many articles appeared in the paper that dealt with religion and temperance. The last issue on record was November 12, 1881.

Sources: Littlefield and Parins, eds., *American Indian and Alaska Native Newspapers and Periodicals, 1826–1924*.

1884 *The Indian Champion* became the first regularly published Choctaw tribal newspaper on February 23, 1884. *The Choctaw News* was the first Choctaw paper to report on Choctaw national government's proceedings, but it lasted for the duration of the government's proceedings. It followed the practice of many tribal papers in being established for the duration of government proceedings. *The Indian Champion,* on the other hand was printed regularly throughout the year. The Choctaw national government appropriated funds for publication so that the tribe would have a reliable source of news.

Sources: Danky and Hady, eds. *Native American Periodicals and Newspapers, 1828–1982*, p. 174; Littlefield and Parins, eds., *American Indian and Alaska Native Newspapers and Periodicals, 1826–1924*, pp. 171–73.

1885 *The Indian* was the first journal published in Canada. It was edited by Peter Edmund Jones (Ojibwa), the son of Peter Jones, the eminent Ojibwa missionary. It was issued bi-monthly from Hagersville, Ontario, from December 30, 1885 to December 29, 1886. It was printed primarily in English, but included some articles in Ojibwa.

Sources: Hodge, *Handbook of American Indians*, p. 233; Wiget, *Dictionary of Native American Literature*, p. 356.

1886 Theodore H. Beaulieu (Chippewa/Ojibwa) and Gustave Beaulieu (Chippewa/Ojibwa) founded *The Progress*, the first private Chippewa-owned publication established to meet the needs of Chippewa people. It was a weekly publication that was, from the beginning, openly critical of the Indian Bureau. The Beaulieu family were prominent in the affairs of Minnesota and were keenly aware of Indian issues and what they thought were inequities in the nature and implementation of Indian policies. T. J. Sheehan, the local Indian agent, pronounced *The Progress* incendiary and revolutionary, and promptly ordered it closed down, which prompted a law suit. In 1887, the U.S. District Court ordered the paper's property restored and compensation made. In October of that same year, printing resumed. The paper was published until July 1889 and was a forerunner of the strongly pro-Indian newspapers of the twentieth century.

Sources: Littlefield and Parins, eds., *American Indian and Alaska Native Newspapers and Periodicals, 1826–1924*, pp. 301–303; Vizenor, Gerald, "A Brief Historical Study and General Content Description of a Newspaper Published on the White Earth Indian Reservation in Becker County, Minnesota" (unpublished typescript), Minnesota Historical Society, 1965.

1889 *The Daily Capital* was the only daily paper published in Indian Territory at the time. It began publication at Tahlequah, Cherokee Nation, November 1889. It was first established as the *Daily Telephone* by Harvey Wirt Courtland Shelton (Cherokee). It appeared only to report the annual session of the Cherokee National Council, and in 1895, it became *The Daily Capital*.

Sources: Littlefield and Parins, eds., *American Indian and Alaska Native Newspapers and Periodicals, 1826–1924*, pp. 123–24.

1893 *The Wah-sha-she* was the first independent newspaper established to meet the needs of the Osage people by the Osage. It was founded by George E. Tinker and other Osage people.

Sources: Littlefield and Parins, eds., *American Indian and Alaska Native Newspapers and Periodicals, 1826–1924*, pp. 379–81.

1893 Norma E. Standley Smiser (Choctaw) became the first Indian woman to edit and publish a newspaper, *The Indian Citizen*, which was established by her father, James Stirman Standley. Smiser published the paper with her husband, Butler Stonestreet Smiser, until 1900 when she assumed sole editorial and management responsibilities. They sold the paper in 1905. In 1889, Smiser's father and her husband bought the paper then called the *Atoka Independent*. The paper published reports on Choctaw and Chickasaw national affairs. Both men were non-Indian but married Choctaw women, and both had become citizens of the Choctaw Nation and served in official capacities; Smiser was admitted to the Choctaw bar and Standley was a national agent for the Choctaw. Standley and

Smiser sought to create a paper that would be loyal to Choctaw interests and would accurately present the Choctaw to the American public.

In August 1893, Standley gave his newspaper interest to his daughter, who then became the associate editor. Under her editorship, the paper maintained its focus on Choctaw affairs. By 1898 Butler Smiser had been given more official duties by the Choctaw government and had less time to devote to the paper. As a result, by 1900 Norma Smiser assumed full editorship and management of *The Indian Citizen.* Under her management the paper reported on Choctaw legislation, citizenship, federal Indian legislation, and U.S. national and international affairs. In 1900 the paper began illustrating its stories and added photographs as well. With the conclusion of Oklahoma statehood and the abolishment of the governments of the Five Civilized Tribes, the paper turned to more general news for a general audience. In 1903, the Smisers sold *The Indian Citizen* to a non-Indian. Ownership and the name of the paper has changed several times, but it continues to be published today by the Atoka Press under its original name, *The Indian Citizen.*

Sources: *American Native Press,* No. 19, Fall 1995; Littlefield and Parins, eds., *American Indian and Alaska Native Newspapers and Periodicals, 1826–1924,* pp. 174–76; Foreman, *Oklahoma Imprints, 1835–1907.*

1903 The Chippewa of White Earth, Minnesota, established their first tribal newspaper, *The Tomahawk,* in 1903. It began as a weekly paper edited by Gustave H. Beaulieu, who was one-quarter Chippewa. For more than twenty years it became the voice of the tribe and took strong stands on political and economic issues of importance to the Chippewa of White Earth. It was the last tribal newspaper established before 1924.

Sources: Littlefield and Parins, eds., *American Indian and Alaska Native Newspapers and Periodicals, 1826–1924,* pp. 50–51.

1908 *The Quileute Independent* was established by Webster Hudson (Quileute) in 1908. It was the first newspaper to serve the needs of the Quileute people in La Push, Washington. In 1910 it was renamed *The Quileute Chieftain.*

Sources: Littlefield and Parins, eds., *American Indian and Alaska Native Newspapers and Periodicals, 1826–1924,* p. 306.

1911 *The Indian Observer* was established in 1911 by August Breuninger in Washington, D.C., urging pan-Indian activism to present the Indian side of the "Indian problem." This has been attributed as the earliest attempt to establish intertribal publications.

Sources: Littlefield and Parins, eds., *American Indian and Alaska Native Newspapers and Periodicals, 1826–1924,* p. 208.

1912 *The Odanah Star* was established in 1912 and edited in 1913 by H. C. Ashmun, the only full-blood Indian editor at that time in the United States.

Sources: Littlefield and Parins, eds., *American Indian and Alaska Native Newspapers and Periodicals, 1826–1924,* pp. 35–36.

1913 *American Indian Magazine* was established as *The Quarterly Journal* by the Society of American Indians. The publication marked the first time a national

Indian organization attempted to publish a periodical "devoted to the interest of the entire race." American Indian-owned and operated, it had on its board some of the best educated and most accomplished American Indian men and women of the period. The articles were intended to educate non-Indians on Indian issues, as well as express the opinions of American Indians. Like most well educated Indians of the time, however, the leading opinions found in the magazine reflected converted Christian assimilationist views.

Sources: Littlefield and Parins, eds., *American Indian and Alaska Native Newspapers and Periodicals, 1826–1924*, pp. 10–19.

1913 Peter Navarre (Prairie Band Potowatomie) became owner of *The Rossville Reporter,* the first newspaper begun by a Prairie-Band Potowatomie. The paper, first established as *The Shawnee County Reporter,* went through several owners before it was purchased by Navarre. While attending Haskell Institute he learned the printing trade. He worked at various printing jobs before buying his own paper. In 1904 he took charge of the White Earth Indian School's paper, *The Chippeway Herald.* Navarre reported on Rossville's community affairs and that of nearby communities. It was a typical small-town newspaper and did not concentrate on Indian affairs. The paper's purpose was to address the social and political needs and interests of the tribe. Navarre published and edited the paper for forty years. In 1953, Navarre sold the paper to Bill and Betty J. Murray. It went through several name changes and owners; in 1984, the paper was published as *The Shawnee County Reporter.*

Sources: Littlefield and Parins, eds., *American Indian and Alaska Native Newspapers and Periodicals, 1826–1924*, pp. 339–340.

1916 Carlos Montezuma (Yavapai; ca. 1867–1923), a well-known physician and American Indian activist, founded *Wassaja,* an anti-government newspaper designed to address Indian issues and to counter the assimilationist rhetoric of educated Indians, such as the members of the Society of Indians. He was a proponent of assimilation and thought it was vital that Indians become well educated so that they could adapt to the non-Indian world. At the same time, he found value and importance in Indian cultures and thought it important that aspects of Indian cultures be retained. Montezuma, a full-blood, was kidnapped at age five, and sold to a photographer for $30. He grew up in white society, being educated and socialized in white values and culture. Montezuma was outspoken on issues such as the attempts by the government to remove the Mojave-Apache from Camp McDowell to Salt River. He opposed allotment and condemned the Curtis Act as a makeshift policy to take care of the temporary "Indian" problems, and neglecting to take care of the real problems. He waged a continuous battle with leaders of the Society of American Indians, convinced that they and other Indian organizations were too influenced by the Indian Bureau. Eventually, they became convinced of his viewpoints. One of the most unique and effective aspects of *Wassaja* was Montezuma's use of a Socratic dialogue to present his point of view regarding current issues. Montezuma conversed with a persona and examined ideas, opinions, and policy. He died on the Ft. McDowell reservation in a brush shelter built especially for him.

Sources: *Biographical Dictionary of Indians of the Americas,* Vol. 1, p. 434; Iverson, *Carlos Montezuma and the Changing World of American Indians;* Littlefield and Parins, eds., *American Indian and Alaska Native Newspapers and Periodicals, 1826–1924,* pp. 382–85; Malinowski, ed., *Notable Native Americans,* pp. 276–77; Waldman, *Who Was Who in Native American History,* pp. 239–40.

1935 *Talking Leaf* was the first urban Indian newspaper. The paper was published by the American Indian Center in Los Angeles, California. It sought to provide local and national news, as well as information about education, career opportunities and it also printed poetry.

Sources: Danky and Hady, eds., *Native American Periodicals and Newspapers, 1828–1982,* p. 405; Littlefield and Parins, eds., *American Indian and Alaska Native Newspapers and Periodicals, 1826–1924,* pp. 407–408.

1937 *The First American* was the first political newsletter edited by a woman, Alice Lee Jemison (Seneca; 1901–1964), who also published it by herself. The paper opposed the Bureau of Indian Affairs (BIA), and Jemison focused on ending its existence. Both the paper and editor were strongly influenced by Carlos Montezuma. In 1934, Jemison was instrumental in founding the American Indian Federation (AIF) and *The First American* became its signature publication. The paper actively supported Indian rights, denounced the Indian Reorganization Act, and reprimanded commissioner John Collier for the disastrous livestock reduction program he forced on the Navajo. The AIF supported treaty rights and land rights. Jemison protested against other forms of negative images of Indians, such as Horatio Greenough's "The Rescue," which depicted an Indian on the verge of killing a white woman. The statue stood on the steps leading to the Capitol rotunda.

In 1940, family responsibilities forced Jemison to stop publication until 1953. With the beginning of termination policy looming, Jemison resumed publication and renewed her strong attacks against federal Indian policies and policymakers. The editor and her supporters predicted the ultimate failure of termination and also that a new Congress would correct the mistakes of the termination policy and Public Law 280 (another target of attack) in another twenty years. Jemison and her colleagues believed strongly in Indian self-determination, but not in termination or self-determination without treaty rights. The publication was suspended in 1954.

Sources: Littlefield and Parins, eds., *American Indian and Alaska Native Newspapers and Periodicals, 1925–1970,* pp. 155–56.

1943 William Morgan (Navajo) translated *Adahooniligii,* the first Navajo language paper. It was edited by Robert W. Young, a linguist. The paper was published from 1943 to 1957 and reported on current events on the Navajo reservation, as well as national and international news. Until 1947, the paper was printed mostly in Navajo, but an English summary was added. As the duration of the publication extended, the Navajo people began submitting more articles and letters. In 1950 the paper's content changed and began to focus on the explanation of federal policies and programs. It also sought to educate the non-English speaking Navajo and to provide a forum for discussion by others. In 1951, Morgan briefly became the editor, which marked the first time a Navajo edited a newspaper.

Morgan and Young went on to collaborate on several Navajo language publications, including a massive dictionary, *The Navajo Language*. The orthography they used is the standard system used by the Navajo today. Morgan received an honorary doctorate from the University of New Mexico.

Sources: Littlefield and Parins, eds., *American Indian and Alaska Native Newspapers and Periodicals, 1925–1970*, pp. 3–4.

1945 The National Congress of American Indians (NCAI) started publishing a newsletter in 1945 and a bulletin in 1947. Both publications were the first postwar efforts, by American Indians, to meet the needs and speak to the concerns of Native peoples.

Sources: Littlefield and Parins, eds., *American Indian and Alaska Native Newspapers and Periodicals, 1826–1924*, pp. 263–64.

1947 *The Smoke Signal*, established in Sacramento, was published by the Federated Indians of California. Its purpose was to report local and national news, provide information about legislation that affected the Indian community, education, and educational opportunities.

Sources: Danky and Hady, eds., *Native American Periodicals and Newspapers, 1828–1982*, p. 386; Littlefield and Parins, eds., *American Indian and Alaska Native Newspapers and Periodicals, 1826–1924*, pp. 388–89.

1959 Dillon Platero (Navajo) became the founding editor of the *Navajo Times Today*, which later became the official tribal newspaper of the Navajo Tribal Council. One of the most important purposes of the paper was to keep students at off-reservation boarding schools informed about the happenings on the Navajo Reservation. Thus, it focused on community activities and news about people. In 1983 it became the first Indian daily newspaper in the United States and it was also the first Indian newspaper to purchase a five-unit newspaper web press, marking the first time a newsprint web was owned by an Indian publication.

Sources: *Biographical Dictionary of Indians of the Americas*, Vol. 2, p. 545; Littlefield and Parins, eds., *American Indian and Alaska Native Newspapers and Periodicals, 1925–1970*, pp. 277–80.

1961 *The Journal of American Indian Education* was the first periodical devoted exclusively to Indian education issues. It was established at Arizona State University by the Center for Indian Education. It has become an internationally circulated publication that includes articles authored by experts from throughout the United States and abroad.

Sources: Littlefield and Parins, eds., *American Indian and Alaska Native Newspapers and Periodicals, 1826–1924*, pp. 220–22.

1962 Howard Rock (Point Hope Inuit; 1911–?) was the first editor of *The Tundra Times*, the first Alaska Native newspaper. With its founding, he became the first Native owner of a newpaper among the Inuit of Alaska. The paper was also the first paper to focus exclusively on Alaska Native issues and concerns. Howard Rock was born on August 10, 1911 in Point Hope. He attended school for a while and then went to Seattle and studied art in Oregon. He began working with jewelry until he was drafted into the U.S. Army Air Corps in 1942. He served in Italy until 1945. Originally the paper was published by Tundra Times, Inc., a combined venture headed by Howard Rock that included Martha Teeluk and Alfred Ketzler. Since 1966 it has been published by the Eskimo, Indian, and Aleut Publishing Company, a joint stock operation. The initial purpose of *The Tundra Times* was to provide a forum to express the perspectives of Native organizations, to keep Native peoples informed on matters and issues relevant to their communities, and to publish informative articles on Arctic culture. In the 1970s the paper expanded to twelve pages, added cartoons and local merchant advertisements; otherwise it maintained its original goals. Today it remains the strongest independent Native voice in Alaska.

Sources: *Biographical Dictionary of Indians of the Americas,* Vol. 2, p. 623; Hirschfelder and Kreipe de Montaño, *The Native American Almanac,* p. 192; Johansen and Grinde, *The Encyclopedia of Native American Biography,* p. 323; Littlefield and Parins, eds., *American Indian and Alaska Native Newspapers and Periodicals, 1925–1970,* pp. 426–27.

1966 The *American Indian News* was the first weekly newsletter published for the readership of the Wind River Reservation.

Sources: Littlefield and Parins, eds., *American Indian and Alaska Native Newspapers and Periodicals, 1826–1924,* p. 30.

1968 The *Indian Archives* was the first newsletter published specifically for prison inmates. Its emphasis was on culture, Native American mythology, history, and the socio-economic conditions among Indian people. The next year it was followed by the *American Indian Cultural Group Newsletter,* another newsletter published by Indian inmates at San Quentin Prison, San Rafael, California, which ran from 1969 to 1972.

Sources: Danky and Hady, eds., *Native American Periodicals and Newspapers, 1828–1982,* p. 171.

1969 *The Council of Women* was the first paper to be published exclusively by women and started as a protest against the male-dominated *Talking Leaf,* the newspaper of the Los Angeles American Indian Center. The women complained that not enough space was given to women's issues and that women were excluded from the production of the paper. *The Council of Women,* which was published on mimeographed sheets of paper, reported on social events such as powwows, problems of the Bureau of Indian Affairs (BIA), and the women's objections to the male-dominated paper. Although it only lasted a short period, it was one of the earliest attempts by women to produce a paper for and by themselves.

Sources: Littlefield and Parins, eds., *American Indian and Alaska Native Newspapers and Periodicals, 1925–1970,* p. 101.

1971 Arthur Raymond (Dakota/Oglala Lakota Sioux) was the first journalist and the first Sioux Indian to be elected to the North Dakota state legislature. Born in Winner, South Dakota, he began his newspaper career at the Mitchell Daily Republic. In 1958, an article he wrote won the Associated Press national first prize and was also chosen by the Pulitzer awards committee for award consideration. In 1971 he became director of Indian studies at the University of North Dakota.

See also: Government: U.S. State, 1971.

Sources: *Biographical Dictionary of Indians of the Americas,* Vol. 2, p. 590.

1976 The *American Indian Libraries Newsletter,* edited by Cheryl Anne Metoyer-Duran (Cherokee), was the first American Indian library newsletter published.

Sources: *Biographical Dictionary of Indians of the Americas,* Vol. 1, p. 422.

1981 Tim Giago (Oglala Lakota Sioux; 1934–) became the owner of *The Lakota Times,* renamed *Indian Country Today.* It represents the nation's largest independently owned American Indian newspaper. Giago was also the first Native American to receive a Nieman fellowship at Harvard University. *Indian Country Today* includes South Dakota, Southwest and Northwest editions. Giago began his journalism career reporting for the *Rapid City Journal* during the 1970s; he became a syndicated columnist, whose columns appear in twenty newspapers in states including Arizona, New Mexico, Colorado, Nebraska, and South Dakota. Giago and *Indian Country Today* have received numerous awards and honors. The paper dominated the South Dakota Press Association's awards for four years in a row, causing the group to reclassify it as a daily paper. In 1985, Giago won a H. L. Mencken Award for column writing but returned it in 1989 because of racist statements found in the writings of Mencken's personal papers.

Sources: Johansen and Grinde, *The Encyclopedia of Native American Biography,* p. 149; Littlefield and Parins, eds., *American Indian and Alaska Native Newspapers and Periodicals, 1925–1970,* pp. 192, 311; Littlefield and Parins, eds., *American Indian and Alaska Native Newspapers and Periodicals, 1970–1985,* pp. 244–45; Malinowski, ed., *Notable Native Americans,* pp. 164–65.

1993 *Windspeaker* became the first national Native newspaper in Canada. It was published in Edmonton, Alberta.

Sources: Champagne, ed., *Chronology of Native North American History,* p. 492.

RADIO

1957 KNDN-AM began broadcasting the radio program *All Navajo, All the Time.* At its inception it broadcast partially in Navajo under KWYK-AM, but today the broadcasts are almost all in Navajo with the exception of some music. It is the only radio station to use Navajo language so extensively.

Sources: Hirschfelder and Kreipe de Montaño, *The Native American Almanac,* p. 196.

1970 The first broadcast license awarded to a tribe (Choctaw) put WYRU-AM of Red Springs, North Carolina, on the air. It directed its programs to a general audience. The effort was a commercial one and producers thought a general audience was the best means to attract advertisers.

Sources: Cook, Ray, Personal communication to Karen Gayton Swisher, December 10, 1996; Keith, *Signals in the Air,* p. 21.

1971 Radio Tuktoyaktuk began broadcasting in English and Inuktitut on January 4, 1971. It was the beginning of Native language broadcasting in Canada.

Sources: Champagne, ed., *Chronology of Native North American History,* p. 383.

1971 For the first time, American Indians participated in Columbia University's summer program in broadcast journalism for members of minority groups. The three students included Lorraine Edmo (Shoshoni/Bannock), Tanna Beebe (Cowlitz), and Donald Savage (Chippewa). Each had worked for radio-TV stations. The eleven-week session provided training in all aspects of broadcast news.

Sources: Dennis, *The American Indian, 1492–1976*, p. 89.

1972 KTDB-FM was the first Indian-owned and operated non-commercial station in the United States that aimed at a Native American audience. It was formerly established at Ramah, New Mexico, but now broadcasts from Pinehill.

Sources: Cook, Ray, Personal communication to Karen Gayton Swisher, December 10, 1996; Hirschfelder and Kreipe de Montaño, *The Native American Almanac*, p. 196; Keith, *Signals in the Air*, p. 21.

1976 The Navajo Radio Network broadcasts its first day of news and public interest programming in the Navajo language. This is the first radio station entirely under Navajo control.

Sources: Champagne, ed., *Chronology of Native North American History*, p. 408.

1977 KMDX-FM was the first Native-owned commercial radio station. It was owned by Gilbert Leivas, a member of the Colorado River Indian Tribes (CRIT).

Sources: Hirschfelder and Kreipe de Montaño, *The Native American Almanac*, p. 196.

1977 Akwesasne Freedom, the first non-licensed Native-run private radio station was established by Ray Cook (Mohawk). It was a small twenty-watt FM transmitter located in a small exiled Mayan village in Guatemala.

Sources: Cook, Ray, Personal communication to Karen Gayton Swisher, December 10, 1996; Keith, *Signals in the Air*, p. 21.

1979 Rosemarie Kuptana (Inuvialuk) hosted the morning and noon Inuvialuktun language programs on the Canadian Broadcasting Corporation's (CBC) Western Arctic—the first Canadian station to offer Native-language programming. In 1982 she joined the Inuit Broadcasting Corporation (IBC) as assistant production coordinator. In 1983 she was elected president of IBC, serving until 1988. Kuptana was awarded the Order of Canada in 1988. In 1991 she was elected president of the Inuit Tapirisut of Canada, becoming active and influential in the constitutional negotiations leading to the Charlottetown Accord in 1992. She was also involved in the Inuit Circumpolar Conference, which included delegates from Canada, the United States, Greenland, and the Soviet Union. In 1991 she wrote *No More Secrets,* a book dealing with child sexual abuse in Native villages.

Sources: Champagne, ed., *Chronology of Native North American History,* p. 328.

1984 CKON-FM was the first and only Native station that received its operating license from a sovereign Indian nation, the Mohawk Nation Council of Chiefs. It was founded by Ray Cook (Mohawk) and Doug George Kanentiio (Mohawk). While the U.S. Federal Communications Commission (FCC) and the Canadian Radio and Television Commission (CRTC) were advised that a license would be issued, the Mohawk Nation did not seek their approval. The Council of Chiefs initiated its action to affirm its sovereign status. The station is built on the U.S.-

Canada border, but on the Mohawk land that encompasses parts of the United States and Canada. Neither the U.S. nor the Canadian governments have interfered. CKON-FM is a commercial community radio station that is totally self-sufficient, and provides twenty-four-hour live programming. It caters to a general audience and is the only local radio station; it has two sister stations—one is one hundred miles away and the other is eighty miles away. CKON-FM is truly the only international radio station operated by Indian people.

Sources: Cook, Ray, Personal communication to Karen Gayton Swisher, December 10, 1996; Johansen and Grinde, *The Encyclopedia of Native American Biography,* pp. 145–47; Wood, Stuart (station manager, CKON-FM, Corwall, Ontario Canada), Personal communication to AnCita Benally, January 1997.

1987 National Native News (NNN) is the first and only radio news service covering Native American issues. It began serving Native communities in Alaska providing thirty stations with news. It expanded to include radio stations in the lower forty-eight states. It has been recognized for providing a valuable service to Alaska Native and American Indian communities by the Alaska State legislature. The station is produced by Alaska Public Radio Network. NNN has been honored with several awards and is produced by Gary Fife (Creek/Cherokee).

Sources: Hirschfelder and Kreipe de Montaño, *The Native American Almanac,* pp. 196, 311; "National Native News Receives Grant," *Navajo Times,* Vol. 30, No. 28 (July 12, 1990), p. 8.

1990 *National Native News,* was the first daily radio news program devoted to American Indian and Alaska Native issues broadcast from Alaska on the National Public Radio network.

Sources: "National Native News Receives Grant," *Navajo Times,* Vol. 30, No. 28 (July 12, 1990), p. 8.

1991 KGHR-FM was the country's first Indian high school radio station, broadcasting from Tuba City, Arizona. It is the town's second radio station and the third one on the Navajo reservation.

Sources: Hirschfelder and Kreipe de Montaño, *The Native American Almanac,* p. 197.

1995 *Native America Calling* was billed as the first electronic talking circle. It is a daily call-in program produced in Albuquerque by the Native American Public Broadcasting Consortium and the Alaska Public Radio Network. Each day two or three guests are hosted by Bernadette Chato (Navajo) and Pam Belgarde (Turtle Mountain Chippewa) to specialize in the day's topic and talk to callers. The program has addressed social issues, education, health, books, and many controversial topics.

Sources: "Resource Guide," *Tribal College,* Vol. 8, No. 2 (Fall 1995), p. 41.

1996 Selena Manychildren (Navajo) and Deenise Becenti (Navajo) were awarded first prize for best newscast in a small market by the New Mexico Broadcasters. The two are newscasters and reporters for the Navajo Nation radio station KTNN, Window Rock, and broadcast the news in Navajo three times a day.

Sources: "Newscasters Earn Long Overdue Award for Talented Work," *Navajo Times,* Vol. 35, No. 19 (May 9, 1996), p. A-6.

TELEVISION

1971 For the first time Inuit villages in the Arctic began receiving television broadcasts. For eighteen hours each day, Inuits were able to view regular television programs.

Sources: Hirschfelder and Kreipe de Montaño, *The Native American Almanac,* p. 186.

1978 The Oglala Sioux tribe announced plans to construct the first Indian owned and operated television station, serving approximately fourteen thousand people who live on the Pine Ridge Sioux Reservation in South Dakota.

Sources: Champagne, ed., *Chronology of Native North American History,* p. 419.

1980 Inuit Tapirisat (Inuit Brotherhood) established Inukshuk, an experimental television station and was given access to a Canadian Broadcasting Corporation (CBC) satellite channel. The station's purpose is to provide regionally oriented programs and the Inuit have used it to broadcast special events such as throat-singing concerts, and instructional segments dealing with such programs as hunting and fire fighting.

Sources: Hirschfelder and Kreipe de Montaño, *The Native American Almanac,* p. 186.

1981 The Inuit Broadcasting Corporation (IBC), the only Native American broadcast network in North America, was established to produce at least five hours of Native-oriented programs per week. The success of Inukshuk demonstrated that there was a market and an audience for Native programs. Consequently the Canadian government licensed a permanent Inuit network. The broadcasts are in Inuktitute and English. Seven communities serve as production sites and receive programs. Programs range from a children's show called *Super Shamou,* to dramatized shows of Inuit stories, to information programs that deal with social issues such as domestic violence.

Sources: Hirschfelder and Kreipe de Montaño, *The Native American Almanac,* p. 187.

1987 Nancy M. Tuthill, (Quapaw/Shawnee) was the first Native American to hold the position of editor in Broadcast Standards and Practices for ABC Television. She has held the position since 1987.

Sources: *Biographical Dictionary of Indians of the Americas,* Vol. 2, pp. 768–69.

1989 Hattie Kauffman (Nez Percé) of ABC News, was the first Indian reporter to appear on national television. In 1981 Kauffman began her career in television journalism in Seattle working for KING-TV. While there she received four Emmy awards. Since March 1990 she has been a consumer affairs correspondent for *CBS News* and she is a frequent substitute anchor for the morning show, *CBS This Morning.* Previously she was a feature reporter for ABC's *Good Morning America* program.

Sources: Hirschfelder and Kreipe de Montaño, *The Native American Almanac,* p. 192; Johansen and Grinde, *The Encyclopedia of Native American Biography,* 196; *Tribune Newspapers* (Mesa, Arizona), February 12, 1996, p. B-4.

1993 The Deadwood Film Festival founded the first national organization of Native American independent film and television producers. The organization's goals are to address the problems of Native production of programs about Native people. They deal with the issue of funding and maintaining authenticity through Native involvement.

Sources: Hirschfelder and Kreipe de Montaño, *The Native American Almanac,* p. 187.

MILITARY

U.S. ARMY SCOUTS

1866 The U.S. War Department organized Indian scouts within the U.S. Army. They were not to exceed one thousand, and they were strictly to act as scouts. Further, they would receive pay equal to that of cavalry scouts. Within one year, 474 American Indians were appointed as scouts. Over the next ten years, the total number reached six hundred. On May 5, 1916, they fought their last battle at Ojos Azules Ranch in Mexico. An Apache scout detachment, part of the Eleventh Cavalry, fought with Pancho Villa's forces. While no Americans, including scouts, died, Villa's force incurred forty-four casualties. The Indian scouts were formally disbanded in 1947 as a distinct element of the U.S. military.

Sources: Champagne, ed., *Chronology of Native North American History,* pp. 197, 314; Dennis, *The American Indian, 1492–1976,* pp. 34, 57.

Among the pictured Company "A" Apache Scouts are at least sixteen Medal of Honor recipients, including Alchesay, who was the first to earn a Medal of Honor and the last to serve as chief of his White Mountain Apache people.

Alchesay, the first Apache to earn a Medal of Honor for serving as scout during the U.S. Army's wars with other Apache groups.

1869 Coruxtechodish, also known as "Mad Bear," (Pawnee) was the first American Indian to be awarded the Medal of Honor, in August 1869, for his service as an Indian scout in the U.S. Army. The original order was for the medal to go to another Pawnee scout, Coruxacahwadde, "Traveling Bear." Because of a mix-up, the medal was awarded to Coruxtechodish. However, when it came time to award the medal, Coruxacahwadde, the originally nominated scout, accepted it.

Sources: Anderson, Jerry (EEO Manager, OASD [FM&P]-ADASD, The Pentagon), Personal communication to AnCita Benally, January 13, 1996; Hirschfelder and Kreipe de Montaño, *The Native American Almanac*, p. 229.

1873 Alchesay (White Mountain Apache) was the first Apache to earn a Medal of Honor for his service as an Apache Indian scout during the U.S. Army's wars with the Apache. He was the last traditionally elected chief of the White Mountain Apache. He became a successful cattle rancher, who encouraged the use of modern methods of raising stock. He also advocated farming and education to Apache youth as vehicles to attaining improved living conditions.

Sources: Anderson, Jerry (EEO Manager, OASD [FM&P]-ADASD, The Pentagon), Personal communication to AnCita Benally, January 13, 1996; *Biographical Dictionary of Indians of the Americas*, Vol. 1, p. 18; Hirschfelder and Kreipe de Montaño, *The Native American Almanac*, p. 229.

Curley, Crow scout for General George A. Custer, Little Bighorn, ca. 1876.

1876 Curley (Crow), a scout for General George A Custer, was the first person to bring news of Custer's demise at the Battle of the Little Bighorn, to the U.S. Army. Although unable to speak English, he was able to convey the news through a series of gestures, drawings, and pantomime. His story, however, was not believed until it was corroborated by white soldiers who brought reports of the battle. In later life he became a celebrity and although he was reluctant to talk about it, he was sought out by historians to retell his story of the battle. He claimed to have been sent away from the battle by Custer before it began and thus did not actually take part in it; he only learned of it. His claim was disputed by aging Lakota warriors who accused him of fleeing in the face of battle. After his retirement as an Army scout, he had a longstanding dispute with the government over his retirement pension, which he finally received in 1923, but died a month after he was approved for retirement pensions. He was buried at the Little Bighorn National Monument.

Sources: Dockstader, *Great North American Indians,* pp. 66–67; Johansen and Grinde, *The Encyclopedia of Native American Biography,* pp. 93–94; Sarf, Michael, *The Little Bighorn Campaign, March–September 1876,* [Conshohocken, Pennsylvania], 1993, pp. 214–16, 263.

MILITARY EDUCATION

1822 David Moniac (Creek) was the first American Indian admitted into the U.S. Military Academy and the first to graduate from it. He became a major in the U.S. Army. He was killed in the Creek War of 1836.

Sources: Anderson, Jerry (EEO Manager, OASD [FM&P]-ADASD, The Pentagon), Personal communication to AnCita Benally, January 13, 1996; Dennis, *The American Indian, 1492–1976,* p. 24.

1913 Joseph J. Clark (Cherokee; 1893-1971), a full admiral in the U.S. Navy, was the first midshipman of American Indian ancestry to attend the U.S. Naval Academy (1913–1917). Born in Pryor, Oklahoma, he served in World War I and later taught at the academy. In 1925, he became a naval aviator and air officer of naval stations. During World War II, he was executive officer of the aircraft carrier *Yorktown* and commanded it until 1943. In 1944, he was promoted to rear admiral, and then vice admiral in 1952. In that office he commanded the first and seventh fleets. During his years of service, he was awarded the Silver Star, the Navy Cross, the Distinguished Flying Cross, and the Legion of Merit. Clark retired in 1953 as a full admiral, the first person of Native American ancestry to attain such a high rank in the U.S. Navy. In 1967, he published his autobiography, *Carrier Admiral.*

Sources: Anderson, Jerry (EEO Manager, OASD [FM&P]-ADASD, The Pentagon), Personal communication to AnCita Benally, January 13, 1996; *Biographical Dictionary of Indians of the Americas,* Vol. 1, p. 132.

1958 Leo Johnson (tribal affiliation unknown) was the first American Indian to matriculate at the U.S. Air Force Academy in Colorado Springs, Colorado, on June 12, 1958. He graduated June 6, 1962, as a commissioned officer and eventually advanced to the rank of captain in the U.S. Air Force. He became an RC 135-M pilot. In his career he received seven Air Medals and an Air Force Commendation Medal.

Sources: Champagne, ed., *Chronology of Native North American History,* p. 333.

1961 M. Victor J. Apodaca Jr. (Navajo) was the first Navajo to graduate from the U.S. Air Force Academy.

Sources: Anderson, Jerry (EEO Manager, OASD [FM&P]-ADASD, The Pentagon), Personal communication to AnCita Benally, January 13, 1996.

1963 Thomas N. Almojuela (Squamish) was the first Northwest American Indian to graduate from the U.S. Military Academy at West Point. He received a congressional appointment to attend West Point in 1963. While at the academy he lettered in four sports and was on the dean's list. He became a captain and served as commander of a tank company in Germany. During the Vietnam War, he flew AHIG Cobra gunships and fought on the ground as well. He received several medals, including a Silver Star, a Bronze Star, an Air Medal with 33 Oak Clusters, and the Army Commendation Medal.

Sources: *Biographical Dictionary of Indians of the Americas,* Vol. 1, p. 19; Champagne, ed., *The Native North American Almanac,* p. 1000; Gridley, ed., *Indians of Today,* p. 71.

1981 Sandra L. Hinds (tribal affiliation unknown) was the first woman to graduate from the U.S. Naval Academy.

Sources: Anderson, Jerry (EEO Manager, OASD [FM&P]-ADASD, The Pentagon), Personal communication to AnCita Benally, January 13, 1996.

1982 Delores K. Smith (Cherokee) was the first American Indian woman to graduate from the U.S. Air Force Academy.

Sources: Anderson, Jerry (EEO Manager, OASD [FM&P]-ADASD, The Pentagon), Personal communication to AnCita Benally, January 13, 1996.

1984 Brigitte T. Wahwassuck (tribal affiliation unknown) was the first American Indian woman to graduate from the U.S. Military Academy.

Thomas N. Almojuela, the first Northwest American Indian to graduate from the U.S. Military Academy, West Point, is pictured with General Colin Powell.

Sources: Anderson, Jerry (EEO Manager, OASD [FM&P]-ADASD, The Pentagon), Personal communication to AnCita Benally, January 13, 1996.

1990 Ted Draper III (Navajo) was not only the first Native American, but the first freshman cadet to attain the rank of sergeant in the history of the U.S. Marine Military Academy in Harlingen, Texas. Previously, he was selected as the Cadet of the Month. From Chinle, Arizona, he is the son of a former Navajo Code Talker.

Sources: *Navajo Times,* Vol. 30, 1990.

AMERICAN REVOLUTIONARY WAR

1770 Crispus Attucks (Natick) was the first American Indian casualty of the pre-revolutionary Boston Massacre. A leader among the Boston patriots, he died along with four others. His mother was Natick, and his father was of African American ancestry. Attucks was a slave until he escaped in 1750. In 1888, the Crispus Attucks Monument was erected on Boston Commons.

Sources: *Biographical Dictionary of Indians of the Americas,* Vol. 1, pp. 32, 120; Katz, *Black Indians,* p. 10; Leitch, *Chronology of the American Indian,* p. 32; Waldman, *Who Was Who in Native American History,* p. 11.

1790 Alexander McGillvray (Creek), a loyalist during the American Revolution, traveled to New York in 1790 to visit George Washington. While there he was given a secret commission as brigadier general and a $100 pension with it. Later he met with the Spanish and disavowed his agreement with the Americans. The Spanish commissioned him a colonel in the Spanish army and provided him with an even larger pension than the Americans had given him. Both the Spanish and Americans hoped to gain his support as they competed for power on the continent, and McGillvray skillfully negotiated with each side, hoping to gain Spanish protection and an American agreement to halt further encroachment into Creek territory. McGillvray was of Creek, French, and Scottish ancestry.

Sources: *Biographical Dictionary of Indians of the Americas,* Vol. 1, pp. 412–13; Edmunds, *American Indian Leaders,* pp. 41–63; Waldman, *Who Was Who in Native American History,* p. 227.

WAR OF 1812

1812 William McIntosh, of Creek and Scottish ancestry, was the first Native American to be commissioned brigadier general in the U.S. Army. He did not actually serve in the American military himself; however, he sent his warriors to fight in the War of 1812, the Creek War, and the First Seminole War. He was a leader of the pro-American White Stick faction of the Creek tribe, who favored the Americans over the British. He was considered a patriot by Americans, but in 1823, and in earlier treaties as well, McIntosh ceded millions of acres to Georgia, an act considered traitorous by Creek leaders. Consequently, the Red Stick faction, which was in control of the recognized Creek tribal government enacted the Broken Arrow Law, which forbade the cession of more Creek land. The council condemned McIntosh and twelve others who had signed the Treaty of Indian

Springs to execution. A party was sent out and carried out the orders of execution. McIntosh was killed with the other signers of the infamous treaty.

Sources: Anderson, Jerry (EEO Manager, OASD [FM&P]-ADASD, The Pentagon), Personal communication to AnCita Benally, January 13, 1996; Waldman, *Who Was Who in Native American History,* pp. 227–28.

CIVIL WAR

1861 Daniel Newman MacIntosh (Creek; 1822–1895), serving as a colonel in the Confederate Army during the Civil War, raised the first Creek Indian Confederate regiment of the war in August 1861 and fought against the Union Creeks led by Chief Opothleyahola at Round Mountain. The regiment was defeated later at Honey Springs, and they remained in the area for the remainder of the war. MacIntosh took part in peace negotiations at Fort Smith and in Washington, D.C. He returned to Oklahoma, where he and his mother had migrated in 1830, during the third Creek removal to Indian Territory. He rebuilt his farm and his property and remained there until his death.

Sources: *Biographical Dictionary of Indians of the Americas,* Vol. 1, p. 381.

1864 Stand Watie (Cherokee; 1806–1871) was the highest ranking military officer of either side during the American Civil War. Jefferson Davis, president of the Confederate States, appointed him as brigadier general in the Confederate Army on May 10, 1864. (Ely Samuel Parker, the first Native American commissioner of Indian affairs, was a close friend of Ulysses S. Grant and penned the final copy of the Confederate army's surrender terms at the Appomattox Courthouse in 1865. Parker became brigadier general in the U.S. Army, but his commission came after the end of the Civil War.) Promotion to brigadier general put Watie in charge of the Confederate Cherokees and members of the Five Civilized Tribes. His primary concern was to protect Cherokee land bordering the western frontier and to guard against Union incursions. Watie was the last Confederate general to concede to the Union Army; he did not surrender until June 23, 1865, at Doaksville, Choctaw Nation, two and a half months after General Lee's surrender.

Sources: *Biographical Dictionary of Indians of the Americas,* Vol. 1, p. 803; Malinowski, ed., *Notable Native Americans,* pp. 450–53; *Self-Guiding Tour for The National Hall of Fame for Famous American Indians and Anadarko Visitors' Center,* p. 4.

1867 Ely Samuel Parker (Seneca; 1828–1895) was the first American Indian to attain the rank of brigadier general in the U.S. Army. During the Civil War he served as military secretary to General Grant and handwrote the articles of surrender that formally ended the Civil War. Although Parker did not begin his formal education until he was twelve, he studied to be a lawyer. However, because of his race he was not considered an American citizen and, therefore, was unable to be licensed to practice law in New York. He then studied to be an engineer and worked in that profession until the outbreak of the Civil War. He volunteered for service, but could not get a military commission from the governor of New York or the secretary of war because of his race. Finally, he was given a commission as captain of engineers. Later that year, he became staff officer to General Ulysses S.

Grant, whom he had met earlier in Illinois. In 1864, Parker was advanced to lieutenant colonel and became Grant's military secretary. On April 9, 1865, Parker penned the final official copies of the surrender terms to the Confederate Army at Appomattox Court House. A startled Robert E. Lee was reported to have shaken hands with Parker commenting, "I'm glad to see one real American," to which Parker replied, "We are all Americans." He was commissioned brigadier general of volunteers at Appomattox, and two years later, on March 2, 1867, he was commissioned brigadier general in the U.S. Army.

Ely Samuel Parker (seated at right), the first Native American commissioner of Indian affairs, penned the final copy of the Confederate army's surrender terms.

Sources: Anderson, Jerry (EEO Manager, OASD [FM&P]-ADASD, The Pentagon), Personal communication to AnCita Benally, January 13, 1996; *Biographical Dictionary of Indians of the Americas,* Vol. 1, p. 349; Liberty, ed., *American Indian Intellectuals,* pp. 15–30; Malinowski, ed., *Notable Native Americans,* pp. 317–19.

WORLD WAR I

1917 More than eight thousand American Indians served in World War I, even though they were not citizens of the United States. Later, this military service became a crucial factor in the congressional decision to extend full American citizenship to all American Indians. The Indian Citizenship Act was passed in 1924.

Sources: Dennis, *The American Indian, 1492–1976,* p. 50.

1917 The Mohawk language was the first Native American language to be used in the modern military of Canada. Elmer Jamieson (Mohawk; 1891–?) was assigned by the Canadian Army to develop a code of using Mohawk after it was discovered that he had been writing letters home in Mohawk. Throughout military history in the North America, various Indian languages have been used to relay messages, orders, or reports; however, a Native language was codified to send military messages for the first time during World War I.

Sources: Champagne, ed., *Chronology of Native North American History,* pp. 243–44.

1918 The Choctaw language was the first American Indian language to be used as part of the U.S. military communications system. Toward the end of World War I, fourteen Choctaw men assigned to the 142nd Infantry Regiment of the U.S. Army were chosen and trained to use their Native language to send messages in several key battles in the Meuse-Argonne campaign in France. This stage of the war was the final big push made by the Germans to penetrate the Allied forces. One Choctaw man was placed in each field company headquarters to handle communications being sent by phone and radio. They wrote field orders that were carried by runners between the various companies. The messages were never decoded by the enemy even when intercepted. In 1986, the Choctaw Nation awarded the families of the Choctaw Code Talkers with the Choctaw Nation's Medal of Honor. It was the first time that the code talkers had been officially recognized. In November 1989, the government of France presented Chief Hollis E. Roberts, chairman of the Choctaw Tribe, with the Chevalier de l'Ordre National du Merite (Knight of the National Order of Merit), the highest honor France can bestow. The Choctaw Code Talkers were honored by the French government at the same time Comanche Code Talkers were given the same honor. The Comanches used their language in the war effort during World War II. Choctaw servicemen also used their language as a code again in World War II.

Sources: Anderson, Jerry (EEO Manager, OASD [FM&P]-ADASD, The Pentagon), Personal communication to AnCita Benally, January 13, 1996; Hirschfelder and Kreipe de Montaño, *The Native American Almanac,* pp. 30, 232.

1921 The Haskell unit of the Kansas National Guard was mobilized for a year of active federal service. The Haskell National Guard was the first and only all-American Indian National Guard organized by the Indian Service. It was organized

TROOP "I" 114TH. CAVALRY CAMP WHITSIDE AUGUST 21 1939.

Troup I, 114th Cavalry Regiment organizing at Haskell Institute was the first and only all-American Indian cavalry organization in the U.S. Army.

on May 4, 1921, and was marshalled into state service and then given federal recognition in the same month. Part of the Fourth Kansas Infantry, it was designated as Machine Gun Company D and received military training like other National Guard units. It built a strong reputation for efficiency and dedication. So impressive was their record that they inspired the formation of an all-Indian Troop C of the 114th Cavalry. The original Machine Gun Company D disbanded in 1934.

Sources: Dennis, *The American Indian, 1492–1976*, p. 55; "Haskell National Guard Battery Mobilized," *The Indian Leader*, (Lawrence, Kansas), December 27, 1940, p. 1; "Saga of All-Indian Cavalry Ended by War," *The Indian Leader* (Lawrence, Kansas), September 23, 1988, p. 1; "Splendid All-Indian Guard Outfits Rose from Units in the Kansas National Guard" (unpublished manuscript; 102nd Military History Department, Haskell Institute, Topeka, Kansas), May 23, 1983; "Twenty Years at Haskell" (unpublished manuscript; 102nd Military History Department, Haskell Institute, Topeka, Kansas), May 23, 1983, p. 1.

1924 Troop C, 114th Cavalry, the only all-Indian cavalry organized in the United States, was organized as a unit of the Kansas National Guard on May 1, 1924. The original unit comprised Haskell students who had no military training. They went on to win numerous awards for being the most efficient, best-disciplined and drilled troop in the state. Considered as Kansas' "show troop," they served as honor guards at important state and national functions and celebrations. At the 1939 New York World's Fair, Troop C was chosen as a special military parade unit to accompany dignitaries and special guests. In that capacity they served as honor guard to King George and Queen Elizabeth of England on their visit. They were trained in military artillery skills and were highly acclaimed. Changing military technology transformed their roles. They remained the most photographed unit but the approaching world war accelerated the dispersal of unit members. On December 23, 1940, the unit was mobilized for a year of active federal service. Their commander was promoted and moved to a new command.

Remaining guardsmen were scattered and finally in 1942, the last of the Indian units were disbanded.

Sources: Dennis, *The American Indian, 1492–1976*, p. 55; "Haskell National Guard Battery Mobilized," *The Indian Leader* (Lawrence, Kansas), December 27, 1940, p. 1; "Twenty Years at Kaskell: Indian Units in the Kansas National Guard" (unpublished manuscript; 102nd Military History Department, Haskell Institute, Topeka, Kansas), May 23, 1983; "Saga of All-Indian Cavalry Ended by War" *The Indian Leader* (Lawrence, Kansas), September 23, 1988, p. 1.

WORLD WAR II

1940 For the first time in U.S. history, American Indians registered for the military draft. In previous American wars, American Indians had been denied commissions and the freedom to enlist in the army. The usual rationale was that American Indians were not citizens; however, with the 1924 Indian Citizenship Act, Indians were eligible for U.S. citizenship. They were, therefore, able to register for the military, and thousands fought in all fronts of World War II. American Indian languages, such as Cherokee, Choctaw, Comanche, Hopi, Kiowa, and Navajo, were used to send and receive orders. None were deciphered by the enemy. Native American men and women proved themselves valuable to the military during World War II.

Sources: Champagne, ed., *Chronology of Native North American History*, p. 301; Dennis, *The American Indian, 1492–1976*, p. 55.

1940s William D. English (Inuit; 1923–) was one of the first pilots to fly the F-27. English served in the U.S. Air Force from 1943 to 1945. In 1945, the military offered him an appointment to West Point, but he turned it down so he could fly commercial aircraft. In 1946, he received his commercial flying license. He has since worked as an American Airline transport pilot examiner for the Federal Aviation Administration (FAA).

Sources: *Biographical Dictionary of Indians of the Americas*, Vol. 1, p. 210; Gridley, ed., *Indians of Today*, pp. 145–46.

1942 Clarence L. Tinker (Osage) was the first Native American to attain the rank of major general in the U.S. Air Force and the highest ranking American Indian in the air force. In May 1942, he became the first American general lost in action in World War II. He received the Distinguished Service Medal posthumously. General Tinker was among the first servicemen to be trained in the air force. Tinker Airfield Base in Oklahoma City was named in his honor.

Sources: *Biographical Dictionary of Indians of the Americas*, Vol. 2, p. 756; Botone, Barnie (director of the Albuquerque Indian Center), Personal communication to AnCita Benally, October 5, 1996; *Self Guiding Tour for the National Hall of Fame for Famous Indians*, p. 7.

Clarence L. Tinker.

1942 The Navajo language was the first Native American language in the United States to be used as a codified military means of communication. As with other American Indian languages used—Choctaw, Comanche, Hopi, and Cherokee— this code was never deciphered by the enemy. In many cases these languages were the only defense between U.S. servicemen and calamity. The Navajo Code Talkers were innovative in that they developed a secret military code and did not merely translate from Navajo to English. About four hundred men were trained to be code talkers and served in the Pacific area; they especially distinguished themselves on Iwo Jima. (The other American Indian languages were used primarily in Europe.) Working around the clock, they sent and received more than eight hundred messages without error. Their contributions remained a military secret until 1966. They were honored in 1968 by the U.S. military. In 1992, the Pentagon honored them by establishing a permanent exhibit at the Pentagon. In 1989, the city of Phoenix dedicated the first permanent tribute to the code talkers.

Sources: Anderson, Jerry (EEO Manager, OASD [FM&P]-ADASD, The Pentagon), Personal communication to AnCita Benally, January 13, 1996; Hirschfelder and Kreipe de Montaño, *The Native American Almanac*, pp. 90, 233–34.

1942 Pascal Cleatur Poolaw (Kiowa) became the most decorated American Indian soldier in U.S. military history. He received a total of forty-two awards and medals, including four Silver Stars, five Bronze Stars, one Air Medal, and three Purple Hearts. He joined the U.S. Army in August 1942 and earned his way to a battlefield commission as a second lieutenant, which he later relinquished. He served in World War II, the Korean Conflict, and Vietnam War, where he died on November 7, 1967. He completed twenty-five years of military service. During World War II, Poolaw had served at the same time as his father, Ralph Poolaw Sr., and his two brothers. His grandfather "Kiowa George" Poolaw had served with the famed All-Indian Cavalry Troop L at Fort Sill from 1893 to 1895.

Sources: Dennis, *The American Indian, 1492–1976*, p. 65; *Self Guiding Tour for the National Hall of Fame for Famous Indians*, p. 4.

1944 Ernest Childers (Creek) was the first member of the Creek Nation and the first American Indian in the twentieth century to receive the Congressional Medal of Honor for valorous actions during World War II. He earned the medal for

Colin Powell with Navajo Code Talkers and their families at the Navajo Code Talker exhibit at the Pentagon in 1992.

actions performed on September 22, 1943, and received it on April 8, 1944. In addition, Childers earned five other decorations for his military service during World War II. He retired as a lieutenant colonel in 1965.

Sources: Anderson, Jerry (EEO Manager, OASD [FM&P]-ADASD, The Pentagon), Personal communication to AnCita Benally, January 13, 1996; *Biographical Dictionary of Indians of the Americas,* Vol. 1, p. 129; Hirschfelder and Kreipe de Montaño, *The Native American Almanac,* p. 229.

1944 Van T. Barfoot (Choctaw) was the first member of his tribe to receive the nation's highest military honor—the Medal of Honor—for his service during World War II. He was cited for his actions on May 23, 1944, and he was awarded on October 4, 1944.

Sources: Anderson, Jerry (EEO Manager, OASD [FM&P]-ADASD, The Pentagon), Personal communication to AnCita Benally, January 13, 1996; Hirschfelder and Kreipe de Montaño, *The Native American Almanac,* p. 229.

ca. 1944 Grace Thorpe (Sauk/Fox) was selected as a member of General Douglas MacArthur's staff for the general's command headquarters in Japan. She served with the Women's Army Corps during World War II and had been serving in New Guinea for more than two years when she was chosen. She returned to the United States in 1950. In the mid-1960s, she began her activist involvement in American Indian causes. She was a major player in efforts to secure land for Deganiwida-Quetzalcoatl University (DQU), an institution that would serve the needs of Native American and Mexican American students. She later took care of public relations for the takeovers on Alcatraz Island and at Ft. Lawton Museum in Washington State. In 1971, she assisted in the founding of the National Indian Women's Action Corps and served as legislative assistant to the U.S. Senate Sub-Committee on Indian Affairs. She also served on the American Indian Policy

Lt. Ernest Childers receiving Congressional Medal of Honor.

Review Board. In 1980, she returned to Oklahoma, where she served as part-time district court judge for the Five Tribes in Stroud, Oklahoma.

Sources: Bataille, ed., *Native American Women*, pp. 259–60; Malinowski, ed., *Notable Native Americans*, p. 433.

Opposite page:
**Grace Thorpe, shown
here in her WAAC uni-
form in 1943, started
her Indian activism in
the 1960s.**

1945 Ernest E. Evans (Pawnee) was the first Pawnee to earn the Medal of Honor in the twentieth century as a member of the regular army. He was honored on November 24, 1945, for actions he performed on October 25, 1944.

Sources: Anderson, Jerry (EEO Manager, OASD [FM&P]-ADASD, The Pentagon), Personal communication to AnCita Benally, January 13, 1996; Hirschfelder and Kreipe de Montaño, *The Native American Almanac*, p. 229.

1945 During World War II more than twenty-five thousand American Indian men and women served in the military. About seventy thousand of them left their reservations for the first time. They served in all branches of the military and participated in action on all fronts. In addition, American Indian languages were used as military communication codes. Hopi, Kiowa, and Navajo soldiers were recruited to develop and use their languages to communicate on the front lines. American Indian service men and women garnered seventy-one Air Medals, fifty-one Silver Stars, forty-seven Bronze Stars, thirty-four Distinguished Flying Crosses, and five Congressional Medals of Honor. In addition, American Indian service in World War II increased awareness of Native Americans to the larger American and international communities. Further, the war experience gave American Indian soldiers off-reservation experience, vocational training, English language skills, and increased political awareness.

Sources: Dennis, *The American Indian, 1492–1976*, p. 56.

1945 Jack Montgomery (Cherokee) was the first Cherokee to be awarded the Medal of Honor. He earned this distinction by his courageous actions on February 22, 1944.

Sources: Anderson, Jerry (EEO Manager, OASD [FM&P]-ADASD, The Pentagon), Personal communication to AnCita Benally, January 13, 1996; Hirschfelder and Kreipe de Montaño, *The Native American Almanac*, p. 229.

1945 John N. Reese (Oklahoma Creek) was the only member of his tribe to earn a Medal of Honor; he was honored for heroic actions performed on February 9, 1945. He received the medal on October 19, 1945.

Sources: Anderson, Jerry (EEO Manager, OASD [FM&P]-ADASD, The Pentagon), Personal communication to AnCita Benally, January 13, 1996; Hirschfelder and Kreipe de Montaño, *The Native American Almanac*, p. 229.

ca. 1945 A decorated U.S. Marine for his service in the Pacific during World War II, Ira Hayes (Pima; 1922–1955) was the only American Indian in the famous image of six U.S. Marines raising the American flag at Mt. Suribachi on Iwo Jima Island, symbolically declaring victory over the Japanese. Three of the men died as a result. The photograph taken by Joseph Rosenthal brought instant fame and public adulation for the three survivors of the incident. Following the publication of the photograph, Hayes was chosen to make a national tour, campaigning for the war effort. A reluctant hero, he found it difficult to be in the spotlight and requested reassignment to the front lines. However, the war was soon over, and he remained stateside. He was modest in regard to his fame and regretted that the U.S. Marines who had died did not receive the same recognition. After the war Hayes returned to the Pima Reservation, but found rural life uncomfortable and began to drift between cities and the reservation. He died in 1955, having succumbed to exposure. A somewhat idealistic account was made of his life after he died. The image of the raising of the flag became a national symbol, and the government commissioned a larger than life bronze statue modeled after it and issued a commemorative stamp of the picture.

Sources: *Biographical Dictionary of Indians of the Americas*, Vol. 1, p. 271; Dockstader, *Great North American Indians;* Malinowski, ed., *Notable Native Americans*, p. 187.

KOREAN CONFLICT

1951 Mitchell Red Cloud Jr. (Winnebago) was the only member of his tribe to earn the Congressional Medal of Honor, which was awarded posthumously for courage, dedication, and self-sacrifice during the Korean Conflict. Without regard for his safety, he warned his comrades of approaching enemy, and while they readied their positions, he fired on the enemy. When he was shot down, he managed to haul himself back up, tie his arm around a tree, and keep firing until he was mortally wounded. For this selfless sacrifice he received the military's highest honor. Red Cloud joined the U.S. Marine Corps in 1941 at the age of sixteen. He served in the Pacific during World War II. He was honorably discharged in 1945, but in 1948 he returned to military service, joining the U.S. Army. He was sent to Korea in 1950 where he died on November 5.

Sources: Anderson, Jerry (EEO Manager, OASD [FM&P]-ADASD, The Pentagon), Personal communication to AnCita Benally, January 13, 1996; Hirschfelder and Kreipe de Montaño, *The Native American Almanac,* p. 229; *Self-Guiding Tour for The National Hall of Fame for Famous American Indians and Anadarko Visitors' Center,* p. 4.

1951 Raymond Harvey (Chickasaw) was the only member of his tribe to be honored with the Medal of Honor for his services during the Korean Conflict. He was awarded the medal on August 2, 1951, for his heroic actions on March 9, 1951.

Sources: Anderson, Jerry (EEO Manager, OASD [FM&P]-ADASD, The Pentagon), Personal communication to AnCita Benally, January 13, 1996; Hirschfelder and Kreipe de Montaño, *The Native American Almanac,* p. 229.

1954 Charles George (Eastern Cherokee) was the only member of his tribe to be given the Medal of Honor for his services during the Korean Conflict. He was awarded this honor on March 18, 1954, for heroic actions on November 30, 1952.

Sources: Anderson, Jerry (EEO Manager, OASD [FM&P]-ADASD, The Pentagon), Personal communication to AnCita Benally, January 13, 1996; Hirschfelder and Kreipe de Montaño, *The Native American Almanac,* p. 229.

VIETNAM CONFLICT

1960s Loretta S. Jendritza (Navajo) was the first Navajo woman to earn the rank of major during her service in the U.S. Air Force. During the Vietnam War, she served as a surgical nurse and worked on medical evacuation flight units. In the 1970s, she was an operating room supervisor at the Air Force Academy Hospital in Colorado Springs, Colorado. She was born in Farmington, New Mexico.

Sources: *Biographical Dictionary of Indians of the Americas,* Vol. 1, p. 317; Gridley, ed., *Indians of Today,* p. 50.

1970s Marcia Ann Biddleman (Seneca; 1945–) was a first lieutenant with the U.S. Marine Corps. During the 1970s, she was the highest ranking woman Marine and the only woman Marine officer to serve as a weather forecaster. In addition, she was the first recipient of the Woman Officer Basic Course Leadership Award. Biddleman attended various military schools before beginning her training at the U.S. Navy Aerographer's Mate School. She served as a drill instructor as well.

Sources: *Biographical Dictionary of Indians of the Americas,* Vol. 1, p. 51; Gridley, ed., *Indians of Today,* p. 434.

PERSIAN GULF WAR

1991 Pfc. Michael A. Noline (San Carlos Apache) was the first Native American casualty of the Persian Gulf War. He was also the first casualty from Arizona. He died January 26, 1991, while returning from a mission on the Kuwaiti-Saudi border. He was laid to rest in Periodot on the San Carlos Apache Reservation.

Sources: Burgis, Mike, and Julie Lobaco, "Apache Community Mourns GIs ," *The Arizona Republic,* January 23, 1991; "Don't Forget Him," *The Phoenix Gazette,* April 16, 1991, p. A-12.

PERFORMING ARTS

DANCE

ca. 1942 Maria Tallchief (Osage; 1925–) was the first Native American and the first American to dance with the Paris Opera. She was also the first American to receive the title of prima ballerina.

See also:Performing Arts: Dance, 1947.

Sources: Champagne, ed., *The Native North American Almanac,* p. 1172.

1947 Maria Tallchief (Osage; 1925–) was not only the first American to dance with the Paris Opera, she also danced with the Ballet at the Bolshoi Theater in Moscow. She later joined the Balanchine Ballet Society (New York City Ballet). She was the first American to receive the title prima ballerina.

Tallchief was born on the Osage reservation and then moved with her family to California where she came under the tutelage of Bronislava Nijinska. She began her career dancing with the Ballet Russe de Monte Carlo where she gained experience as a soloist. However, it was not until she and George Balanchine teamed together, that she achieved her greatest success. He created ballets for her that focused on her strengths and artistic gifts, making her one of the most renowned dancers of her time. *Firebird,* which he created for Tallchief, became her signature role and the one for which she is best known. She married Balanchine in 1946 and divorced him four years later, however, they maintained a professional relationship.

During Tallchief's career, she received many awards and honors including the Indian Achievement Award and an honorary life membership from the Indian Council Fire in 1967, and the induction into the Oklahoma Hall of Fame in 1968. In 1996 she earned further distinction by becoming the first Native American woman to become a Kennedy Center honoree. She received the award alongside Johnny Cash, another performing artist of American Indian descent. In 1967, with her sister Marjorie Tallchief, Rosella Hightower, and Moscelyne Larkin she appeared in *Four Moons,* a ballet created to celebrate the sixtieth year of Oklahoma statehood. The ballerinas were also honored with a mural on the ceiling of the Oklahoma State Capitol building.

Sources: Bremser, ed., *International Dictionary of Ballet,* Vol. 2, pp. 1379–82; Champagne, ed., *The Native North American Almanac,* p. 1172; Gridley, *Indians of Today,* p. 292; Livingston, *American Indian Ballerinas,* p. 193; Malinowski, ed., *Notable Native Americans,* pp. 421–22.

1957 Ballerina and choreographer Moscelyne Larkin (Shawnee/Peoria) established the Oklahoma Indian Ballerina Festival. During her career, Larkin danced with the original Ballet Russe, the Ballet Russe de Monte Carlo, and the Danilova Company in South America.

Sources: *Biographical Dictionary of Indians of the Americas,* Vol. 1, p. 350.

MARJORIE TALLCHIEF

1957 Marjorie Tallchief (Osage) was the first American invited to join the Paris Opera Ballet as *premiere danseuse etoile;* she was also the first American to dance at the Bolshoi Theatre in Moscow. She is the younger sister of Maria Tallchief and like her was an internationally acclaimed ballerina. Critics at first frowned at her lack of emotional drama despite great technical skill, but later acclaimed her as one of the most lyrical and versatile ballerinas. In fact she became known for her great expressive powers. She also became known for her acrobatic elasticity and the high speed *fouettes* that became her trademark. In 1948 she danced in George Balanchine's *pas de trois classique* alongside Andre Eglevsky and Rosella Hightower, another Native American dancer. It is one of the few known times that two Indian ballerinas danced in the same piece. She has danced for presidents and kings and queens—twice at the White House for Presidents John F. Kennedy and Lyndon Johnson.

Maria Tallchief.

Sources: Bremser, ed., *International Dictionary of Ballet,* Vol. 2, pp. 1382–84; Koegler, *Dictionary of Ballet,* p. 407; Livingston, *American Indian Ballerinas,* pp. 193, 199; Gridley, *Indians of Today,* p. 294.

ca. 1962 World-famous ballerina Rosella Hightower (Choctaw; 1920–) founded her own dance school, the Center of Classical Dance in Cannes. Hightower danced with several dance groups including: the Ballet Russe de Monte Carlo; the American Ballet Theatre (as a soloist); the Ballet Russe; the Grand Ballet of the Marquis de Cuevas (Grand Ballerine); the Ballet Theatre of Lucia Chase; and the Threatre of the Champs Elysees.

Sources: *Biographical Dictionary of Indians of the Americas,* Vol. 1, p. 278; Livingston, *American Indian Ballerinas,* pp. 159–61.

1967 *Four Moons,* was the only ballet written especially for American Indian ballerinas. It was choreographed for four of the world's most famous Indian ballerinas—Maria Tallchief, Marjorie Tallchief, Rosella Hightower, and Moscelyn Larkin. The score was written by Louis Ballard, a Quapaw/Cherokee composer. Its theme is based on Indian mythology and it is the only ballet written and danced by American Indians to showcase Indianness. It was performed in celebration of the sixtieth year of statehood for Oklahoma.

Sources: Gridley, *Indians of Today,* pp. 469–70.

1981 Rosella Hightower (Choctaw; 1920–) was the first American and the first Native American to direct the Paris Opera Ballet. As director, she initiated controversial innovations that departed dramatically from the usual customs of ballet.

She assailed the hierarchical star system; she wanted all dancers to have dance time so they could develop and improve their skills; she initiated a three-tiered system of programming, which allowed one-third of the company to perform in the opera house, one-third to tour, and one-third to perform voluntary *group de recherches* in modern works. In Hightower's first year, she directed *Hommage au ballet* and featured a rare on-stage appearance by the entire opera company. The dramatic changes she brought put her at the forefront of the ballet world.

In 1975 the French government presented Hightower with the Chevalier de la Legion d'Honneur, the Officier de la Legion d'Honneur in 1988, and the Grand

Louis W. Ballard, musician/composer, whose unique compositions include ceremonial-type undertones.

Prix national de danse in 1990. As a dancer Hightower danced with the original Ballet Russe with Rudolf Nureyev. In 1967 she was one of four ballerinas to appear at the premier of *The Four Moons* in Tulsa. Along with Maria Tallchief, Majorie Tallchief, and Moscelyne Larkin, she was honored with a mural painted on the ceiling of the Oklahoma State Capitol building. Since retiring from dancing, Hightower has established Le Centre de Danse Classique in Cannes, a residential school that includes academic training as well as dance.

Sources: *Biographical Dictionary of Indians of the Americas,* Vol. 1, p. 278; Bremser, *International Dictionary of Ballet,* Vol. 2, pp. 662–65; Livingston, *American Indian Ballerinas,* pp. 266–68; Malinowski, ed., *Notable Native Americans,* pp. 195–96.

The American Indian Dance Theater performs an Eagle Dance.

1988 *In the Land of Spirits,* was the first Canadian Native ballet produced. John Kim Bell (Mohawk) co-composed the ballet as part of a fund-raising concert for the Canadian Native Arts Foundation established by Bell in 1988. The purpose of the organization was to provide Native American students with scholarships in the arts. Bell was convinced that sponsors would be more willing to participate if they contributed to fund-raising performances rather than just giving money. With that in mind he composed *In the Land of Spirits,* and it debuted at the National Arts Centre in Ottawa. It was a great artistic and financial success. It later became the first recorded Native ballet.

Sources: Champagne, ed., *Chronology of Native North American History,* p. 325; Champagne, ed. *The Native North American Almanac,* pp. 1009–1010; Malinowski, ed., *Notable Native Americans,* pp. 29–30.

1996 Spirit Walker was the first American Indian dance troupe to tour foreign military bases. They have visited Iceland, England, Scotland, Germany, and Norway, performing pow wow dances.

Sources: "Warm Springs Dance Troup Tours European Military Bases," *Indian Country Today,* Vol. 16, No. 20 (November 11–18, 1996) p. B-2.

FILM

1894 The first movie to focus on an American Indian subject was *The Ghost Dance,* filmed in West Orange, New Jersey, by Thomas A. Edison Films, which produced other documentaries about American Indians, including *Moki Snake Dance,* filmed in 1901. These forty- to ninety-second moving images provided Americans with their first view of Indian ceremonial dances.

Sources: Champagne, ed., *Chronology of Native North American History,* p. 245; Hirschfelder and Kreipe de Montaño, *The Native American Almanac,* p. 177; Washburn, *Handbook of North American Indians,* pp. 177, 609.

1909 James Young Deer (Winnebago) was the first Indian man to act in a film. He acted in *The Mended Lute* and *The True Heart of an Indian*—both filmed in 1909. He made an additional film in 1911, *The Yaqui Girl.* He was married to Princess Red Wing, who was also featured in the movie.

Sources: Champagne, ed., *Chronology of Native North American History,* p. 265; Hirschfelder and Kreipe de Montaño, *The Native American Almanac,* p. 182.

1911 A group of Indians expressed strong disapproval to the Bureau of Indian Affairs (BIA) about the inaccurate portrayal of Indians in movies, marking the first time Indians collectively protested the entertainment industry. They further protested the use of non-Indians to portray Indians. BIA commissioner Robert G. Valentine concurred, and promised to assist in eliminating objectionable representation of Indians. In 1914 Native actors threatened to strike if the movie industry did not improve their portrayal. At a meeting of the Society of American Indians, Chauncey Yellowrobe objected to what he considered an inaccurate, falsified version of the Battle of Wounded Knee in 1890. In 1979 the American Indian Theatre Guild stated that little had changed in over fifty years.

Sources: Hirschfelder and Kreipe de Montaño, *The Native American Almanac,* p. 178.

1912 By agreement between Thomas H. Ince, producer for Bison-10 Motion Picture Co., and the U.S. government, a large number of Oglala Sioux were taken from Pine Ridge to a film studio in the Santa Monica Mountains. For three years they acted in more than eighty westerns. It was the first large group of American Indians to act in films.

Sources: Champagne, ed., *Chronology of Native North American History,* p. 270.

1950 The first film to treat American Indians as more than one-dimensional characters was released and proclaimed as honest in its depiction of Indian history. *Broken Arrow* is the story about the friendship between Chiricahua Apache chief Cochise and Thomas Jeffords, an Indian agent. The film also includes the element of interracial marriage (Jeffords marries an Apache woman), which was considered highly controversial for its time. The only Indian actor with a significant part was Iron Eyes Cody.

Sources: Champagne, *Chronology of Native North American History,* p. 323; Sonneborn, *Performers,* pp. 43–52.

1951 Victor Daniels (Cherokee), also known as Chief Thunder Cloud, has appeared in twenty-seven movies, more than any other Indian actor. Daniels has appeared in such movies as *Geronimo* (1939), in which he had no speaking lines appeared in such movies as *Geronimo* (1939), in which he had no speaking lines but only provided menacing expressions as a backdrop. He did not receive credit under either his stage name or his real name.

Sources: Hirschfelder and Kreipe de Montaño, *The Native American Almanac,* p. 180.

1970 "Chief" Dan George (Squamish; 1899–1981) was the first Native American and the first Canadian Indian nominated for an Oscar for best supporting actor for an American film. He started his film career at the age of sixty. In 1971 George won the New York Film Critics Award and the National Society of Film Critics Award for best supporting actor in *Little Big Man.* During his career he worked to improve the portrayal of Indians in films.

Sources: *Biographical Dictionary of Indians of the Americas,* Vol. 1, p. 240; Hirschfelder and Kreipe de Montaño, *The Native American Almanac,* p. 180; Malinowski, ed., *Notable Native Americans,* pp. 158–159.

1975 The American Indian Film Festival opened in Seattle, Washington, on March 14, 1975. It is the oldest and the most well-known international film forum dedicated to the presentation of American and Canadian Indians in cinema. Michael Smith (Sioux) is the founder and director.

Sources: Champagne, ed., *Chronology of Native North American History,* p. 403.

1990 The National Film Board of Canada announced the creation of Studio One, a studio designed for use by indigenous peoples to develop media that will provide accurate portrayal of Native peoples. It was the first organization to devote its attention exclusively to training Native artists in the film industry.

Sources: Champagne, ed., *Chronology of Native North American History,* p. 476; Hirschfelder and Kreipe de Montaño, *The Native American Almanac,* p. 187.

1992 The first major international platform of Native American cinema was held in Munich Germany at the Tenth Annual Munich Filmfest. Such films as *Surviving Columbus* (George Burdeau), *Wiping the Tears of Seven Generations* (Gary Rhine and Fidel Moreno), *Itam Hakim, Hopiit* (Victor Masayesva, Jr.), and *The Honor of All* (Phil Lucas) were honored.

Sources: Champagne, ed., *Chronology of Native North American History,* 1994. p. 488.

TELEVISION FILM AND SERIES

Early-1970s Film and television actor James Garner (Cherokee; 1928–) has starred in several television series, including *Maverick* during the late-1950s, and in the early-1970s, *Nichols* and *The Rockford Files,* for which he earned two Emmys. In addition he served in the armed forces during the Korean Conflict, where he was wounded in action, receiving a Purple Heart.

Sources: *Biographical Dictionary of Indians of the Americas,* Vol. 1, p. 235.

1979 Jay Silverheels (Mohawk; 1912–1980) was the first American Indian awarded a star on the Hollywood Walk of Fame. Silverheels played "Tonto" on *The Lone Ranger* television series during the 1950s. Aware of the misrepresentation of Indians in the entertainment industry, he created the Indian Actors Workshop in an attempt to increase American Indian opportunities in Hollywood.

Sources: Champagne, ed., *The Native North American Almanac*, p. 1160; Hirschfelder and Kreipe de Montaño, *The Native American Almanac*, p. 180.

Jay Silverheels, the first American Indian awarded a star on Hollywood's Walk of Fame.

1983 *I'd Rather Be Powwowing,* was the first television documentary produced by an all-Indian crew, which included George Horse Capture (Gros Ventre; 1936–) as producer, Larry Littlebird (Santo Domingo Pueblo) as director; and Larry Cesspooch (Ute) as the sound director. The film is about a young man following the powwow circuit.

Sources: Hirschfelder and Kreipe de Montaño, *The Native American Almanac,* p. 186; Malinowski, ed., *Notable Native Americans,* pp. 200–201.

MUSIC

1895 Though Europeanized, music of the Omaha was the basis for Anton Dvořák's *The New World Symphony.* The selections included such familiar ballads as "Land of the Sky Blue Waters" and "At Dawning." It has become the stereotypical melody of white conceptions of Indian music.

Sources: Dennis, *The American Indian, 1492–1976,* p. 46.

1914 Ada Navarrate (Maya) was the first Native American to enter the international opera world, winning acclaim as a soprano. Also known as Tappan de Carrasco, she was born in Merida, the capital of the state of Yucatan, Mexico. She debuted in Mexico City in 1914 and made her international debut with the Boston Opera Company in 1917. She retired in 1936.

Sources: *Biographical Dictionary of Indians of the Americas,* Vol. 2, p. 466; Leitch, *Chronology of the American Indian,* p. 192.

1926 Tsianina Redfeather Blackstone (Creek; ca. 1882–1985) sang the title role in *Shanewis: The Robin Woman,* the first American opera with a modern setting that was produced in two consecutive seasons at the Metropolitan Opera in New York City. It was written by "Indianist" composer Charles Wakefield Cadman, who said that it was loosely based on Blackstone's life. Although she was not highly praised for her mezzo soprano voice, critics commented on her strong personality. In 1918 she volunteered to entertain troops in Europe. After the Armistice was signed, she returned to her music career. She retired in the 1930s and then became active in Indian concerns. She died in 1985.

Sources: Bataille, ed., *Native American Women,* p. 29; Lamawaima, Tsianina (niece of Tsianina Redfeather Blackstone, and professor of Native American studies, University of Arizona, Tucson), Personal communication to Karen Gayton Swisher, September 1996.

1949 Russell "Big Chief" Moore (Pima) was a well known jazz trombonist and leading American Indian musician who played with some of America's greatest jazz bands and artists. His talent for music was apparent in childhood. He made his own music with pipes, making so much noise that his parents hid them to have some peace. His father died when Moore was eleven, and he was sent to Chicago to live with an uncle who happened to be a music teacher. There he learned to play several instruments. Throughout his career he performed solo and with his own band at various times. He played with some of the greatest jazz musicians, such as Lionel Hampton (1935) and Louis Armstrong (1943–45). He played first trombonist in Armstrong's band and later was featured on Satchmo's

Hello Dolly album. Moore was internationally known and he travelled with an international jazz band in Europe, North Africa, and other parts of the world. He traveled to France, where he performed at the Paris Jazz Festival in 1949, likely being the only American Indian to do so. Moore also had the honor of playing at two presidential inaugural balls.

    See also: Performing Arts: Music, 1960.

Sources: *Biographical Dictionary of Indians of the Americas,* Vol. 1, p. 443.

1951 Ed Lee Natay (Navajo; d. 1967) was the first Navajo and the first Native American to record for Canyon Records in Phoenix, Arizona. Initially Canyon Records was asked to record Natay for a production by the Phoenix Little Theater. Taken with Natay's rich voice, Canyon Records owners Ray and Mary Boley asked to record his voice. The result was the first recording of Indian music produced by Canyon Records, *Natay, Navajo Singer.* The eight songs that comprise this album were recorded in a ballet studio. With its release, the Boleys created Canyon Records, which had been known as Arizona Recording Productions, and began concentrating on American Indian music. Canyon Records became the first recording company to specialize in Indian music for a Native American audience and for commercial purposes. Before his death in 1967, Natay made an additional recording. Forty-six years later Canyon Records released a twenty-CD package featuring music from the original album and from his last recording.

    Natay was the son of a Navajo leader and medicine man. He attended school in Fort Defiance, Arizona, and Santa Fe, New Mexico. After completing his schooling, he became one of the first Native Americans to work as an instructor in the public high schools of New Mexico. In 1996 Ray Boley established a music schol-

Ed Lee Natay, Navajo recording artist, shown with with Canyon Records founder Ray Boley in 1951.

arship at Northern Arizona University in his and Ed Lee Natay's name for American Indian students studying music.

Sources: "Canyon Records Celebrates 45 Years with Concert Series," *Arizona Native Scene,* Vol. 2, No. 17, 1996, p. 8; "Canyon Records—Voice of the People," Phoenix, Arizona (promotional material).

1958 Keely Smith (Cherokee; 1935–) became the first woman of Native American descent to win a Grammy award. She was also an actress and appeared on national television variety shows. She was active in the Los Angeles American Indian Center.

Sources: *Biographical Dictionary of Indians of the Americas,* Vol.2, p 700.

1960 Louis W. Ballard (Quapaw/Cherokee; 1931–) wrote the first modern American Indian ballet, *Koshare,* which premiered in Barcelona, Spain, in 1960. In 1972, his composition, *Desert Trilogy* was nominated for a Pulitzer Prize in music. In the same year he was the first musician to receive the Indian Achievement Award from the Indian Council Fire. He is one of the foremost Indian musical composers in the United States. He received his M.A. in music from the University of Oklahoma in 1967. Ballard creates a unique blend of the ceremonial music he grew up with, into ballets, chamber, orchestral, and choral music compositions.

Sources: *Biographical Dictionary of Indians of the Americas,* Vol. 1, p. 36; Hirschfelder and Kreipe de Montaño, *The Native American Almanac,* pp.168, 173; Gridley, ed., *Indians of Today,* p. 242; Malinowski, ed., *Notable Native Americans,* pp. 22–23.

1960 Russell "Big Chief" Moore (Pima) was the first Native American musician to play at a presidential inauguration. He played at inaugural ball for John F. Kennedy and in 1964, for Lyndon B. Johnson. He also performed at other White House functions. He was a jazz trombonist and is one of the earliest Native Americans to become a professional jazz musician. He played with some of the most well-known musicians in jazz; and in 1949 he participated in the Paris Jazz Festival, likely being the only Indian to do so.

Sources: *Biographical Dictionary of Indians of the Americas,* p. 443; Gridley, *Indians of Today,* p. 175; Hirschfelder and Kreipe de Montaño, *The Native American Almanac,* p. 172.

1962 Wayne Newton (Powhatan/Cherokee; 1942–) was the first Native American entertainer to be featured on televised variety shows. He appeared on the *Jackie Gleason Show,* the *Ed Sullivan Show,* and the *Danny Kaye Show.* Newton began his career appearing on a radio show with his brother. After moving to Phoenix, Arizona, he performed on his own radio show. He was "discovered" by Gleason who invited him to appear on his show. Newton went on to become the most successful and popular nightclub performer in Las Vegas. In addition to his singing career he has appeared in several movies including a James Bond feature, *License to Kill.* He has supported Indian organizations and expressed pride in his heritage.

Sources: *Biographical Dictionary of Indians of the Americas,* Vol. 2, pp. 472–73.

ca. 1969 Robbie Robertson (Mohawk; 1943–) was the first Native American to become a prominent rock musician and became the first Indian to win several honors for his music. He is best known for his work in The Band. He was born July 5, 1943, in Toronto, Ontario, Canada. He spent his childhood living in the city, but also spent time with his mother's family on the reserve. In 1968 he changed the name of his rock band from Hawks to The Band, and recorded his first album, *Music from Big Pink*. His second album went gold and included such songs as "The Night They Rode Old Dixie Down," and "Up on Cripple Creek." The Band was the first U.S. rock group to be featured on the cover of *Time* magazine, January 12, 1970. Another album *Rock of Ages* produced another gold record. The Band broke up in 1976; Robertson is now a solo artist.

Sources: *Biographical Dictionary of Indians of the Americas,* Vol. 2, pp. 618–20; "Down to Old Dixie and Back," *Time,* January 12, 1970, pp. 42–46.

1970s Jesse Edwin Davis III (Kiowa; 1945–1988) was a prominent rock guitarist. He worked as backup for Bob Dylan, John Lennon, Willie Nelson, and Marvin Gaye. He played lead guitar for "Last Train to Clarksville" (by the Monkees) and "Doctor My Eyes" (by Jackson Browne). Davis also performed at the Concert for Bangladesh. During the 1980s he joined activist, writer, and musician John Trudell (Lakota Sioux), providing musical accompaniment to Trudell's poetry. Their album, *aka Grafitti Man,* was released in 1986.

Sources: *Biographical Dictionary of Indians of the Americas,* Vol. 1, p. 180; Wright-McLeod, Brian, "Movers, Shakers, Hit-Makers and Heartbreakers," *Aboriginal Voices,* Vol. 4, No. 2 (April/May/June 1997), pp. 14–15.

1972 Louis W. Ballard (Quapaw/Cherokee; 1931–), one of the foremost American Indian musical composers in the United States, was the first musician to receive the Indian Achievement Award of the Indian Council Fire. Ballard uniquely blends the American Indian ceremonial music he grew up with into ballets, chamber, orchestral, and choral music compositions. He earned his M.A. in music from the University of Oklahoma in 1967. Ballard has received numerous awards and commissions, including a nomination for a Pulitzer Prize for his *Desert Trilogy.*

Sources: *Biographical Dictionary of Indians of the Americas,* Vol 1, p. 36; Champagne, ed., *The Native North American Almanac,* p. 1006; Gridley, ed., *Indians of Today,* pp. 242–43.

1975 Wayne Newton (Powhatan/Cherokee; 1942–) was named the Male Entertainer of the Year by the Academy of Variety and Cabaret Artists, thereby becoming the first person of Native American descent to be so honored.

Sources: *Biographical Dictionary of Indians of the Americas,* Vol. 2, pp. 473–74.

Loretta Lynn.

1980 Loretta Lynn (Cherokeel; 1935–) has become the most honored woman artist of Native American descent in the country/western music business. In 1967, 1972, and 1973, she was named Country Music Award's Female Vocalist. In 1972 she was named Entertainer of the Year, and won four top-duet awards. In 1971 she received a Grammy Award and in 1978 she was awarded an American Music Award. In 1980, she was named the Entertainer of the Decade. Lynn is also a very accomplished business woman. She owns three publishing companies, a rodeo, a western store, and a talent agency. In 1976 she published her autobiography, *Coal Miner's Daughter,* which later became a movie. Lynn has often expressed pride in her Cherokee ancestry; two of her great-grandmothers were full-blood Cherokees.

Sources: *Biographical Dictionary of Indians of the Americas,* Vol. 1, p. 378; Lynn, Loretta., with George Vecsey, *Coal Miner's Daughter,* Chicago: Regnery, 1976.

1980 John Kim Bell, (Mohawk; 1952–) has accomplished a number of firsts. He became the first Native North American to become a symphony orchestra conductor in 1980. Bell, who was born on the Kahnawake Mohawk Reserve near Montreal, became the youngest professional conductor in the United States after he was hired as an assistant conductor for a touring Broadway company. Following his appointment he studied at the Academia Musicale Chigiana in Sienna, Italy, where he received a certificate of performance in 1981. The Canadian Broadcasting Company (CBC) featured him in a documentary. Thereafter, Bell was deluged with letters from Native parents wanting to know how their children could access opportunities in the music field. Sympathetic to the queries, Bell formed the Canadian Native Arts Foundation in 1985 with his own funds to provide Native youth with scholarships in the arts.

Sources: Champagne, ed., *The Native North American Almanac,* p. 1009; "Maestro with a Mission," *MacLean's,* January 18, 1988, pp. 6–7; Malinowski, ed., *Notable Native Americans,* pp. 29–30.

1991 Daryl H. Benally (Navajo) was the only Navajo and the only Native American to be chosen to tour with the New Mexico Ambassador of Music '91 Europe Musical Tour. The tour group consisted of high school musicians from throughout the state. Benally attended Gallup High School in Gallup, New Mexico, and played the French horn, participating in the high school marching and orchestra bands. A member of the National Honor Society, he has proclaimed himself a math "nut."

Sources: "Music Helps Student See the World," *Navajo Times,* Vol. 31, No. 27 (July 3, 1991), p. A-8.

1996 Johnny Cash (Cherokee; 1932–) was the first Native American to win major honors in the country/western music business. At one time he had his own variety series on television. Cash has had several songs that have sold over a million records; for example, "I Walk the Line." In 1996 he, along with another Native American performer, Maria Tallchief, was a Kennedy Center honoree. He and Tallchief are the only Native Americans to be so honored.

Sources: *Biographical Dictionary of Indians of the Americas,* Vol. 1, p. 116.

1996 Robert Moore (Sicangu Lakota Sioux) was the first Native American to sing at a national political convention. He sang the national anthem at the Democratic convention in Chicago on August 26, 1996.

Sources: Shoemaker, Darrell. "Sicangu Songbird Sings at National Convention," *Indian Country Today,* Vol.16, No. 11 (September 9–16, 1996) p. A-3;

THEATER

1844 George Henry (Ojibwa), also known as Maungwudaus, formed the "Wild Indian" troupe and traveled throughout the United States, Great Britain, France, and Belgium in 1844 and 1845. His acting troupe was the first one organized by an Indian and composed of Indians. Henry was the half-brother of American Indian missionary Peter Jones, who found the troupe to be a great embarrassment. In addition to performing for white audiences, Henry wrote travelogues, *Remarks*

Concerning the Ojbway Indians, by One of Themselves, Called Maunguwdaus, Who Has Been Travelling in England, France, Belgium, Ireland, and Scotland, published in 1847, and *An Account of the Chippewa Indians, Who Have Been Travelling Among the Whites in the United States, England, Ireland, Scotland, France and Belgium,* published in 1848. Both are commentaries and impressions of Henry as he observed European white people and their peculiar customs in the countries they visited. It was one of the first publications by Indians about white people.

Sources: *Dictionary of Native American Literature,* p. 148; Wiget, ed., *Dictionary of Native American Literature,* p. 48.

1931 Rollie Lynn Riggs (Cherokee; d. 1954) wrote *Green Grow the Lilacs,* which was produced by the Theatre Guild in New York City in 1931 and was named one of the ten best plays on Broadway. It was later adapted by Richard Rodgers and Oscar Hammerstein into the musical *Oklahoma!* Riggs is considered one of the greatest writers of folk drama and the most eminent of Native American playwrights.

Riggs' mother died when he was a young child and his father's remarriage brought hardships for him. He was often mentally and emotionally abused by his stepmother and although he eventually went to live with an aunt, the experience was traumatic. Consequently, his writings examine issues of betrayal by women, rebellious youth, and loss of innocence. Riggs was extremely proud of his Native heritage and as a youth was fascinated with Cherokee music, which led him to learn tribal chants.

Riggs wrote only one play oriented toward Indian issues, *The Cherokee Night,* which addresses mixed-blood Cherokees and their struggle for acceptance and the right to an identity. Although Broadway producers were not interested, it may have been Riggs' greatest artistic achievement. In his other plays, he addressed topics that were prohibited in his day, such as incest and suggestions of sexuality. In many areas, he was ahead of his time in exploring various aspects of the human character. Riggs himself was gay, but kept it secret. During World War II he served in the U.S. Army. He died in 1954.

Sources: *Biographical Dictionary of Indians of the Americas,* p. 617; Wiget, ed., *Dictionary of Native American Literature,* pp. 289–93; Witalec, ed., *Native North American Literature,* pp. 549–56.

1956 Arthur Smith Junaluska (Cherokee; 1918–) organized the first American Indian drama company. He was also the first Indian ever to perform in a Shakespearean repertory company. In addition, he founded the American Society for Creative Arts. Junaluska was educated at the Cherokee Indian School and then attended several colleges in the United States before enrolling at the London School of Medicine. While doing medical research he modified a serology test, which became a commonly used technique by commercial blood banks. He planned a career in medicine until he became interested in theater. As a member of the performing arts community, Junaluska has written plays, directed, performed, choreographed, and taught acting. His most notable contributions include a ballet production *Dance of the Twelve Moons,* and the plays *Shackled, The Medicine Woman,* and *The Grand Council of Indian Circle.* Many of his works focus on Indian themes, and present sensitive and realistic portrayals. He has also created non-Indian drama and has served as a consultant for stage plays, movies, radio, and television productions.

Sources: *Biographical Dictionary of Indians of the Americas,* p. 327; Gridley, *Indians of Today,* p. 152.

1986 Playwright, director, and producer Tomson Highway (Cree; 1951–) became artistic director of the Native Earth Performing Arts, Toronto's only professional theater company for Indians. He works to help Indian writers get their work seen. Highway is famous for his plays *The Rez Sisters* (1986) and *Dry Lips Oughtta Move to Kapuskasing* (1989). *The Rez Sisters* won the Dora Mavor Moore Award for best new play in Toronto and placed runner-up for the Floyd S. Chalmers award for outstanding Canadian play for 1986. It was also nominated for Canada's Governor General's Literary Award in 1988. Further, *The Rez Sisters* was the only Native film, and one of two Canadian films, represented in the Edinburgh International Festival.

Sources: *Biographical Dictionary of Indians of the Americas,* Vol. 1, p. 278; Champagne, ed., *Chronology of Native North American History,* p. 324; Malinowski, ed., *Notable Native Americans,* pp. 196–97; Witalec, ed., *Native North American Literature,* pp. 325–32.

RELIGIOUS LIFE

1500s The use of peyote among indigenous peoples was first recorded by the Spanish in the 1500s. The Chichimec were reported to use peiotl, as they called it, for protection from danger. In 1620 the Spanish issued an edict forbidding the use of the plant. Farther north in 1649, in the southwest United States area, the Carizzo were reported to be using it in all night ceremonies that included drumming. The practice spread to southern Plains tribes such as the Lipan Apache, Tonkawa, the Kiowa, and Kiowa Apache. The expansion of the religion involved key Indian leaders, such as Quannah Parker. The movement culminated in the 1918 formation of the Native American Church, a religion that combines tribal religions and elements of Christian concepts with the use peyote as a sacrament. It has been a controversial religion because of its use of peyote, which contains a hallucinogenic drug.

Sources: Davis, ed., *Native America in the Twentieth Century,* pp. 446–49; Dennis, *The American Indian, 1492–1976,* p. 36; Hirschfelder and Molin, *The Encyclopedia of Native American Religions,* pp. 213–15.

1500s An official campaign, the Extirpacion de Idolatrias, was launched to eradicate indigenous religions, customs, and practices in the Andes. The 1540s witnessed the beginning of efforts to eliminate ceremonial rites. In 1551, the First Counciliar Council of Lima declared all pre-Christian Indians damned. The campaign had limited success as Indian people continued to maintain their religions and cultures.

Sources: Greenleaf, Richard E., "Persistence of Native Values: The Inquisition and the Indians of Colonial Mexico," *Journal of the Americas,* Vol. 3, No. 3 (January 1994), pp. 351–76.

1522 The first recorded trial of an Indian before the Mexican Inquisition was that of Marcos of Acolhuacan. He was tried for the crime of concubinage.

Sources: Greenleaf, Richard E., "Persistence of Native Values: The Inquisition and the Indians of Colonial Mexico," *Journal of the Americas,* Vol. 3, No. 3 (January 1994), pp. 351–76.

1560s *Takiy onkoy* (dancing sickness), a religious movement, was initiated in the southern Andes. Leaders admonished followers to reject Spanish customs and culture and called for a return to native traditions, particularly the cult of *wak'as* (ancestor worship).

Sources: Wearne, *Return of the Indian, Conquest and Revival in the Americas,* p. 195.

1587 On August 13, 1587, Manteo (Hatteras) was christened Lord of Roanoke and of Dosamonquepeak, the Indian town located on the mainland opposite Roanoke Island. It was the earliest recorded Protestant service on American soil. He was a guide and interpreter for Sir Walter Raleigh's colonies in North Carolina. He went to England twice and assisted Ralph Lane and John White when they tried to establish settlements.
Sources: *Biographical Dictionary of Indians of the Americas*, Vol. 1, p. 392; Dennis, *The American Indian, 1492–1976*, p. 3.

1615 Roman Catholic Recollet missionaries arrived in New France and were accepted as emissaries from the French traders, whom the Indians had accepted as partners. This was the first time a community of Indians gave access to Europeans into their society. It began a long association of Catholic missionization among the Native peoples.
Sources: Champagne, ed., *The Native North American Almanac*, p. 104.

1629 Spanish Catholic missionaries established churches at Acoma, Hopi, and Zuñi pueblos.
Sources: Champagne, ed., *Chronology of Native North American History*, p. 56.

1634 The French Jesuit missionaries established their first mission at Ihonatiria, a Huron village. The Jesuits replaced the Recollets and implemented a policy of living among Indian groups to encourage conversion. At the same time, the Recollets favored a practice of living apart from the Indians and encouraging them to settle among the French instead.
Sources: Champagne, ed., *Chronology of Native North American History*, p. 57.

1643 Hiacoomes (Wampanoag, 1610–1690) became the first American Indian in North America to be converted to Christianity. Hiacoomes was also the first Indian ordained a Christian clergyman, in 1670.
Sources: *Biographical Dictionary of Indians of the Americas*, Vol. 1, p. 275.

1651 Waban (Nipmuc) became the first Massachusetts chief to embrace Christianity, after responding to John Eliot's missionizing efforts. When the Praying Town of Natick was established, Waban moved his people there, where they lived as Christians with other "Praying Indians." Waban also agreed to send one of his sons to a colonial school. Waban became one of the principal leaders in the "Praying" community and encouraged his constituents to maintain peaceful relations with the Europeans. He was one of the residents who warned the English colonists of the impending attack by Metacom, also known as King Philip. However, Waban may have been among those falsely accused of complicity with the Wampanoag; he was imprisoned during the conflict. He returned home from his imprisonment ill and died sometime the following year.
Sources: *Biographical Dictionary of Indians of the Americas*, Vol. 1, p. 392; Hirschfelder and Molin, *The Encyclopedia of Native American Religions*, p. 309; Hodge, *Handbook of American Indians North of Mexico*, pp. 884–85; Stoutenburgh, *Dictionary of the American Indian*, pp. 330–31.

1657 Skanudharova (Huron) is believed to have been the first Native American woman to enter Catholic religious life.
Sources: Hirschfelder and Molin, *The Encyclopedia of Native American Religions*, p. 267.

1660 The first Indian church in New England was established by John Eliot. The church was built in Natick, Massachusetts, for the benefit of newly converted Christian Indians. It was hoped that by having their own communities they would learn the civilized arts of the English people while not actually living among the whites. At the same time, they would be removed from the bad influences of their former Indian communities.

Sources: Dennis, *The American Indian, 1492–1976,* p. 12.

1667 Iroquois converts settled at La Prairie (Caughnawaga) near Montreal. This began a series of missionary settlements as the Jesuits tried to organize converted Indians into European-like communities.

Sources: Champagne, ed., *The Native North American Almanac,* p. 106.

1670 Hiacoomes (Wampanoag) preached his first sermon as an ordained minister to the Wampanoag people on Martha's Vineyard. He was the first Indian preacher ordained through the missionary program of John Eliot; he was ordained by Eliot and John Cotton.

Sources: *Biographical Dictionary of Indians of the Americas,* Vol. 1, p. 275; "Hiacoomes," in *The American Indian;* Hirschfelder and Kreipe de Montaño, *The Native American Almanac,* p. 302; Hirschfelder and Molin, *The Encylopedia of Native American Religions,* p. 119.

ca. 1680s Pope (San Juan Pueblo) was one of the first North American Indians to successfully lead a revolt based on religious persecution. In 1680, he planned and led the Pueblo Revolt against the Spanish occupiers of the Southwest. From the beginning of Spanish occupation, Pueblo villages were denied the right to practice their ancient religious traditions and were forced to accept Christianity. Kivas were raided and religious objects destroyed and desecrated by Catholic priests. Villagers were forced to pay heavy tribute to the Spanish military, the civilian governor, and Catholic priests. The final act of desecration came when priests ordered the destruction of sacred masks and the flogging of religious leaders. Pope and his followers vowed to rid themselves of the Spanish and carried out the revolt. For thirteen years, the Pueblo villages were free of Spanish domination. Pope did not live long after the insurrection.

Sources: *Biographical Dictionary of Indians of the Americas,* Vol. 2, pp. 560–70; Champagne, ed., *The Native North American Almanac,* pp. 1135–36; Walker, *American Indian Lives,* pp. 6–13.

ca. 1740s Delaware Prophet (Delaware), or Neolin, also known as "The Enlightened One," established a revivalist religion among the Delaware and other peoples of the Ohio valley. He claimed that, through a mystical experience, he was given revelation by the Master of Life in Heaven to be shared with the people. The Master of Life revealed to him that whites had corrupted the balance of life and were preventing themselves from reaching heaven. Therefore, Indians were to reject white ways and customs, especially trade goods, such as guns and alcohol. The Prophet told of a great war in which the Indians would overpower whites. Influenced by the Prophet's teachings, Ottawa leader Chief Pontiac mounted a large-scale, but futile, attack, known as Pontiac's Rebellion, against the British in 1763.

Sources: *Biographical Dictionary of Indians of the Americas,* Vol. 1, p. 184; Champagne, ed., *Native America,* p. 511; Leitch, *Chronology of the American Indian,* p. 117; Malinowski, ed., *Notable Native Americans,* pp. 114–16.

1752 The first Moravian missionaries (Protestant missionaries from Germany) and traders arrived in North America among the Inuit of Labrador.

Sources: Champagne, ed., *The Native North American Almanac,* p. 107.

Mid-1700s Aspenquid (Abenaki) was one of the first American Indians converted to Christianity by French missionaries. He preached widely throughout northern New England and eastern Canada to other Indians. After his death, his memory was honored with the dedication of Aspenquid Day by the town of Halifax, Nova Scotia.

Sources: "Aspenquid," in *The American Indian; Biographical Dictionary of Indians of the Americas,* Vol. 1, p. 26; Hirschfelder and Molin, *The Encyclopedia of Native American Religions,* p. 7; Hodge, *Handbook of American Indians North of Mexico,* p. 101.

1765 Samson Occom (Mohegan) was the first Native American to preach to a white audience in Europe. A Christian clergyman, Occom was also instrumental in raising the necessary funds to establish Dartmouth College. He and Reverend Nathaniel Whitaker toured England to raise money for Eleazer Wheelock's Indian Charity School. Occom delivered more than three hundred sermons, collecting over $12,000. Wheelock used the money to move the school to New Hampshire and rename it Dartmouth College. Opposed to the move, Occom ended his relationship with Wheelock especially after the decision was made not to recruit American Indian students. He then concentrated on working with American Indian people. In 1785 Occom established Brothertown, a community of Christian Indians from various tribes. Occom was an outspoken critic of white treatment of Indians and wrote many treatises on the issue. He addressed Indian issues from a scholarly and philosophical perspective. His most famous piece is *A Sermon, Preached at the Execution of Moses Paul, an Indian.* He is also considered North America's first literary scholar.

See also: Education, 1754; Literature, 1772.

Sources: *Biographical Dictionary of Indians of the Americas,* Vol. 2, p. 482; Champagne, ed., *Native America,* p. 82; Malinowski, ed., *Notable Native Americans,* pp. 293–96; Witalec, ed., *Native North American Literature,* pp. 482–85.

1769 In an effort to civilize the Indians of southern California, the Spanish established the San Diego mission, the first of twenty-one missions where Indians from many tribes and bands would be resettled. The missions were intended to be agrarian settlements for Christianized Indians. They were located a day's journey apart along the El Camino Real, the route between San Diego and San Francisco. The missions included two friars who monitored the mission, and a military garrison. Indians who resided there were required to provide work and services for the mission.

Sources: Dennis, *The American Indian, 1492–1976,* p. 16; Champagne, ed., *Chronology of Native North American History,* p. 96; Hirschfelder and Kreipe de Montaño, *The Native American Almanac,* p. 303.

1799 Handsome Lake (Seneca; ca. 1735–1815), also known as Tenskwatawa, established the Handsome Lake Religion, or Longhouse Religion. He claimed that during a serious illness brought about by alcohol and sickness, four spirits revealed the will of the Creator, or *Gaiwiio,* "Good Word," to him. Their message included three important components: the imminence of world destruction; the definition of sin; and the prescription for salvation. These components comprised the core of a new faith that revitalized the way of life for its Native American followers. In addition, Handsome Lake was instructed by the spirits to reject many white customs, especially the consumption of alcohol. He taught purification through adhering to traditional beliefs and practices, valuing one's family, and sharing the land. His personal reformation played a crucial role in the resurgence of the Seneca and Iroquoian traditional cultures. A popular figure among his people, Handsome Lake was elected to the Seneca Tribal Council in 1801. In this capacity he represented his people in lobbying for land rights. The religion of Handsome Lake still thrives, combining elements of Quakerism with Iroquoian beliefs. Followers worship one God. The code of Handsome Lake was published in 1850.

Sources: *Biographical Dictionary of Indians of the Americas*, Vol. 1, p. 262; Champagne, ed., *Native America*, pp. 464, 513; "Handsome Lake," in *The American Indian.*

1830 White Thunder (Cheyenne) was the Keeper of the Sacred Arrows when the bundle was captured by the Pawnee in a battle, the only such catastrophe in recorded Cheyenne history. A series of disasters plagued the tribe thereafter, even after new arrows were made. In 1835, White Thunder, accompanied by a Cheyenne delegation and carrying only a pipe, traveled to a meeting with the Skidi Pawnee. At the end of the meeting the Cheyenne were able to recover one of the original sacred arrows. White Thunder, who later died in battle with the Pawnee, was identified as the only Keeper of the Sacred Arrows to be killed by enemies of his people. He did not choose a successor.

Sources: Hirschfelder and Molin, *The Encyclopedia of Native American Religions*, p. 320.

1833 Peter Jones (Ojibwa, 1802–1856) was Canada's first fully ordained minister, becoming a Methodist minister in 1833. He and his brother, John, also provided the first translation of the Bible into Ojibwa. In addition, in 1827, Jones became the first Native Methodist missionary to the Ojibwa. Jones was known by the name Kahkewaquonaby (Sacred Feathers) until age sixteen when his Welsh father baptized him, giving him the name Peter. He grew up to become a political leader and devout Christian. He was elected chief of two Ojibwa bands, including his own Credit River Missisauga Band. He vigorously maintained that Indians could achieve what whites could if allowed proper education, housing, and title to their lands. He traveled to several large cities to advocate for Indian rights, petitioning for land. Working to protect economic interests of his people, he strove to develop a solid financial foundation for his band's settlement. An author, Jones wrote many religious and secular works. His autobiography, *Life and Journals of Kah-ke-quo-na-by*, and *History of the Ojibway Indians* are the most well known. His photograph is recognized as the earliest surviving print of an Indian. He died in 1856 in Brantford, Ontario, and in 1857 the Ojibwa people erected a monument in his honor.

Sources: Champagne, ed., *The Native North American Almanac*, p. 1080; Dockstader, *Great North American Indians*, pp. 126–27; Malinowski, ed., *Notable Native Americans*, pp. 215–16.

1833 Jesse Bushyhead (Cherokee; d. 1844) was the first member of his tribe to be ordained a Baptist minister. He became a devout Christian after he attended school in Tennessee, where he studied the Bible and became convinced of the necessity of baptism by immersion. In 1830, Bushyhead was baptized by a Tennessee Baptist preacher. In 1832, he was recommended and accepted for the position of assistant missionary with the Baptist Board of Foreign Missions, where he served for eleven years. After his ordination, he established a church at Amohee and ministered in evangelism and the translation of religious works into Cherokee. He completed a translation the book of Genesis, which was published in the *Cherokee Messenger*. In addition to his activities as a minister, he served as a justice in the Cherokee Supreme Court. In 1838 and 1839, he was chosen by the Cherokee with Evan Jones, his mentor, to lead Cherokee groups to Oklahoma. In Oklahoma, he founded the National Temperance Society among the Cherokee and served as its first president. He died in 1844, after a career of influencing many of his people to accept Christianity.

Sources: Hirschfelder and Molin, *The Encyclopedia of Native American Religions*, p. 33; "Jesse Bushyhead," in *The American Indian*.

1840 Joseph Napeshnee (Mdewakanton Dakota Sioux; d. 1870) was the first full-blooded Dakota male to convert to Christianity when he became a member of the Presbyterian church. He later served as a ruling elder in the church for almost ten years. He was baptized at Lac Qui Parle, Minnesota, when he was about forty years old and became an extremely devout Christian, who refused to return to the religion of his tribe. Napeshnee became the leading farmer among his people and befriended white residents during the 1862 Dakota War. He served as an Indian scout for several years before returning to Lac Qui Parle, where he died in July 1870.

Sources: Hirschfelder and Molin, *The Encyclopedia of Native American Religions*, p. 192; Stoutenburg, *Dictionary of the American Indian*, p. 275; Williamson, Thomas S., "Napeshneedoota: The First Male Dakota Convert to Christianity," *Minnesota Historical Collections*, 1880.

1850 Henry Budd (Cree), also known as Sakacewescam, was the first North American Indian to be ordained a deacon and then a priest by the Church of England. As a young child of eight, Budd was taken from his home at Norway House West in Manitoba by Reverend John West to be educated at Red River in present-day Winnipeg. He was baptized on July 21, 1822, and renamed after a Church of England clergyman. In the same year, his mother and sister joined him at Red River. Budd remained in the mission school until 1828. He then became a schoolmaster and married. He also farmed and evangelized to the Cree, Ojibwa, and mixed-bloods. In 1850, he began serving the church as a deacon. In 1853, he was ordained to the priesthood and appointed minister of the first Anglican mission north of Red River—The Pas' Devon Mission—in 1867. At The Pas he trained teachers and established a church government. Budd was known as an articulate and eloquent preacher and called the "Praying Chief" by his congregation. His diary was published in 1974.

Sources: Hirschfelder and Molin, *The Encyclopedia of Native American Religions*, p. 29.

1854 Paul Mazakutemani (Mdewakanton Sioux; d. 1885), with his brother Cloudman (Mdewakanton Sioux), was one of the founders of Hazelwood Republic and was elected as its first president. One of the first students to attend

Opposite page:
The earliest known photograph of a North American Indian, Rev. Peter Jones (The Waving Plume), ca. 1845, by David Octavius Hill.

164

Lac Qui Parle Mission School, Mazakutemani learned to read and write Dakota along with adopting other skills. In 1851, he was one of the signers of the Treaty of Traverse des Sioux, in which most of Santee Sioux homeland in the Mississippi Valley was ceded. The agreement caused friction among tribal members. Hazelwood Republic was founded to accommodate the Dakota, like Mazakutemani, who had accepted Christianity and the white way of life. Individual ownership of farms was encouraged, and the bylaws of the Republic demanded abandonment of tribal customs and the adoption of Euro-American dress. During the Dakota War of 1862, Mazakutemani worked to maintain peace and negotiate for the release of white prisoners and later served as a scout for the U.S. Army. He wrote a narrative about the war, which was later translated by Stephen Return Riggs for the Minnesota Historical Society. Mazakutemani died on January 6, 1885, still active in religious affairs.

Sources: *Biographical Dictionary of Indians of the Americas*, Vol. 1, p. 175; Hirschfelder and Molin, *The Encyclopedia Native American Religions*, pp. 175–76; Waldman, *Who Was Who in Native American History*, pp. 11, 226.

1855 Allen Wright (Choctaw; 1825–1885) was the first American Indian from Indian Territory to receive a M.A. from the Union Theological Seminary of New York City. He was ordained to the Presbyterian ministry and became an honorary member of the American Board of Commissioners of Foreign Missions. Active in tribal affairs, Wright was elected to the Choctaw House of Representatives and the Senate and eventually became tribal treasurer. He served in the Civil War on the Confederate side, after which he was elected principal chief of the Choctaw for two terms. A negotiator of treaties for the Choctaw and Chickasaw nations, he suggested the name Okla-homma for the proposed lands to be used as Indian Territory in the West. During his political activity, Wright remained active in church affairs and translation work. He translated the Chickasaw constitution and codes of law into English and the Psalms from Hebrew to English. He also produced *Chahta Lekiskon*, a Choctaw dictionary, in 1880. Like many other American Indian clergymen, Wright sought to bridge the gap between Indian and white cultures.

Sources: "Allen Wright," in *The American Indian; Biographical Dictionary of Indians of the Americas*, Vol. 2, p. 843; Hirschfelder and Molin, *The Encyclopedia of Native American Religions*, p. 332; Waldman, *Who Was Who in American Indian History*, p. 393.

1855 James Bouchard (Delaware; 1823–1889) was the first American Indian to be ordained a Roman Catholic priest. His mother was Monotowa, a French captive, who was killed in 1834 by the Lakota. His father was Kistalwa, a Delaware chief. Bouchard first joined the Presbyterian church while attending mission schools in Ohio; however, he converted to Catholicism in 1846. He then began preparing for the Jesuit priesthood. After his ordination he was assigned to work with miners in California. In addition to his spiritual ministry, he gave lectures on his Native heritage.

Sources: "James Bouchard," in *The American Indian;* Hirschfelder and Molin, *The Encyclopedia of Native American Religions*, p. 26; Waldman, *Who Was Who in Native American History*, p. 36.

1865 John B. Renville (Santee Dakota Sioux; d. 1903) was the first Dakota to be ordained a minister by the Presbyterian church. He was the son of Joseph

Renville, who translated the Bible into Dakota. Renville was educated at the mission school established by Thomas S. Williamson before he went to college in Illinois. He served as a teacher at the Upper Sioux Agency in Minnesota Territory. He died in 1903 on the Sisseton Reservation in South Dakota, where the Santee were relocated.

Sources: Hirshfelder and Molin, *The Encyclopedia of Native American Religions,* p. 238.

1872 David Grey Cloud (Santee Dakota Sioux; d. 1890) was the first missionary of the Dakota Native Missionary Society. He received his license to preach in 1872 and was ordained a minister the following year. In 1862, he was imprisoned for his role in the Dakota War. While in prison, he was converted to Christianity by Dr. Thomas S. Williamson. He spent the remainder of his life working among his people as a missionary. He died in 1890 at the Sisseton Agency in South Dakota.

Sources: "David Grey Cloud," in *The American Indian;* Hirschfelder and Molin, *The Encyclopedia of Native American Religions,* p. 108.

1873 Enmegahbowh (Ojibwa/Ottawa) assisted in the founding of a school to train American Indian clergy of the Episcopal church in 1873. Formerly a Methodist minister, he was ordained an Episcopal preacher at Gall Lake in 1858. Enmegahbowh served among the Ojibwa in Minnesota throughout most of his ministry. He was assigned to Gall Lake in Minnesota in 1858 and remained there until the 1862 Santee Sioux-Minnesota conflict known as the Dakota War. In 1869, he moved the Gall Lake mission to the White Earth Reservation, where he established a training school in 1873. He remained active in ministering among American Indian people.

Sources: *Biographical Dictionary of Indians of the Americas,* Vol. 1, pp. 210–11; "Enmegahbowh," in *The American Indian;* Hirschfelder and Molin, *The Encyclopedia of Native American Religions,* p. 78; Waldman, *Who Was Who in Native American History,* p. 106.

1881 David Pendleton Oakerhater (Cheyenne; d. 1931) was the first American Indian ordained an Episcopal deacon. As an officer of the Bowstring Soldier Society of the Cheyenne, he participated in the Red River War. As a result he was taken prisoner and incarcerated at Fort Marion in St. Augustine, Florida. While there he became convinced by Richard H. Pratt of the advantages of Euro-American civilization. Upon release from prison he and Zotom, another former prisoner were trained as missionaries. In 1878, he was baptized and renamed David Pendleton, taking the surname of his sponsor. After he was ordained an Episcopal deacon, on June 7, 1881, he served at the Whirlwind Mission of the Holy Family in Indian Territory, present-day Oklahoma, where he ministered for the next fifty years. He died on August 31, 1931. In 1985, the Episcopal church included his name on its calendar of saints.

Sources: Hirschfelder and Molin, *The Encyclopedia of Native American Religion,* p. 200.

1881 For the first time, Indians were explicitly forbidden to practice their religions by order of President Chester A. Arthur, who authorized the secretary of the Interior to ban the practice of dances, rites, and customs that were "contrary to civilization." The ban resulted in imprisonment and punishment for many Indians on reservations as well as those away at boarding schools. It led to such conflicts as the Massacre at Wounded Knee in 1890. The ban was not completely lifted until 1934;

Opposite page:
American Indian
children view a statue
of Kateri Tekakwitha,
the seventeenth-century
Indian girl who may
be raised to sainthood,
at the Shrine of Our
Lady of Martyrs,
Auriesville, New York.

and it was not until 1978 when President Jimmy Carter signed the Native American Religious Freedom Act that religious freedom was guaranteed for Native Americans.

Sources: Dennis, *The American Indian, 1492–1976*, p. 42.

ca. 1881 John Slocum (Squaxin) founded Tschadam, the Indian Shaker Religion. When he was approaching middle age he had a near-death experience. He claimed that he had gone to the "promised land," where he was instructed to return to earth and carry out a mission to spread the news of salvation to the Indians. The new religion that resulted from his mystical experience combined elements of Native religions and Christian concepts, and its membership was exclusive to Indians. Within a year, Slocum became seriously ill again. While recovering he observed his wife shaking as she approached him, which he perceived as a sign of divine power. Thereafter, a state of "shaking" during meditation became important in the religion. Shaking was thought of as a means of the worshipper to shake off his or her sins.

The Indian Shaker religious movement developed during an assimilationist political trend of working to eradicate Indian religions and cultures in America. Although the religion was officially outlawed, it spread quickly to many other Indian reservations in the Pacific Northwest. After Slocum's death, his wife, Mary Thompson Slocum, continued the religion's message and practice and added new rituals, such as wearing special clothing, setting the tableware in a particular arrangement, and making clockwise movements during worship. She was reportedly disillusioned with the waning of devotion to the religion and with the internal conflicts that afflicted its church. However, the religion is still practiced.

Sources: Hirschfelder and Molin, *The Encyclopedia of Native American Religions*, p. 268; Johansen and Grinde, *The Encyclopedia of Native American Biography*, pp. 358–59; "John Slocum," in *The American Indian*.

KATERI TEKAKWITHA (1656–180)

Kateri Tekakwitha

1884 Kateri Tekakwitha (Mohawk; 1656–1680), also known as the "Lily of the Mohawks" and La Sainte Savvagesse, was the first Native American to be venerated by the Roman Catholic church. Born in 1656 in Osernenon, in what is now the state of New York, she was orphaned at an early age; she was severely scarred by smallpox and had impaired eyesight. She was baptized Easter Sunday in 1656 and took a vow of chastity in 1679. Extremely devout, she led a Spartan life, which probably led to her early death at age twenty-four. Tradition has it that right before her death, her scars disappeared and her face became radiant. In 1884 the Jesuits submitted her name for canonization. In 1932 her name was formally presented to the Vatican; in 1943 she was venerated, and in 1980 Kateri was beatified, or declared blessed. While most historians are convinced of her authenticity, at least one individual, K. I. Koppedrayer, doubts her existence. More than fifty biographies and more than one hundred articles have been published about her.

Sources: Champagne, ed., *Native America*, p. 510; Malinowski, ed., *Notable Native Americans*, p. 430; Mathes, Sherie, "American Indian Women and the Catholic Church," *North Dakota History*, Vol. 47 (1980), pp. 20–25

1890   Edward Cunningham (Métis; 1862–1920) became the first Canadian Métis to be ordained as a Roman Catholic priest. He was born in Edmonton, Alberta, on July 5, 1862, into a family of eleven children. He began his education at St. Albert then attended the University of Ottawa from 1882 to 1885. At Lachine in Quebec, he served his novitiate before continuing his religious training at St. Joseph in Ottaway. He was ordained by Monsignor Vital-Justin on March 19, 1890. His service was mainly with the Piegan people. He died in Edmonton, Alberta, on July 21, 1920.

Sources: Hirschfelder and Molin, *The Encyclopedia of Native American Religions*, p. 61.

1890   Josephine Crowfeather (Hunkpapa Lakota Sioux; 1867–1893), also known as Mother Mary Catherine and Sacred White Buffalo, was the first full-blooded Sioux woman to become a nun. As a newborn, her father carried her into battle. Because she was unharmed, she was thereafter thought to possess special spiritual powers and was named after the most revered deity in Lakota religion, White Buffalo Calf Woman. She began her religious training in 1888 under the guidance of the Reverend Francis M. Craft. Crowfeather took her vows in 1890 after completing her studies at Avoca, Minnesota, where she studied with five other Lakota women. In 1893, Mother Catherine died from tuberculosis.

Sources: Bataille, ed., *Native American Women*, pp. 222–23; Ewans, Mary, "The Native Order: A Brief and Strange History," in *Scattered Steeples, the Fargo Diocese*, edited by Jerome D. Lamb, et al., pp. 10–23; Mathes, Valerie Sherer, "American Indian Women and the Catholic Church, *North Dakota History*, Vol. 47 (1980), pp. 20–25.

ca. 1891   Josephine Crowfeather (Hunkpapa Lakota Sioux; 1867–1893), also known as Mother Mary Catherine and Sacred White Buffalo, and the Reverend Francis M. Craft (Iroquois) founded the first Indian Christian sisterhood, the Congregation of American Sisters. Crowfeather, who was also the first Sioux woman to become a nun, served as the founding prioress-general and assumed the title "Mother." Both Crowfeather and Craft nurtured the vision of seventeenth-century Algonquian convert Kateri Tekakwitha to establish an order devoted exclusively to training Indian women for a religious life so they could work among their own people. Additional goals were to prepare Indians for citizenship, teach them English, and serve as leaders. The women religious were taught the rudiments of medicine and nursing, skills they used often. In 1898, when the Spanish-American War began, Craft offered the services of the sisters to care for the ill and wounded. They were accepted and several were commended for their work. Lack of adequate financial support and the dispersal of many of the sisters after the war left too few members for ecclesiastical support and Craft abandoned the ambition. As late as 1942 three members were still alive. Most of the others abandoned religious life. Other orders like the Sisters of the Blessed Sacrament took Indian nuns and trained them to serve Indian communities.

Sources: Bataille, ed., *Native American Women*, pp. 222–23; Ewans, Mary, "The Native Order: A Brief and Strange History," in *Scattered Steeples, the Fargo Diocese*, edited by Jerome D. Lamb, et al., pp. 10–23; Mathes, Valerie Sherer, "American Indian Women and the Catholic Church," *North Dakota History*, Vol. 47 (1980), pp. 20–25.

1900   Henry H. Lowry (Lumbee) became the first presbyter of the Lumbee Methodist Conference. In 1900, the Lumbee Methodist Conference was organized after Lowry had led a group away from the established Methodist church. The purpose of the group was to promote Lumbee self-determination. The group was expelled and forbidden to baptize new members or to conduct marriage ceremonies. The group named itself the Holiness Methodist Church of the Lumbee River Annual Conference, also known as the Lumbee Methodist Conference. The organization grew, and by 1974 it had planted seven churches. Lowry's work in the church was continued by some of his children.

Sources: Hirschfelder and Molin, *The Encyclopedia of Native American Religions,* p. 164.

1903   Cornelius Hill (Oneida) was the first Oneida to become an ordained Episcopal priest. He began his religious education at Nashotah House seminary in Wisconsin when he was twelve years old. He was ordained a deacon on June 27, 1885, and in 1903 he was ordained to the priesthood. During his life he served in public office as well, leading opposition to the policies of allotment of tribal lands. His struggle to prevent the loss of Wisconsin Oneida land was futile, however. In the church Hill served as an interpreter and organist. He died in 1907, well respected and esteemed by the Oneidas he served.

Sources: Hirschfelder and Molin, *The Encylopedia of Native American Religions,* p. 120.

1903   Albert Negahnquet (Potawatomi) was the first full-blooded American Indian to be ordained a Roman Catholic priest. The Benedictine monks at a Sacred Heart mission recognized his potential and encouraged his entrance into the priesthood. He was ordained a priest by the College of the Propaganda Fide in Rome. After returning to the United States he worked among American Indian people, first in Oklahoma and then in Minnesota. Although he was a devout Catholic and served the church well, he was laicized in 1941. No explanation was given for the demotion, but it was suggested that cultural conflict and racism within the church may have affected Negahnquet's priesthood.

Sources: *Biographical Dictionary of Indians of the Americas,* Vol. 2, p. 470; Hirschfelder and Molin, *The Encyclopedia of Native American Religions,* p. 197; "Negahnquet," in *The American Indian.*

1910   Plains Indians were forbidden to perform the Sun Dance ceremony. The Bureau of Indian Affairs (BIA) deemed the body piercing during the dance too extreme.

Sources: Dennis, *The American Indian, 1492–1976,* p. 48.

1912   Edward Ahenakew (Plains Cree; 1885–1961) became the first American Indian to be ordained an Anglican minister. He was later well known for his writings; *Voices of the Plains Cree* was published posthumously in 1974.

Sources: Champagne, ed., *Chronology of Native North American History,* p. 997.

1914   Jonathon Koshiway (Sac/Fox; d. 1971) founded the First Born Church of Christ, the second peyote church and the first one to be legally incorporated. He worked for more than forty years promoting the peyote religion. Born on the Sac and Fox Reservation in Kansas, Koshiway attended Chilocco Indian School and the Haskell Institute. He was said to be very interested in religion and studied the Bible and Christianity, becoming acquainted with the Presbyterian church, and the beliefs of Jehovah's Witnesses and the Reorganized Church of Jesus Christ of

Latter-Day Saints (Mormans). After becoming familiar with the religious use of pey-ote in 1903 and learning the Otoe peyote ceremony, Koshiway began proselytizing about the spiritual use of peyote among the Winnebago, Omaha, Menominee, and Navajo through the forum of the Native American Church. Among followers he was known as the "Grand Old Man of Peyote." He died in 1971.

Sources: Hirschfelder and Molin, *The Encyclopedia of Native American Religions,* p. 151.

1918 The Native American Church (NAC), the first American Indian church, was organized and incorporated on October 10, 1918, in Reno, Oklahoma. Mack Hoag (Cheyenne) and other members of the emerging Peyotist religion from the Otoe, Ponca, Comanche, Kiowa and Apache tribes initiated the formal establish-ment of what became known as the Native American Church. There was much opposition to NAC from Christian religious organizations as well as from well educated Indians. The move to organize was a means to gain legal recognition and protection. Yet, despite its incorporation, it took several key court decisions to finally legitimize the religion. The church has since spread to many states and to Indian tribes outside of the Plains people. Today it remains controversial but mostly to non-Indians, especially legislators.

Sources: Davis, ed., *Native America in the Twentieth Century,* pp. 446–49; Dennis, *The American Indian, 1492–1976,* p. 50; Hirschfelder and Molin, *The Encyclopedia of Native American Religions,* pp. 193–94.

1921 Nelson Gorman and Alice Peshlakai (Navajo) founded the first Presbyterian mission at Chinle, Arizona. Peshlakai translated English hymns into Navajo, while Gorman worked as a trader and cattleman. Gorman and Peshlakai are the parents of Carl Nelson Gorman and the grandparents of R. C. Gorman, both highly acclaimed artists.

Sources: Champagne, ed., *The Native North American Almanac,* pp. 1064–65; Hirschfelder and Molin, *The Encyclopedia of Native American Religions,* p. 151; Malinowski, ed., *Notable Native Americans,* p. 168.

1938 The first successful efforts to repatriate Native American sacred objects to their rightful caretakers occurred when the sacred Midipadi (or Waterbuster Clan) Bundle was returned to the Hidatsa people. In 1907, it was sold to anthropologist Gilbert L. Wilson, who later gave it to George Heye, founder of the Museum of the American Indian in New York City. The sale was agreed to by Wolf Chief, the son of Small Ankle, the last Keeper of the Bundle. Traditionally, new keepers belonged to the Midipadi clan, designated by the former keeper, requiring a token payment. The bundle was believed to provide guidance in the founding of new villages. At the time of Small Ankle's death in 1888, no Midipadi member had "bought" the bundle. Also, during this period missionaries were encouraging the destruction of Native sacred bundles and objects, and the government had out-lawed the practice of American Indian religions. Further, Wolf Chief was not a member of the Midipadi, having inherited his mother's clan, and had converted to Christianity. Uncomfortable with the idea of destroying or abandoning the bundle, he agreed to sell it instead. Since the bundle was the property of the Midipadi clan and not the personal property of an individual, the sale created furious opposition among clan members. After Wolf Chief died in 1934, the

Midipadi clan petitioned for the bundle's return. After four years the Museum of the American Indian reluctantly returned the sacred bundle to the clan and to the Hidatsa in 1938.

Sources: Gilman and Schneider, *The Way to Independence,* pp. 296–301; 314–15; Hirschfelder and Molin, *The Encyclopedia of Native American Religions,* pp. 268, 315.

ca. 1941 James C. Ottipoby (Comanche) was the first member American Indian to be commissioned in the Army Chaplain Corps. He served during World War II. He was also the first of his tribe to receive a college degree. He graduated from Hope College, in Holland, Michigan, with a B.A.

Sources: Dennis, *The American Indian, 1492–1976, p. 142.*

1943 Phillip B. Gordon (Ojibwa) was the first ordained American Indian to offer the invocation for a session of the U.S. House of Representatives. In addition, for many years he was the only American Indian Catholic priest in the country. He began his education at St. Mary's Mission School on the Bad River Reservation in Wisconsin. Following his seminary education, he was ordained in 1913. He then served as a part-time chaplain at Carlisle Indian School, after which he was given a two-year assignment working with the Bureau of Catholic Indian Missions, visiting Indian schools and other agencies in the Midwest. He also served as chaplain at Haskell Institute, where he began advocating for better living conditions for American Indian students. His activism put him at odds with his superiors and he was transferred and unable to work with Indian communities again until 1918. He again became politically active. In 1923, he was appointed to the Committee of One Hundred, whose members were appointed by the secretary of the Interior to study federal Indian policy. In that capacity he worked toward citizenship for all Indians. Among the honors he received are an honorary degree from the College of St. Thomas in St. Paul, Minnesota, in 1933, and the Indian Council Fire Indian Achievement Award in 1942. He was invited to offer the opening prayer at the convening of the U.S. House of Representatives on July 11, 1943. He died in 1948.

Sources: Hirschfelder and Molin, *The Encyclopedia of Native American Religions,* pp. 104–105.

ca. 1947 Roe B. Lewis (Pima/Tohono O'odham) was the first American Indian to be ordained a minister in the United Presbyterian church and to have a complete college and seminary education. He was also the first Indian minister of his church to have a doctorate of divinity degree. In 1956 he became a staff member of the Board of National Indian Missions of the United Presbyterian Church. He is an advocate of providing opportunities for Indian youth. In 1966 he was awarded the Indian Council Fire Achievement Award, and given an honorary membership. He is a member of the Southwestern Regional Conference and was the first Indian to be elected president. He is a member of several religious organizations, including the Cook Christian Training School in Tempe, Arizona.

Sources: Gridley, ed., *Indians of Today,* pp. 390–91; Lewis, Robert (family member), Personal communication to AnCita Benally, March 1997; Robbins, Eunice (registrar, Cook College and Theological School, Tempe, Arizona), Personal communication to AnCita Benally, March 1997.

1952 Gloria Ann Davis (Navajo/Choctaw) was the first American Indian to enter the Order of the Blessed Sacrament in the Roman Catholic church. In her ministry she has served mostly elementary-age, minority children in Arizona, Louisiana, and Pennsylvania. On the Navajo Reservation she broadcast a regular program in Navajo on the station KGAK and worked at St. Michael School for Girls.

Sources: Hirschfelder and Molin, *The Encyclopedia of Native American Religions,* p. 64; Gridley, ed., *The Indian Today,* pp. 64–65.

1954   Vine Deloria Sr. (Yankton Dakota Sioux; 1901–1990) was the first Indian ever appointed to a national executive post in the Episcopal church. He was appointed to the Episcopal National Council in New York City as Indian secretary for the church and was put in charge of all Indian missions. He found the urban assignment frustrating, however, as it was nearly impossible for him to assist the Indian people and returned to ministering among them. Deloria ministered through the Episcopal church for thirty-seven years relishing the assignments given him to work with them. His first twenty years of ministry was among the Indian people of South Dakota, where he often served as the spokesperson for Indian Episcopalians to non-Indians. Following his brief service for the national office, he returned to serving Indian people, first in Iowa and then in South Dakota again when he was appointed archdeacon of the Niobrara Deanery. He retired in 1968, although he continued to serve as priest for St. Paul's Episcopal mission in Vermillion. He died in 1990, having earned the respect of both Indians and whites.

Sources: *Biographical Dictionary of Indians of the Americas,* Vol. 1, p. 185; Champagne, ed., *The Native North American Almanac,* p. 1044; Malinowski, ed., *Notable Native Americans,* pp. 121–22; Gridley, ed., *Indians of Today,* pp. 345–46; Paulson and Moses, *Who's Who among the Sioux,* p. 59.

1956   Frank Takes Gun (Crow) was elected as the first president of the newly named and organized Native American Church (NAC) of North America. It had been previously known as the Native American Church. A devout follower of NAC of North America, Takes Gun devoted his time to permanently guaranteeing freedom of religion to NAC members. He was convinced that to gain legitimacy for the use of peyote it was essential that NAC groups incorporate under the various state laws. He also worked with tribal governments to legitimize the church on their respective reservations. He actively participated in convincing the Navajo Tribal Council to legalize peyotism in 1967. When Navajo NAC members were arrested for possession of peyote, he sought the assistance of the American Civil Liberties Union (ACLU). Consequently, several of the early cases regarding peyotism's legitimacy became landmark court decisions that guaranteed religious freedom for NAC members. While Takes Gun devoted much of his attention to legalizing peyotism on the Navajo Reservation, the eastern and northern NAC membership took exception to his preoccupation with the Navajo. Further in 1958 he passed a resolution to hold elections every six years rather than every two. Opposition was strong and resulted in a split in the national organization. In 1972, James Atcitty was elected president of Takes Gun's organization and he reunited the two factions.

Sources: Aberle, David F., "Peyote Religion Among the Navajo," in *Handbook of North American Indians,* Vol. 10: *History of Indian-Whie Relations,* edited by Alfonso Ortiz, pp. 566–68; Hirschfelder and Molin, *The Encyclopedia of Native American Religions,* pp. 291–92.

1957 Peter Kelly (Haida; 1885–1966) was a Haida chief and a Protestant minister. Kelly received a doctor of divinity, the first Canadian Native American west of the Rockies to earn this distinction. In 1957 he became the first Native president of a provincial conference when he was elected president of the United Church in British Columbia.

Sources: *Biographical Dictionary of Indians of the Americas*, Vol. 1, p. 331.

1967 The Navajo Tribal Council granted members of the Native American Church (NAC) the right of religious freedom. It was the first time that a non-Navajo religion was granted such a right when the Council passed CO-63-67 on the premise of honoring basic Navajo human rights, which included freedom of religion. After twenty-seven years of arrests, confiscation of religious paraphernalia and court hearings Navajo Peyotists could practice their religion free from the fear of arrest. Two days later on October 11, 1967, resolution CO-65-67 was passed, allowing the sale, use, and possession of Peyote in the Navajo country by NAC members, but prohibited non-members from doing the same. The latter resolution was an effort to protect as well as regulate the use and possession of peyote.

Sources: Aberle, David F., "Peyote Religion Among the Navajo," in *Handbook of North American Indians*, Vol. 10: *History of Indian-White Relations*, edited by Alfonso Ortiz, pp. 558–69; Davis, ed., *Native America in the Twentieth Century*, pp. 282–83; Hirschfelder and Molin, *The Encyclopedia of Native American Religions*, p. 291.

1972 Harold Stephen Jones (Santee Dakota Sioux; 1909–) became the first American Indian to be consecrated as suffragan bishop of the Episcopal Diocese of South Dakota. With financial support from the Episcopal church, he completed his seminary training at Seabury Seminary in Evanston, Illinois. He began work on the Pine Ridge Reservation in South Dakota working primarily with the Sioux. He later became priest of the parish at Wahpeton where he served as a youth counselor to an Indian and non-Indian congregation. In 1968, he was assigned to the Good Shepherd Episcopal Mission at Fort Defiance on the Navajo Reservation. He was elected bishop soon thereafter. In his ministry Jones worked to help Indian and non-Indian groups understand each other.

Sources: *Biographical Dictionary of Indians of the Americas*, Vol. 1, p. 320; Dennis, *The American Indian, 1492–1976*, p. 95; Hardy, Margaret (lay pastor, Good Shepherd Episcopal Mission, Fort Defiance, Arizona), Personal communication to AnCita Benally, March 1997.

1975 Frank Fools Crow (Oglala Lakota Sioux) was the first Native American leader of a Native religion to offer the invocation at the convening of the U.S. Senate. Fools Crow said the prayer in Lakota and it was translated into English. He is from Kyle, South Dakota, and is a Lakota holy man and ceremonial leader. Fools Crow began studying to be a holy man when he was thirteen years old under the direction of his uncle, Stirrup, who took him on his first vision quest in 1905. In 1913, he conducted his first Kettle Dance, a ritual taught him by his grandparents. In 1914, Stirrup asked permission from Fools Crow's father to train him as a holy man who would conduct Yuwipi ceremonies to cure illnesses. The responsibilities included refraining from taking sides in political issues, and abstinence from alcohol, womanizing, and fighting. In 1917 he joined the Catholic church but continued to practice his tribal religion. In 1973 during the Wounded Knee takeover, he negotiated with federal agents and American Indian Movement

(AIM) members for a peaceful end. His efforts paid off and the confrontation came to a close. In 1975, while leading a delegation to Washington, D.C., to discuss the Fort Laramie treaty of 1868, he was invited to pray at the Capitol. In 1979, his biography written by Thomas E. Mails, *Fools Crow,* was published fulfilling the instructions of his 1965 vision quest that a person would come to whom he should disclose certain information.

Sources: "Frank Fools Crow," in *The American Indian;* Hirschfelder and Molin, *The Encyclopedia of Native American Religions,* pp. 91–92; Hirschfelder and Kreipe de Montaño, *The Native American Almanac,* p. 310.

1976 George P. Lee (Navajo) was the first Native American to be appointed to the highest offices of the Church of Jesus Christ of Latter-Day Saints (LDS or Mormons). He was appointed as a full-time member of the First Quorum of the Seventy, a prestigious assembly that works closely with the president of the church, the Quorum of Twelve Apostles, and other high-ranking leaders in administering the affairs of the church. Until his removal and excommunication in 1989, he was the highest ranking Native American in the church. His removal was the first imposed on a high ranking official in over forty-six years.

Lee was an early enrollee of the LDS Indian Student Placement Program, an educational program that put Indian children in LDS homes during the school year. A devout Mormon, he served a two-year mission and then attended Brigham Young University where he earned a bachelor's degree and a doctorate in educational administration; he earned his M.A. from Utah State University. He received several honors, including a fellowship from the U.S. Office of Education, 1970–1971, a Ford Foundation fellowship award, and the Spencer W. Kimball Lamanite Leadership Award. In 1987 he published his autobiography, *Silent Courage.* His 1989 excommunication came about because of apostasy and conduct unbecoming a member of the church, according to the church's press release. Lee countered that severance from the church came because of doctrinal differences and disagreement over the role of American Indians in the religion.

Sources: Davis, ed., *Native Americans in the Twentieth Century,* p. 115; "Excommunicated Navajo Mormon Left Searching for Answers to His Future," *Navajo Times,* Vol. 27, No. 37 (September 14, 1989), p. 1; "George P. Lee," in *The American Indian;* Hirschfelder and Molin, *The Encyclopedia of Native American Religions,* p. 175.

1986 Donald E. Pelotte (Abenaki) was the first Native American to be ordained bishop in the Roman Catholic church, on May 6, 1986, at Red Rock State Park in Gallup, New Mexico. He began his religious training at age fourteen when he entered the seminary. He received a Ph.D. in theology from Fordham University. In 1986 he became coadjutor of the Gallup diocese. His elevation to bishop made him the highest ranking American Indian in the Catholic church. Apache and Zuñi dances and gifts of pottery and sacred corn were included along with a Mass and tribal chants and prayers as part of the ordination celebration. He published *John Courtney Murray, Theologian in Conflict,* which was awarded *America* magazine's October Catholic Book Club Selection for 1986. It is used widely in seminary classes to study the conflicts between secular and religious issues.

Opposite page:
Charles J. Chaput, the
first American Indian
named archbishop.

Sources: Hirschfelder and Molin, *The Encyclopedia of Native American Religions,* p. 210; "Pelotte Becomes Third Bishop of Local Diocese," *Navajo Times,* Vol. 30, No. 13 (March 29, 1990), p. 2.

1990   Steven Tsosie Plummer (Navajo) was ordained as the first Navajo bishop of the Episcopal church on March 10, 1990. The ordination was conducted by the Most Reverend Edmond Lee Browning, presiding bishop of the national church. Plummer was the fifth Indian to be consecrated in the church and is one of the top ranking Indian religious leaders in the world. Once a school dropout, he began his religious training at Cook Christian Training School in Tempe, Arizona. He eventually attained a college degree. Plummer was also the first Navajo to be ordained to the priesthood in the Episcopal church in June of 1976. He was ordained to the diocenate in 1975.

Sources: "Indian Named Bishop," *Navajo Times,* Volume 26, No. 27 (July 7, 1988), p. 8; "Plummer Ordained as First Navajo Bishop," *Navajo Times,* Vol. 30, No. 11 (March 15, 1990), p.1; Robbins, Eunice (registrar, Cook College and Theological School, Tempe, Arizona), Personal communication to AnCita Benally, March 1997.

1997   Charles J. Chaput (Prairie Band Potawatomi) was the first American Indian named archbishop when he assumed leadership of the Denver archdiocese of the Catholic church. He was named bishop by Pope John Paul II, as Roman Catholic Bishop of Rapid City, South Dakota in 1988. He previously held the position of provincial minister of the Capuchin Province of Mid-America in Denver, Colorado.

Sources: "Indian Named Bishop," *Navajo Times,* Vol. 26, No. 27 (July 7, 1988), p 8; Lopez, Aaron J., "Native American Ready for Duty as Archbishop," *Lawrence Journal-World,* April 6, 1997, p. 128.

INDIAN RIGHTS
AND ACTIVISM:
500 YEARS OF STRUGGLE

1500s Prophet, statesman, and lawgiver, Deganawida (Huron), along with Hiawatha (Mohawk or Onondaga), prophet and orator, endeavoring to unite the entire human race, worked to establish one confederation based on the principles of equity and righteousness two centuries before the great "Age of Enlightenment." It is unclear whether the underlying ideas of the Iroquois League, or Iroquois Confederacy, originated with Deganawida or Hiawatha; one account teaches that Deganiwida was the protege of Hiawatha, and another describes Hiawatha as merely a mouthpiece for Deganwida, who was a stutterer. Whichever account is accurate, they both describe the league's purpose as a means to ending warfare, enmity, and strife among Iroquois peoples and replacing disaccord with an alliance based on equity and righteousness. The Great Law, a code of the confederacy, further provided clear instructions on the political structure of the league, assigning specific roles and council seats to each member and designating how many chiefs each member tribe would have. The ideas underlying the foundation for the Iroquois League were summed up with three sets of double principles: 1) equity and justice and righteousness in conduct, thought, and speech; 2) physical strength, civil authority, and inner spiritual power; 3) sanity of mind and physical health and peace among individuals and groups. Initially five Iroquois tribes joined: the Onondaga, Mohawk, Seneca, Oneida, and Cayuga. At a later date the Tuscarora became the sixth member. Some historians claim that the constitution on which the United States was founded was influenced by the league. Although there is much debate over the validity of such a claim, there are remarkable similarities between the U.S. constitution and the organization and ideas of the league. Unique to the league, however, was the role of women in choosing chiefs who would preside at the council; clan mothers chose chiefs, and chiefs answered to them. By 1677 the Iroquois League had developed into the most powerful North American Indian alliance, lasting into the twentieth century.

Sources: *Biographical Dictionary of Indians of the Americas,* Vol. 1, p. 182; Champagne, ed., *Native America,* p. 511; Leitch, *Chronology of the American Indian,* p. 82; Malinowski, ed., *Notable Native Americans,* pp. 113–14.

1501 Slavery began for Native people of Labrador and Newfoundland when the Portuguese, led by Gasper Cortes-Real, captured two shiploads of individuals to sell into slavery.

Sources: Champagne, ed., *Chronology of Native North American History,* p. 63; Francis, *Native Time,* p. 28.

1524 The kidnapping of a small child from an old woman was reported in a letter sent to King Francis I of France by Verrazano, an Italian explorer. It was the first reported abduction of Native Americans from what would become the United States by representatives of the French government. Verrazano's men attempted at the same time to abduct a young woman, but failed when she screamed and successfully fought against them.

Sources: Dennis, *The American Indian, 1492–1976*, p. 1; Wood, Peter H., "Indian Servitude in the Southeast," in *Handbook of North American Indians*, Vol. 10; *History of Indian-White Relations*, edited by Alfonso Ortiz, p. 407.

ca. 1586 Ensenore (Secotan) greeted the first English settlers on Roanoke Island. As chief of a tribe near Albemarle Sound (in present-day North Carolina), he offered his friendship and led his people in planting extra corn for the starving newcomers.

Sources: *Biographical Dictionary of Indians of the Americas*, Vol. 1, p. 211; Hodge, *Handbook of American Indians North of Mexico,*, pp. 426–27; Thatcher, *Indian Biography*, pp. 110–11.

1621 Massasoit (Wampanoag; ca. 1600–1661), also known as Woosamequin and sachem of one of the most powerful Indian confederacies located in what is now known as the southeast New England region, met with the settlers for the first time in 1621. Massasoit worked to maintain good relations with the pilgrims as a means of giving his people an advantage against the Narragansett tribe across the bay. However, this friendship ultimately resulted in the loss of Wampanoag land through the first treaty between the Wampanoag and the pilgrims. The agreement came prior to a peace agreement that would last for more than fifty years and ended with "King Philip's War." The peace treaty was made April 1, 1621 at Strawberry Hill, otherwise known as Plymouth, Massachusetts

Sources: *The American Indian; Biographical Dictionary of Indians of the Americas*, Vol. 1, p. 400; Champagne, ed., *Native America*, p. 81; Dennis, *The American Indian, 1492–1976*, p. 5; Leitch, *Chronology of the American Indian*, p. 93.

ca. 1623 Chickataubut (Massachusetts, d. 1633) was probably the first Native American to fight to protect grave sites. He was a sachem who went to war against a Weymouth colony (Massachusetts) because of the colonists' desecration of Indian graves, including that of his mother.

Sources: *Biographical Dictionary of Indians of the Americas*, Vol. 1, p. 125; Waldman, *Who Was Who in Native American History*, p. 65.

1627 Captured Carib Indians were brought to Virginia as slaves for the first time. They escaped to the Powhatan Confederacy.

Sources: Champagne, ed., *Chronology of Native North American History*, p. 56.

1633 The first land allotment policy was established by the General Court of Massachusetts Colony, a precedent that would be long lasting and far-reaching. The General Court further centralized Indian policy by giving the central government authority to handle Indian affairs rather than allowing local jurisdiction.

Sources: Champagne, ed., *Chronology of Native North American History*, p. 56; Dennis, *The American Indian, 1492–1976*, p. 6.

1637 With the defeat of the Pequot Confederacy, the most dominant Indian confederacy, the balance of power shifted significantly from American Indian nations to the English. The Pequot, who occupied a strategic area abundant with wampum and fur-bearing animals, were blamed for killing Englishmen who were hunting for Indian slaves. Determined to avenge their deaths, the English enlisted the aid of several Indian tribes, including the Narraganset, another powerful Indian confederacy and longtime adversaries of the Pequot. The English set fire to the palisaded Pequot fort at Mystic River and killed more than seven hundred men, women, and children. Severely crippled, the Pequot Nation was forced to agree to terms of peace that were harsh and aimed at disempowering them. The conflict became known as the Pequot War.

Sources: Champagne, ed., *Chronology of Native North American History,* p. 57; Champagne, ed., *The Native North American Almanac,* p. 23; Leitch, *Chronology of the American Indian,* p. 94.

1638 The Quinnipiac Nation concluded the first agreement that provided for reserved land exclusively for American Indians. A "reservation" was set aside for the Quinnipiac Nation. The terms of the agreement designated that the Quinnipiac could retain only twelve hundred acres of their original land base. Further, they subjected themselves to English rule and promised to convert to Christianity. The terms of the settlement with the Puritans of Connecticut further decreed that they could not sell or leave their reservation or allow foreign Indians to enter. They were forbidden to buy guns, powder, or whiskey. They did promise to be under the protection of the colony.

Sources: Champagne, ed., *Chronology of Native North American History,* p. 23; Champagne, ed., *The Native North American Almanac,* p. 59; Hirschfelder and Kreipe de Montaño, *The Native American Almanac,* p. 301.

1641 The Dutch of New Amsterdam changed their original policy of paying for the heads of Native Americans and instead began a policy of offering bounty rewards for scalps.

Sources: Dennis, *The American Indian, 1492–1976,* p. 7.

1673 The first transaction between American Indian people and the Pennsylvania colony was recorded on February 8, 1673. A tract of land (seven hundred acres) was exchanged for drink, coats, lard, powder, two knives, and some paint.

Sources: Dennis, *The American Indian, 1492–1976,* p. 9.

1681 Nanagoucy (Mahican) initiated one of the first efforts of pan-Indian unity when he began a discussion of an intertribal confederacy as he traveled throughout the Ohio country. French allies supported the idea. By 1683 there were three hundred lodges housed by Illinois, Miami, and Shawnee close to French trading centers. Soon there were almost four thousand Illinois, Miami, Wea, Kilaica, Shawnee, Pepikokia, Piankeshaw, and Ouabona gathered as well. The French, for their part, built a fort nearby.

Sources: Champagne, ed., *Chronology of Native North American History,* p. 74.

1686 The first of many "walking purchases" was concluded between the Delaware and William Penn on behalf of Pennsylvania colonists. A "walking purchase" referred to the amount of land a man could walk in a given number of days. The distance covered was the amount of land granted. William Penn was granted the forty miles of land he was able to walk in a day and a half. In 1737, when the treaty was renegotiated, professional walkers were hired who could cover sixty-seven miles in a day and a half.

Sources: Leitch, *Chronology of the American Indian,* p. 112.

1751 The Pima Nation rebelled against the Spanish for their continued injustices against them. As a result the Spanish built a presidio at Tubac and fortified it with a garrison of fifty men.

Sources: Dennis, *The American Indian, 1492–1976,* p. 13.

1758 A group of Christian Indians from different tribes agreed to reside on the first state reservation, established on August 29, 1758, by New Jersey legislators. Brothertown, which comprised sixteen hundred acres, was set aside for the settlement and exclusive use of Indians. About two hundred Native persons were relocated there, most of them Lenape and Unami. Brothertown remained an Indian community until it was sold in 1801. Some remnants of the community relocated to the Lake Oneida Reservation in Wisconsin.

Sources: Dennis, *The American Indian, 1492–1976,* p. 14; Hirschfelder and Kreipe de Montaño, *The Native American Almanac,* p. 303; Kane, *Famous First Facts,* p. 311; Leitch, *Chronology of the American Indian,* p. 116.

1768 The first free and independent community on the North American Continent was established through the Treaty of Fort Stanwix. In this treaty, the Six Nations ceded land between the Ohio and Tennessee rivers to the English. The founding of Watauga Commonwealth and the Independent Civil Government was the earliest recorded civil grant.

Sources: Dennis, *The American Indian, 1492–1976,* p. 14; Hirschfelder and Kreipe de Montaño, *The Native American Almanac,* p. 303; Leitch, *Chronology of the American Indian,* p. 116.

1775 For the first time the Continental Congress decreed its jurisdiction over American Indian nations by setting up three departments of Indian Affairs—North, South, and Midcentral. Each one was organized to be headed by a commissioner.

Sources: Champagne, ed., *Chronology of Native North American History,* p. 99; Dennis, *The American Indian, 1492–1976,* p. 16; Leitch, *Chronology of the American Indian,* p. 122.

1775 For the first time, the Continental Congress officially appropriated $500 for the education of American Indian youth at Dartmouth College in New Hampshire. Five years later the amount was increased to $5,000.

Sources: Dennis, *The American Indian, 1492–1976,* p. 16.

1775 The Six Nations opened peace negotiations for the first time with the newly appointed commissioners of the new republic of the United States. The agreement included the employment of two blacksmiths to be located among the Indians, and the opening of trade.

Sources: Dennis, *The American Indian, 1492–1976,* p. 16.

1778 The Delaware negotiated the first treaty between the United States and an Indian nation on September 17, 1778. It was the first of 370 treaties that would be concluded between the United States and indigenous nations of North America. In this first treaty, the Delaware were offered the prospect of statehood, but it would never be carried through. On the eve of the American Revolution, the Delaware proposed that they become the fourteenth colony to be added to the original thirteen colonies. Until the post-Civil War era, U.S. Indian policy would be based on treaty agreements. In 1871 treaty making with Indian tribes was officially abolished when a rider to an appropriations bill was passed. Since 1871, dealings between American Indian tribes and the federal government have been conducted through congressional acts, executive orders, and executive agreements.

Sources: Champagne, ed., *Chronology of Native North American History,* p. 103; Dennis, *The American Indian, 1492–1976,* p. 17; Leitch, *Chronology of the American Indian,* p. 123.

1786 The first federal Indian reservation was established on August 7, 1784.

Sources: Dennis, *The American Indian, 1492–1976,* p. 19.

1794 The Oneida, Tuscarora, and Stockbridge tribes concluded the first Indian treaty with the new republic of the United States, which included a provision for education. The treaty promised to provide a teacher to instruct young Indian men in the professions of miller and sawer. In later treaties, provisions were made specifically for education, or agreements were made to provide some kind of "civilizing" program. Education was viewed as the key to assimilating Indians into European American society. Thus, monetary appropriations toward Indian education became crucial to U.S. expansion goals. Today the Bureau of Indian Affairs (BIA) provides federal educational services to American Indians.

Sources: Champagne, ed., *Chronology of Native North American History,* p. 114; Dennis, *The American Indian, 1492–1976,* p. 21.

1814 The end of the War of 1812 permanently precluded any future possibilities of alliance between Indian nations and any European power. Hereafter, Indian nations within the borders of the United States dealt only with the government of the United States. Indian tribes lost their political, economic, and military leverage.

Sources: Champagne, ed., *Chronology of Native North American History,* p. 129; Dennis, *The American Indian, 1492–1976,* p. 23.

1827 The Cherokee Nation adopted its first modern constitution, organizing a constitutional tribal government and establishing itself as an independent and sovereign entity. Modeled after the U.S. constitution, the Cherokee constitution was in development for ten years before its formal adoption. Progressive and farsighted as it was, though, the state of Georgia took action to nullify it, claiming jurisdiction over all people within the state border and refusing to acknowledge Indian tribes as separate, sovereign nations. As gold was discovered, Georgia declared all Cherokee lands to be under its control. State legislative actions nullified all ordinances put into effect by the Cherokee government, even declaring that the Cherokee could not testify against whites. It was the first step in Georgia's efforts to extinguish Cherokee title to lands in the state. As a working government document, the Cherokee constitution would soon become ineffective.

Sources: Champagne, ed., *Chronology of Native North American History,* p. 143; Dennis, *The American Indian, 1492–1976,* p. 26; Leitch, *Chronology of the American Indian,* p. 143.

1830 For the first time the U.S. government legally adopted a policy of removing American Indian tribes from their lands when Congress passed the Indian Removal Act. Much of the efforts to extinguish indigenous title to lands was in response to Cherokee efforts to legally protect their lands. The act forbade the appropriation of land without the consent of the people; however, state and federal officials often negotiated agreements with non-legitimate representatives of Indian governments. The Cherokee pro-removal faction led by John Ridge signed agreements with the state of Georgia and ceded all Cherokee lands, but his faction did not legitimately represent the Cherokee Nation. Consequently, the Cherokee Nation condemned the actions of Ridge and the pro-removal faction and ordered their execution for treasonous acts. Most members of the faction were killed. President Andrew Jackson, who supported and advocated Indian removal, steadfastly argued that the demise of savage nations and the expansion of a progressive white civilization were inevitable.

Sources: Leitch, *Chronology of the American Indian,* p. 144; Nies, *Native American History,* p. 244.

1832 The U.S. Supreme Court decision in the *Worcester v. Georgia* case repudiated the state's claim of jurisdiction over the Cherokee. It was the first time that a Supreme Court ruling recognized the sovereignty of American Indian nations. Supreme Court Chief Justice John Marshall wrote that refusal to acknowledge the Cherokee Nation as a sovereign nation defied the federal government's authority to regulate relations with the Cherokee. He acknowledged that the actions of Georgia were hostile to treaty agreements which established territorial boundaries and guaranteed respect to Cherokee land claims. The Cherokee were, nevertheless, divested of their lands, and in 1834 their removal, known as the "Trail of Tears," began under the direction of General Winfield Scott. More than four thousand people died from the hardships they endured during removal.

Sources: Leitch, *Chronology of the American Indian,* p. 147.

1835 *The Cherokee Phoenix,* the first American Indian newspaper in North America (established in 1828), was also the first to be denied freedom of the press when it incited the displeasure of the Georgia governor in 1835, who enlisted the aid of the state militia to close it down. This was one step of several that Georgia used to finalize the removal of the Cherokee and the other Civilized Tribes from their homelands in Georgia. In the spring of 1838 federal troops were sent to remove the Cherokee to Indian Territory.

Sources: Dennis, *The American Indian, 1492–1976,* p. 27; Hirschfelder and Kreipe de Montaño, *The Native American Almanac,* p. 304; Littlefield and Parins, eds., *American Indian and Alaska Native Newspapers and Periodicals, 1826–1924,* pp. 84–92.

1854 The first policy of American Indian preference in hiring was put into practice as the Indian Bureau began favoring applicants of one-quarter or more Indian blood over non-Indian applicants with equal qualifications for employment within the Indian Office. This policy was implemented through the twentieth century. Today more than half the employees of the Bureau of Indian Affairs (BIA) are of American Indian or Alaska Native ancestry.

Sources: Dennis, *The American Indian, 1492–1976*, p. 32.

1861 The Confederate government established its first Bureau of Indian Affairs (BIA). General Albert Pike of Arkansas was appointed to head the office. During the Civil War many American Indians took a prominent role in the conflict. Stand Watie (Cherokee), the highest ranking American Indian in the Confederate Army, would be the last general to surrender to the Union. For Indians, fighting for the South was more than an expression of American political convictions; they fought for their homeland.

Sources: Dennis, *The American Indian, 1492–1976*, p. 33.

1863 The Cherokee Nation was the first prominent Indian Nation to sever its ties with the Confederate states and abolish slavery. Despite this separation, many Cherokees still fought on the Confederate side during the American Civil War. Prominent Cherokee Stand Watie rose to the highest military rank in the Confederate Army. Former slaves became citizens in the Cherokee Nation.

Sources: Leitch, *Chronology of the American Indian*, p. 160.

1867 The Medicine Lodge Peace Treaty negotiations represented the largest gathering of American Indians and whites in the history of U.S.-Indian relations. The treaty council was convened near the Medicine River in Kansas Territory. It created Indian Territory out of the area south of the Kansas border, in present-day Oklahoma.

Sources: Leitch, *Chronology of the American Indian*, p. 162.

1868 American Indians were specifically denied the right to vote by the Fourteenth Amendment, Section 2, in the clause specifically stating that non-tax paying American Indians were excluded. Some American Indians were not granted the right to vote until 1948. Each state denied or extended the franchise to Indians at its discretion. Some states required private ownership of land, others required off-reservation residency. Still others demanded proof of literacy or English proficiency.

Sources: Dennis, *The American Indian, 1492–1976*, p. 35.

1869 For the first time civilian reformers were given an official role in the formation and implementation of U.S. Indian policy. President Ulysses S. Grant established the Board of Indian Commissioners, giving it the authority to implement his Indian policy. The commission was the result of disclosures of widespread corruption in the Indian Office. The Board of Indian Commissioners comprised wealthy, prominent civilians who had advocated reform of the Indian Office. During its tenure, the Board of Indian Commissioners sought assimilationist reforms and supported such policies as the Dawes (General Allotment) Act. It was abolished in 1933.

Sources: Champagne, ed., *Chronology of Native North American History*, p. 203; Dennis, *The American Indian, 1492–1976*, p. 34; Leitch, *Chronology of the American Indian*, p. 165.

1870 Christian denominations were officially designated to implement U.S. Indian policy when President Ulysses S. Grant passed control of Indian agencies from army officers to Christian denominations through an order known as the Indian Peace Policy. It was a response to reformers, who had long pointed to the discrepancy of having army officers administering Indian policy as they were assigned to fight them. Congress acknowledged the criticism and passed a law prohibiting army officers from being appointed as Indian agents.

Sources: Champagne, ed., *Chronology of Native North American History,* p. 205; Leitch, *Chronology of the American Indian,* p. 167; Nies, *Native American History,* pp. 278–79.

1872 American Indians were mentioned for the first time in an American political party platform when the Republican Party stated that it initiated a humane policy toward Indians. It was a reference to President Ulysses S. Grant's Indian Peace Policy which gave Christian denominations control of implementing the Christianization and civilization of Native peoples under the assumption that churches would be more benevolent, humane, and honest in their dealings with disadvantaged people. In 1884, the American Prohibition National Party would mention American Indians in its platform, declaring that American Indians and the Chinese ought to be treated with equality with European Americans. It would not be until 1928 that a political party mentioned American Indians in its platform again.

Sources: Leitch, *Chronology of the American Indian,* p. 168.

1878 The first appropriations to establish an Indian police force at each Indian agency were granted by the U.S. Congress. Later the Office of Indian Affairs as administrator of reservation life established Courts of Indian Offenses and Indian Police. Staffed with hand-picked Indians, the courts and police replaced traditional law and authority.

Sources: Champagne, ed., *The Native North American Almanac,* p. 452; Dennis, *The American Indian, 1492–1976,* p. p. 40; Washburn, *Handbook of North American Indians,* pp. 229, 233.

1879 Standing Bear (Ponca; 1829–1908), a chief, was the first Native American to be declared "a person within the meaning of the law." The Indian Bureau had refused to compensate him and his people for wrongs, because American Indians were "not persons within the meaning of the law." His legal victory made it possible for the Ponca to regain some of their homeland as a permanent reservation in 1858, but a blunder by government surveyors resulted in designation of Ponca land to the Sioux. Despite protests, the Ponca were removed to Indian Territory. At least one-fourth of the tribe died as a result of harsh conditions on their new reservation, and the death rate did not abate. One of those casualties was Standing Bear's son. In January 1879, with sixty-six followers, Standing Bear began a trek back to the Niobrara (Ponca homeland) to bury his son. However, General George Crook was sent with orders to return them to Indian Territory. They were captured and incarcerated at Fort Omaha, where they were visited by newspaper journalist Thomas H. Tibbles, who arranged for two lawyers to represent them in court. They managed to have a writ of habeas corpus issued. The federal government protested that such a writ could not be issued, because American Indians were not "persons within the meaning of the law." The case (*Standing Bear v.*

Crook) received national attention and became a landmark in the history of Indian rights. Judge Elmer S. Dunday ruled that indeed American Indians were "persons within the meaning of the law," and that in peace time they could not be imprisoned or removed against their will. The Ponca were given back a few hundred acres of their traditional homeland, but the Commissioner of Indian Affairs specified that the decision applied only to Standing Bear and his small group and not to the rest of the tribe. The government was fearful that other tribes would be able to legally and successfully petition for a return of their home-

Standing Bear, the first Native American legally declared "a person," a distinction that enabled the Ponca to regain some of their homeland.

lands as well. After the trial, Standing Bear went on a national tour with Susette and Francis La Flesche and Tibbles. (This was the beginning of activism for both of the La Fleshes.) Standing Bear died in 1908.

Sources: *The American Indian; Biographical Dictionary of Indians of the Americas*, Vol. 2, p. 711; Champagne, ed., *Native America*, p. 271–72.

1882 The Indian Rights Association was organized in Philadelphia by non-Indian reformers concerned over the administration of U.S. Indian policy and the plight of American Indian peoples. Composed primarily of well-educated upper middle class men and women advocating assimilationist policies, the group's primary goals were to secure citizenship, deeds to private ownership of land, civil rights, and improved education for Indian people. They supported such policies as the Dawes (General Allotment) Act of 1887. Such groups as the Indian Rights Association greatly influenced the direction of Indian policy in the late nineteenth century.

Sources: Leitch, *Chronology of the American Indian*, p. 176.

1883 The first Mohonk Conference was held in Lake Mohonk, New York. The conference was attended by prominent citizens who were also social activists. At the Mohonk Conference, they gathered to discuss issues and concerns relating to American Indians. The meetings were sponsored by Robert K. Smiley, a member of the U.S. Board of Indian Commissioners. American Indians were not among the participants.

Sources: Leitch, *Chronology of the American Indian*, p. 177.

1884 The aboriginal land rights of the Inuit in Alaska were recognized by a congressional act on May 17, 1884, when the U.S. Congress provided for a civil government in Alaska. Specific definitions were not outlined, but officially and legally, Native rights were acknowledged. The act left congressional action of conferring title to land in the future. Until the Alaska Native Claims Settlement Act in 1871, the Inuit had not relinquished their land rights. On the basis of this congressional acknowledgment, other Native Americans—American Indians and the Aleutian—were able to maintain their land rights as well.

Sources: Dennis, *The American Indian, 1492–1976*, p. 43; Leitch, *Chronology of the American Indian*, p. 177.

1887 The Dawes (General Allotment) Act went into effect on February 7, 1887. It authorized the President to subdivide American Indian lands among tribal members and then sell the surplus to whites. The purpose was to force American Indians to abandon their communal lifestyle and adopt a settled agrarian life. The ultimate goal was to permanently assimilate Indians into white society. Indian tribes lost millions of acres of land; some individuals lost their status as members of their Indian tribes along with their rights and privileges. American Indians were not consulted as allotment policy was being drafted, and most did not consent to it when it was ratified.

Sources: Champagne, ed., *Native America*, p. 237; Dennis, *The American Indian, 1492–1976*, p. 44; Leitch, *Chronology of the American Indian*, p. 180.

1888 American Indian women were offered citizenship for the first time. Under a provision of a congressional act, women who married U.S. citizens were extended the privilege of U.S. citizenship.

Sources: Leitch, *Chronology of the American Indian,* p. 180.

1893 The first congressional appropriations for Indian water development came as a result of water scarcity for livestock on the Navajo Reservation.

Sources: Dennis, *The American Indian, 1492–1976,* p. 46.

1911 The Indian Protection Service (Servico de Proteccao aus Indios) was founded in Brazil in an effort to safeguard indigenous peoples against extinction by the military and Candido Mariano da Silva Rondon, a prominent political figure.

Sources: Leitch, *Chronology of the American Indian,* p. 189.

1911 Charles Alexander Eastman (Santee Dakota Sioux, 1858–1939) was one of the founders and the first president of the Society of American Indians, the first Indian organization that had exclusive Native American membership. In 1911 Eastman (born Ohiyesa, "the winner") represented American Indians at the First Universal Race Congress in London. He graduated from Dartmouth College in 1887 and Boston University Medical School in 1890. He was an articulate Indian rights activist, author, lecturer, and physician. The ease with which he conducted himself amazed politicians, academics, and other whites. Emerging from a traditional background, where he was immersed in Dakota culture, he moved to the boardrooms and lecture halls of high white society. Active in Indian rights issues, he sought to promote American Indians when he could. He later helped organize the Boy Scouts of America and the Campfire Girls of America and is credited with incorporating ideas from American Indian lore to each organization. In 1933 he was honored with the first Indian Achievement Award. He died in 1939 at the age of eighty.

Sources: *The American Indian; Biographical Dictionary of Indians of the Americas,* Vol. 1, p. 206; Malinowski, ed., *Notable Native Americans,* pp. 137–39.

1926 Gertrude Simmons Bonnin (Yankton Nakota Sioux; 1875–1938), also known as Zitkala-Sa, and Raymond Bonnin (Yankton Nakota Sioux) organized the Congress of American Indians (NCAI). It was the only nationally organized reform group with exclusive Indian membership. Gertrude Simmons Bonnin became its first president. NCAI devoted its efforts to improving the condition of American Indians, so they could become better American citizens. The central theme of Bonnin's work was to convince American Indians to support Indian rights issues, and to create a pan-Indian consciousness at a time when Indian tribes and Indians in general were more concerned with their respective tribal issues and did not give as much attention to pan-Indian issues as Bonnin would like to have seen. However, it may have been her forceful character and strong leadership style that dissuaded other tribal leaders from full participation. Bonnin was a strong advocate of fostering pride in American Indian heritage and culture, and she was influential in securing significant reforms in American Indian policy. In addition, she was an expert violinist and musical composer. In 1913 she co-authored an opera, *Sun Dance.* To this date it is the only opera co-authored by a

Gertrude Simmons Bonnin.

Native American. The NCAI dissolved in 1938 upon Bonnin's death. In 1944, another pan-Indian organization, The National Congress of American Indians (also NCAI), found a political climate more conducive to pan-Indianism and became successful in addressing general Indian issues.

Sources: *Biographical Dictionary of Indians of the Americas*, Vol. 1, p. 82; Bataille, ed., *Native American Women*, p. 32; Champagne, ed., *Native America*, pp. 183–84; Dockstader, *Great North American Indians*, pp. 40–41; Malinowski, ed., *Notable Native Americans*, pp. 42–45.

1928 The Navajo Tribal Council amended the council regulations to allow Navajo women the right to vote. While women had always been an integral part of the political process, Anglo American tradition assumed that only men could vote. Although it required special action, it is significant that the Navajo government acted as quickly as it did to extend the franchise to women. Other tribes waited as late as the 1960s to give women the right to vote.

Sources: Shepardson, Mary, "Development of Navajo Tribal Government," in *Handbook of North American Indians*, Vol. 10: *History of Indian-White Relations*, edited by Alfonso Ortiz, pp. 624–35.

1928 Henry Roe Cloud (Winnebago, 1886–1945), an educator and activist who worked to improve the federal government's treatment of American Indians, co-authored the "Meriam Report" in 1928 as a member of the Institute for Government Research survey team. The report, which became cited frequently later, detailed American Indian problems, including the destitution caused by the Dawes (General Allotment) Act of 1887 (in which Indians lost millions of acres of land). In 1931, Cloud became the first American Indian superintendent of Haskell Institute. In 1935, he received the third Indian Achievement Medal of the Indian Council Fire. He was appointed supervisor of Indian education by the Bureau of Indian Affairs (BIA) in 1936.

Sources: *Biographical Dictionary of Indians of the Americas*, Vol. 1, p. 133; Dockstader, *Great North American Indians*, pp. 51–52; Malinowski, ed., *Notable Native Americans*, pp. 80–82.

1940s Pomo Women's Club, also known as Pomo Mothers' Club, participated in and supported a successful lawsuit filed by Steven Knight against a Ukiah, California, theater that denied American Indians the right to sit on its lower level. The court declared it an infringement of civil rights to enforce this policy, deeming it discriminatory. To avoid lawsuits, other business owners ended their "No Indians Allowed" policies. The Pomo Women's Club was established in 1940 and disbanded in 1957.

Sources: Bataille, ed., *Native American Women*, p. 5; Davis, *Native America in the Twentieth Century*, p. 458.

1944 Louis R. Bruce (Mohawk/Dakota Sioux) was co-founder and first executive secretary of the National Congress of American Indians (NCAI). Having served as chairman of the President's Advisory Committee on American Indian Affairs, he was appointed the third American Indian to head the Bureau of Indian Affairs (BIA) in 1969. During his tenure at the BIA he attempted to hire American Indians to top administrative positions and strived to transform the BIA from a service agency to a management agency with Indians in charge. He was dismissed from the BIA after the American Indian Movement (AIM) occupation of the BIA headquarters in 1972.

Sources: *Biographical Dictionary of Indians of the Americas*, Vol. 1, p. 98; Champagne, ed., *The Native North American Almanac*, p. 1021; Malinowski, ed., *Notable Native Americans*, pp. 56–58.

1944 Napoleon B. Johnson (Cherokee) helped establish the National Congress of American Indians (NCAI) and went on to serve nine consecutive terms as a representative in the organization. In addition, Johnson would serve as an Oklahoma Supreme Court justice.

Sources: *Biographical Dictionary of Indians of the Americas*, Vol. 1, p. 319; Gridley, ed., *Indians of Today*, p. 94.

1944 D'Arcy McNickle (Flathead; 1904–1977) helped found the National Congress of American Indians (NCAI). The NCAI was designed to speak on behalf of all tribes to local governments and the federal government. McNickle worked for the Bureau of Indian Affairs (BIA) as a field representative and assistant to Commissioner John Collier and as director of Tribal Relations. In addition, McNickle served as program director for the Center for History of the American Indian at the Newberry Library in Chicago. The center was later renamed after him.

See also: Tribal Government: American Indian, 1952.

Sources: *Biographical Dictionary of Indians of the Americas*, Vol. 1, p. 414.

1948 A veteran of the U.S. Marines during World War II, Miguil Trujillo (Isleta Pueblo) won a lawsuit against the state of New Mexico that effectively gave American Indians the right to vote in that state. New Mexico was found to be in violation of the Fifteenth Amendment.

Sources: "An Unsung Hero Who Fought for the Pueblo's Right to Vote," *Indian Country Today*, Vol. 16, No. 10 (September 2–9, 1996), p. A-4; Leitch, *Chronology of the American Indian*, p. 221.

1960 The Lumbee Indians were perhaps the first Native people to actively combat discrimination in the American public school systems. Lumbee brothers Eugene and James Chance were fined $150 and $100, respectively, for trying to enroll their children in a segregated, whites-only public high school. They were not protesting school segregation, but the refusal of the school board to build a school closer to their community. The closest Indian school was thirty miles away.

Sources: Dennis, *The American Indian, 1492–1976*, p. 62.

1961 Herbert Blatchford (Navajo) was the founder and first executive director of the National Indian Youth Council (NIYC), an organization of young Native students, who revolted against the more conservative organizations led by older and more cautious American Indian leaders. NIYC was the first pan-Indian organization founded by American Indian youth. It became the defining group behind the Red Power movement of the late 1960s and the 1970s. Blatchford was also editor of the organization's journal, *The Aborigine*.

Sources: *Biographical Dictionary of Indians of the Americas*, Vol. 1, p. 77; Davis, *Native America in the Twentieth Century*, pp. 404, 536; Washburn, ed., *Handbook of North American Indians*, p. 316.

1965 The Zuñi tribal elections were marked by two significant firsts: Zuñi women were allowed to vote for the first time; and the 1965 elections marked the first time the method of secret ballots was used in Zuñi elections.

Sources: *Biographical Dictionary of Indians of the Americas*, Vol. 1, p. 355.

1965 LaDonna C. Harris (Comanche; 1931–) helped organize the Oklahomans for Indian Opportunity. In addition, she began serving as its first president from 1965, a post she would hold until 1968, when President Lyndon B. Johnson appointed her to the National Council on Indian Opportunity. In 1969, Harris founded the Americans for Indian Opportunity. Based in Washington, D.C., the organization was designed to provide information resources for American Indians and serve as a liaison or advocate on their behalf.

Sources: *Biographical Dictionary of Indians of the Americas,* Vol. 1, p. 268.

1966 Emil Notti (Athabascan; 1933–), the first Alaska Native to receive an honorary doctorate from Alaska Methodist University, organized the Alaska Federation of Native Associations (AFN) and officiated as its first president. AFN was founded in response to the exclusion of Alaska Natives in the negotiations and settlement of Native land claims by the U.S. Department of Interior, the Bureau of Indian Affairs (BIA), Alaska State officials, and U.S. legislative representatives. Notti was one of the most instrumental leaders who worked for the passage of the Alaska Native Claims Settlement Act. Born in Koyukuk, Alaska, on March 11, 1933, Notti attended Mt. Edgecombe Indian School and received a B.S. from Northrop Institute of Technology. Active in Alaska Native issues, Notti has worked as a field representative for Alaska Human Rights Commission and as a coordinator of the Alaska State Community Action Program, Inc. He has functioned as president of Cook Inlet Native Association and served with the Alaska Conservation Society.

Sources: *Biographical Dictionary of Indians of the Americas,*, Vol. 2, p. 481; Davis, ed., *Native America in the Twentieth Century,* pp. 11, 21; Gridley, ed., *Indians of Today,* p. 105.

LaDonna Harris, founder of the Americans for Indian Opportunity in Washington, D.C.

AMERICAN INDIAN MOVEMENT (AIM)

1968 The American Indian Movement (AIM), founded by Dennis Banks (Anishinabe Ojibwa; 1932–), Clyde Bellecourt (Ojibwa; 1939–), and others, was the first confrontational American Indian rights organization that utilized methods of public protests, marches, and demonstrations to bring public attention to Indian issues. The first annual convention of AIM was held at Camp Owendigo, Minnesota, on October 13–15, 1971. AIM emerged from the core of the Red Power movement of the 1960s and 1970s, which worked to raise public awareness of the plight of American Indians in modern society. Its reputation for radical activity has made AIM the most well-known American Indian rights organization today. Pan-Indian in nature, AIM has chapters in urban centers and reservations and includes members from each Native American nation. During the 1970s AIM organized a number of highly publicized protests, including the 1972 "Trail of Broken Treaties" march to Washington, D.C., the subsequent week-long occupation of the Bureau of Indian Affairs (BIA) headquarters, and the 1973 takeover of the site of the 1890 Wounded Knee massacre on the Pine Ridge Reservation. Although AIM has been instrumental in educating mainstream America on Indian issues and effecting change, the radical nature of some of its activities has raised controversy among American Indians; not all endorse AIM's political rhetoric or its methods of activism.

Sources: *Biographical Dictionary of Indians of the Americas*, Vol. 1, p. 46; Hirschfelder and Kreipe de Montaño, *The Native American Almanac*, p. 309; Malinowski, ed., *Notable Native Americans*, pp. 23–25.

1968 Dennis J. Banks (Anishinabe Ojibwa; 1932–) co-founded the American Indian Movement (AIM) in 1968 with Clyde Bellecourt (Ojibwa; 1939–) and others. Bellecourt served as AIM's first director. His experience with the judicial system convinced Banks of the inconsistency in how justice was meted out to American Indians. He served a term of two and a half years in the Minnesota State Penitentiary for robbery, while his white accomplice was freed, serving no time. Following his release, he further noted the abuse of the civil rights of American Indians and the economic and social inequities they must endure. With Bellecourt and George Mitchell, he formed the American Indian Movement, not only to protest injustices, but also to bring about change and to force issues of Indian rights into the open. Banks and AIM participated in the 1969 Alcatraz Island takeover in San Francisco, the 1972 "Trail of Broken Treaties" to Washington, D.C., and the subsequent Bureau of Indian Affairs (BIA) headquarters takeover. He was also a leader of the 1973 armed takeover of the Wounded Knee massacre site on the Pine Ridge Reservation. A participant in the courthouse fight in Custer, South Dakota, which resulted in the burning of the courthouse building and rioting, he was indicted, convicted, and sentenced to fifteen years in prison on charges of arson and assault. Banks, however, fled to California, where he was given amnesty

Dennis J. Banks

Clyde Bellecourt.

by Governor Edmund G. Brown. Banks remained in California until 1983. While in California Banks earned an associate of arts degree and taught at Deganawida-Quetzolcoatl University (D-QU), later becoming the first Native American Chancellor of D-QU. When Brown's term expired, the Onondaga Reservation granted Banks sanctuary, and he volunteered his services during his stay. In 1984 he surrendered to South Dakota authorities and was given a three-year sentence. After serving part of his sentence, he was paroled in 1985. In 1978 Banks founded the organization, Sacred Run, which has organized a series of spiritual runs totaling more than forty-three thousand miles in North America, Japan, Europe, Australia, and New Zealand. In 1992 he led the "Walk for Justice" from California to Washington, D.C. Banks has remained an activist for American Indian causes.

See also: Indian Rights and Activism, 1968.

Sources: *Biographical Dictionary of Indians of the Americas,* Vol. 1, p. 39; Champagne, ed., *The Native North American Almanac,* p. 78; Hirschfelder and Kreipe de Montaño, *The Native American Almanac,* p. 309; Malinowski, ed., *Notable Native Americans,* pp. 23–25.

1971 The National Tribal Chairmen's Association, the first organization seeking to unite sitting tribal leaders, was formed. Leaders from fifty reservations and twelve states met to discuss how reservation people could impact national Indian policy. A prevailing concern among tribal leaders was that urban Indians and young militants were steering the course of Indian policy and neglecting the needs and concerns of reservation people.

Sources: Champagne, ed., *Chronology of Native North American History,* p. 384.

1971 The Native American Rights Fund (NARF), the first legal organization established by American Indians for the exclusive purpose of defending and prosecuting Indian rights cases, was founded. The specific goals of the NARF were maintaining and ensuring tribal existence, promoting the human rights of Indian citizens, protecting tribal resources, and developing Indian law. Since its inception, NARF has won many court cases, brought attention to crucial issues affecting Indian tribes and citizens, and facilitated the development of legislation for the benefit of Indian nations, such as the Native American Graves Protection and Repatriation Act. In 1992 NARF was co-recipient of the Carter-Menil Human Rights Foundation Prize in recognition of its work on behalf of.Native Americans.

Sources: Champagne, ed., *Chronology of Native North American History,* p. 83; Champagne, ed., *The Native North American Almanac,* pp. 64–66, 222; Hirschfelder and Kreipe de Montaño, *The Native American Almanac,* p. 309.

1971 Alaska Natives agreed to the Alaska Native Claims Settlement Act (ANCSA). It was the first time a congressional act attempted to compensate Alaska Natives for their lands, giving them title to forty-four million acres of land and settling the debate over Alaska Native land rights. In addition, $962.5 million was divided among thirteen regional corporations. Each corporation's membership was extended to Natives and their heirs until 1991. The land was divided among two hundred villages and the regional corporations that held surface rights. While the settlement acknowledged Native land rights, it was not without controversy. Natives lost access to many more acres of land for hunting and fishing rights. Critics charged that not enough protection was provided to ensure that land would remain in the ownership of Native Americans. Twenty years later, President Ronald Reagan signed into law the 1991 amendment to ANCSA to correct such problems as land rights and ownership protection that arose from administering ANCSA. The amendment was written after numerous meetings: fifteen congressional hearings, seven Alaska Federation of Natives conventions, and five Native leadership retreats. It provided for protection of corporate stock and Native land ownership.

Sources: Champagne, ed., *Chronology of Native North American History,* p. 385; Champagne, ed., *The Native North American Almanac,* pp. 67, 491, 297–300, 505, 924; Hirschfelder and Kreipe de Montaño, *The Native American Almanac,* pp. 309–310, 311.

1973 The restoration of the Menominee Indian Tribe of Wisconsin made it the first terminated tribe to regain its reservation status. In 1954, the Menominee tribe was the first tribe to be terminated by an act of the U.S. Congress. As soon as its termination status was official activists began efforts to repeal the act. With termination the Menominee lost thousands of acres of land, including prime lakefront property. Among those working diligently to return federal recognition to the Menominee was Ada Deer (Menominee). On December 22, 1973, President Richard Nixon signed the law that repealed Menominee termination status.

Sources: Champagne, ed., *Chronology of Native North American History,* p. 328; Champagne, ed., *Native America,* p. 35; Champagne, ed., *The Native North American Almanac,* pp. 438, 502, 505; Malinowski, ed., *Notable Native Americans,* pp. 111–113.

1973 Barnie Botone (Blackfoot/Kiowa) became the first American Indian to be trained and hired as a locomotive engineer. Previously Indians were hired as laborers but none as an engineer or in a management position. He is the great-great-grandson of Kiowa War Chief Lone Wolf, who as a prisoner of war was sent

Dennis Banks helped lead the 1972 "Trail of Broken Treaties" march to Washington, D.C.

Russell Means, a major player in the American Indian Movement (AIM).

to Florida on a train. When Botone's grandmother learned that he was going to be a locomotive engineer, she cried at the irony of it. As a small girl she saw her grandfather sent away on a train, and now her grandson would operate trains. Botone vowed to be the best engineer ever. He remained with the Santa Fe Railroad for twenty-three years and earned that many years of seniority. He later became president of the Brotherhood of Locomotive Engineers, and vice-president of the New Mexico Federation of Labor. He credits affirmative action for his employment as a locomotive engineer.

Sources: Botone, Barnie (director, Albuquerque Indian Center, Albuquerque, New Mexico), Personal communication to AnCita Benally, October 2, 1996; Weahkee, Cheryl (secretary, Alburquerque Indian Center), Personal communication to AnCita Benally, October 2, 1996.

1973 On February 23, 1973, activists Dennis J. Banks (Anishinabe Ojibwa; 1932–), Clyde and Vernon Bellecourt (Ojibwa), and Russell C. Means (Lakota Sioux; 1939–), assisted by nearly two hundred armed supporters, including many members of the American Indian Movement (AIM), occupied the community of Wounded Knee, South Dakota—site of the infamous 1890 massacre of some 350 Sioux men, women, and children by the U.S. military. The occupation, which was in protest of the corruption and nepotism of elected council head of the Pine Ridge Reservation, Richard Wilson, lasted ten weeks. It ended in a negotiated settlement and withdrawal of both sides and eventually led to an investigation into tribal government. Highly publicized in the national media, the siege became known as "Wounded Knee II" and, unlike the 1969 occupation of Alcatraz Island and the 1972 takeover of the BIA offices in Washington, D.C., in which national support waned, the Wounded Knee occupation garnered continued support of many non-Indians.

Opposite page:
Russell Means addressing crowd at a 1970 Thanksgiving Day protest in Plymouth, Massachusetts.

Sources: Champagne, ed., *Chronology of Native North American History*, p. 393–94; Malinowski, ed., *Notable Native Americans*, p. 23–25, 269–71.

1978 The first negotiated settlement between state officials and an eastern American Indian tribe was completed. The settlement was between the Narragansett Indians and the state of Rhode Island. It returned to the Narragansett eighteen hundred acres of land. The tribe sued the state for taking thirty-five hundred acres, which violated the 1790 Trade and Intercourse Act.

Sources: Champagne, ed., *Chronology of Native North American History,* pp. 414, 422.

1978 On May 18, 1978, the U.S. Supreme Court upheld the right of Santa Clara Pueblo to determine who is rightly a member of the tribe in the case *Santa Clara Pueblo v. Martinez.* It was the first time the Supreme Court acknowledged the right of American Indian nations to specify their membership. In this case a Santa Clara woman sued for the right to enroll her children on the tribal census rolls. The Pueblo, however, being patrilineal, denied membership, arguing that its rules allowed only descendants of male members to enroll. Martinez appealed to the higher court, claiming a case of gender discrimination. The court ruled against her argument and affirmed the right of American Indian tribes to conduct their internal affairs autonomously, including whom they admit into membership.

Sources: Champagne, ed., *Chronology of Native North American History,* p. 417; Champagne, ed., *The Native North American Almanac,* pp. 484–85; Hirschfelder and Kreipe de Montaño, *The Native American Almanac,* pp. 49–50.

1978 After years of fighting for the right to practice their Native religions, American Indians were guaranteed freedom of religion by the American Indian Religious Freedom Act (AIRF), which was signed into law by President Jimmy Carter. While other Americans have enjoyed freedom of religion as guaranteed by the U.S. Bill of Rights, Native Americans have struggled for the right and the freedom to perform their religious practices. This act specifically guaranteed religious

Russell Means and K. Frizzell signing settlement at Wounded Knee in 1973.

freedom for all indigenous peoples in the United States and in effect rescinded all earlier legislation to curb, deny, or abolish the existence and practice of Native American religions. However, it did not provide legal mechanisms to enforce the act. Later amendments to the act, such as one in 1994, put these in place.

Sources: Champagne, ed., *Chronology of Native North American History,* p. 418; Champagne, ed., *The Native North American Almanac,* pp. 79, 460; Hirschfelder and Kreipe de Montaño, *The Native American Almanac,* p. 310.

1978 On November 8, 1978, the Indian Child Welfare Act (ICWA) was signed into law. This act was designed to prevent the placement of American Indian children in non-Indian homes. It also granted to various tribal governments the right to protect families by ensuring that American Indian children would be placed with other tribal members. In the past, states had placed children without regard to cultural compatibility. Further, many abuses occurred during the illegal adoption of children without the knowledge of their parents or other relatives.

Sources: Champagne, ed., *Chronology of Native North American History,* p. 419; Hirschfelder and Kreipe de Montaño, *The Native American Almanac,* p. 310.

1978 The Mashpee Wampanoag lost the first case of any eastern tribe filing a suit under the terms of the 1790 Trade and Intercourse Act. In *Mashpee Tribe v. Town of Mashpee,* the tribe's suit was dismissed by a federal district court because they were not a tribe when they filed suit in 1976. The Mashpee had hoped to regain lands they had lost.

Sources: Champagne, ed., *The Native North American Almanac,* p. 78; Davis, ed., *Native America in the Twentieth Century,* p. 684; Hirschfelder and Molin, *The Encyclopedia of Native American Religions,* p. 301.

1980 Owanah Anderson (Choctaw; 1926–) was the only American Indian representative to the Commission on Security and Cooperation held in Madrid,

Russell Means with Dennis Banks and other AIM members after dismissal of charges in 1973 Wounded Knee takeover.

Spain. Best known for her work in advancing issues concerning American Indian women, Anderson had established, in 1979, the Ohoyo Resource Center to offer assistance to Native women in pursuing their educational and professional goals. In 1982, she published, *Ohoyo One Thousand: A Resource Guide of American Indian/Alaska Native Women.* In 1981, Anderson received the Ann Roe Howard Award from Harvard University Graduate School of Education. In 1984, she became a member of the North Texas Women's Hall of Fame. In 1987, she was honored by the National Coalition of Women of Color. Since the 1980s, Anderson has been working closely with the Episcopal church in assisting Native Americans and indigenous peoples worldwide.

Sources: Bataille, ed., *Native American Women,* pp. 10–11; Champagne, ed., *The Native North American Almanac,* p. 1001; Malinowski, ed., *Notable Native Americans,* pp. 13–14.

1984 For the first time in 146 years, on March 25, 1984, members of the Eastern Cherokee and the Cherokee Nation of Oklahoma held a joint meeting at the Cherokee sacred grounds in Red Clay, Tennessee. They agreed to remain separate but would meet annually to discuss common concerns.

Sources: Champagne, ed., *Chronology of Native North American History,* p. 445; Davis, ed., *Native America in the Twentieth Century,* p. 98; Hirschfelder and Kreipe de Montaño, *The Native American Almanac,* p. 311.

1988 For the first time in modern history American Indian leaders met with the president of the United States, on December 12, 1988. The meeting was intended to be a forum to discuss careless, offhand remarks made by President Ronald Reagan regarding Native Americans. The remarks made by Reagan raised concern among Indian leaders of the obvious misinformation about Native peoples among the Reagan administration regarding their current political, cultural, and social state of affairs.

Sources: Champagne, ed., *Chronology of Native North American History,* p. 458.

1989 Winona LaDuke (Ojibwa) was one of the first American Indians to receive the Reebok Human Rights Award, recognizing human rights activists under the age of thirty. Trained as an economist she has published extensively on economic development, environmental issues, and legal issues as they affect Native Americans. She has actively defended the rights of all Indian peoples and focused on groups such as the Navajo Big Mountain resistance group in Arizona. With the monetary award she received from Reebok she initiated the White Earth Recovery Project. The effort was devoted to retrieving some of the 830 thousand acres promised to the White Earth Reservation. Also active in women's issues, LaDuke has been a member of the Women of Red Nations (WARN), president of the Indigenous Women's Network, and representative of the International Council of Indigenous Women.

Sources: Bataille, ed., *Native American Women,* p. 145.

Opposite page:
Rigoberta Menchu from Guatemala, the youngest person ever to win the Nobel Peace Prize, is shown at a United Nations press conference.

1992 Rigoberta Menchu (K'iche' Maya) was the first Native American to be honored with the Nobel Peace Prize. She was nominated for her work among indigenous people in Guatemala. Menchu published several books, including her autobiography, *Let Me Speak,* in which she told of the Guatemalan people's struggle for human rights and her involvement in that fight.

Sources: "Guatemala," *Microsoft Encarta,* Microsoft, 1994; Menchu, Rigoberta, *Let Me Speak;* Wearne, *Return of the Indian,* pp. 1, 187–88.

1993 After more than a century of effort, the Lumbee tribe of Cheraw Indians of North Carolina was finally recognized by the U.S. House of Representatives on October 28, 1993. Although the state of North Carolina had formally recognized the Lumbee as an Indian tribe since 1885, the Department of the Interior has opposed federal recognition since 1890.

Sources: Champagne, ed., *Chronology of Native North American History,* p. 494; Davis, ed., *Native America In the Twentieth Century,* pp. 196, 322–23.

1993 On December 9, 1993, Carrie and Mary Dann (Shoshoni) became possibly the first American Indian women recipients of the 1993 Right Livelihood Award, also known as the alternative Nobel Peace Prize. They shared the cash award with other award recipients from Israel, Zimbabwe, and India. They were cited for courage in asserting their rights to protect their land and that of other indigenous peoples. In 1983 they were two of seventeen women honored by the Wonder Women Federation in New York City. They have opposed the U.S. federal government by defending their right to occupy their lands since 1972. A 1966 Indian Claims Commission decision awarded Western Shoshoni lands that extinguished title to several million acres, some of which the Danns continue to occupy.

Sources: Champagne, ed., *Chronology of Native North American History,* p. 497; Davis, ed., *Native America in the Twentieth Century,* p. 307; Hirschfelder and Kreipe de Montaño, *The Native American Almanac,* p. 311.

SCIENCES

PHYSICAL SCIENCES

ca. 7500 B.C.E. Beans: a wide variety of beans are indigenous to the Americas. They have served as a great source of protein for Indians for centuries.

Sources: Weatherford, *Indian Givers*, p.72.

ca. 7500 B.C.E. Corn: an indigenous staple food of America's Native peoples. It was not eaten much by Europeans initially. Instead they used it primarily for animal food.

Sources: Weatherford, *Indian Givers*, p. 73.

ca. 7500 B.C.E. Potatoes: American Indians produced high yields of potatoes from small plots of land. The potatoes were grown in different colors and sizes.

Sources: Weatherford, *Indian Givers*, pp. 62, 77.

ca. 7500 B.C.E. Sunflowers: indigenous to the Americas, this plant was domesticated in the northern plains of what is known as present-day United States. Able to flourish in a cold climate, the sunflower plant was introduced to Russia where it became the major oil producing plant. Previous to its introduction, Russians had no oil producing plant and had to rely on animal fats. Today Russia is the leading producer of sunflower oil.

Sources: Weatherford, *Indian Givers*, pp. 72–73.

ca. 450 B.C.E. The Hohokam of present-day Arizona were the first to develop acid-etching techniques on shells. Their use of this technique pre-dated European techniques by 450 years; etching of iron swords was done just before the time of Christ. In China, etching on bronze appeared about 250 B.C.E. Hohokam peoples applied wax or pitch to areas on a shell they did not want corroded by acid, then acid was applied and allowed to corrode the shell material. The wax or pitch was then removed, revealing intricate designs. Most likely acid from fermented saguaro cactus fruit was used as the corrosive acid with which to etch. Shells were probably obtained as a trade item. Other Native groups and communities, even those who lived near the ocean, did not work with etched shells and it appears that acid etching on shell was uniquely Hohokam.

Sources: *Ancient America Series: More Than Bows and Arrows* (film), Thirteenth Regional Corporation/Camera One, 1994; Haury, *The Hohokam, Desert Farmers and Craftsmen*, pp. 318–19

ca. 300 B.C.E. The Maya were the first to invent the concept of zero and put it to practical use, before any other civilization in the world. Zero was not used widely in Europe for at least another one thousand years. By discovering this concept, they were able to construct enormous buildings with great precision. Other mathematical achievements, such as astronomical measurements, came from using the concept.

Sources: *Ancient America Series: More Than Bows and Arrows* (film), 13th Regional Corporation/Camera One, 1994; Jimenez, *The Mexican American Heritage,* p. 33.

765 C.E. Representatives from each of the major Maya centers assembled at Copan to adjust their calendars and correct accumulated errors, and perhaps to synchronize and standardize them. Carved texts have been found at Copan, which suggest that this city was a center of astronomy during the Classic period, 300–900 C.E.

Sources: Leitch, *Chronology of the American Indian,* p. 29.

1091 The Aztec established 1091 as the base of their calendar. Like the Maya calendar it was based on a fifty-two-year cycle. Dates were calculated by measuring the time that had elapsed from the beginning of each period. Different from the Gregorian calendar, which determined time elapsed from one original base date, names were given to each fifty-two-year period to distinguish them from each other.

Sources: Leitch, *Chronology of the American Indian,* p. 36.

1524 Chontal Maya traders gave Hernan Cortes the first Native-made map seen by Europeans of the inland trading routes along the gulf coast of the modern state of Tabasco in Mexico. Painted on cotton cloth, the map was a highly accurate depiction of four hundred miles of roads. The Chontal Maya traded extensively along the coast from Xicalanco (Tabasco, Mexico) to Nito (Honduras).

Sources: Leitch, *Chronology of the American Indian,* p. 67.

1542 Big Eyes (Wichita) provided a crude map for Hernando de Soto that linked, for the first time, a continuous span of the width of North America so that its size could be estimated. Captured by the Teja and sold to the Tigueux Indians of Arizona who came in contact with Francisco de Vasquez de Coronado's expedition, Big Eyes was so named because of two lines of tattoos under her eyes. During a skirmish with the expedition Big Eyes was captured and became the property of Juan de Zaldivar, a captain under Coronado. She accompanied the expedition to the panhandle of Texas where she made her escape. She rejoined her people, and in 1542, they came into contact with de Soto's expedition. Historical questions persist about Big Eyes' story, but her adventures linked the New World expeditions of the French and Spanish, connecting the expanse of North America for Europeans for the first time.

Sources: Bataille, ed., *Native American Women,* p. 22.

1700s Mayta Capac (Inca) was the Inca ruler responsible for major developments in the construction technology of bridges and walls. The earliest known Inca suspension bridge, over the Apurimac River, was constructed during the reign of Mayta Capac.

Sources: *Biographical Dictionary of Indians of the Americas,* Vol. 1, p. 406.

ca. late-1700s The Palouse people, now known as the Nez Percé, were reported by Lewis and Clark to be selectively breeding Appaloosa horses. This breed of horse was strong enough to survive cold mountain winters, which was why they were favored by Native peoples of the North. Mountain men spoke often of the "Palouse horse." Eventually these spotted horses became known as Appaloosas. In the 1990s the Nez Percé began to breed and raise Appaloosas again as part of a community project to teach cultural values while engaging in economic development.

Sources: Simonelli, Richard, "Return of the Appaloosa," *Winds of Change,* Vol. 6, No. 4 (Autumn 1991), pp. 26–27; Slatta, *The Cowboy Encyclopedia,* p. 186.

1839 For the first time since Europeans had seen the ancient Maya ruins, the Maya were given credit for the construction of the abandoned cities. John Lloyd Stephens, an American lawyer, and Frederick Catherwood published a book entitled *Incidents of Travel in Yucatan,* which publicized the Maya ruins. The Lost Ten Tribes of Israel, or other imaginary builders, had been previously credited with the construction of the ancient cities.

Sources: Leitch, *Chronology of the American Indian,* p. 151.

1877 The first systematic investigation of an Indian archaeological site in Argentina was the excavation of a prehistoric tumulus at Campana on the Parana River. It was conducted by Estanislao Zeballos and Pedro Pico.

Sources: Leitch, *Chronology of the American Indian,* p. 172.

1889 Susan La Flesche (Omaha; 1865–1915) was the first Indian woman to become a physician. La Flesche, the daughter of Omaha chief Joseph La Flesche, received her medical degree from the Women's Medical College, Pennsylvania, in 1889. She enrolled at Hampton Normal and Agriculture Institute in 1884. While there she was contacted by the Connecticut Indian Association, which funded her medical schooling. After completing the program she returned to Nebraska and won a government appointment as the first Indian and the first woman to hold the position. In 1893 she resigned to nurse her ailing mother and in 1894 she married Henry Picotte (Yankton Sioux). La Flesche-Picotte was active in the affairs of her tribe especially in speaking out against the use of liquor. She further advocated education and assimilation, stands that were unpopular among many members of her tribe. She continued her interest in health and hygiene and in 1913 she established the first Indian hospital in Walkthill, Nebraska. La Flesche-Picotte also had a change of heart in supporting the assimilationist rhetoric and policies imposed on American Indians. In 1915 she openly supported the Peyote Religion, which would become the Native American Church in 1918. She further began to criticize the condescending paternalism of white reformers. In her lifetime she served as a physician, but also as an outspoken Indian rights activist.

Sources: Champagne, Ed., *The Native North American Almanac,* pp. 1087–88; Johnson and Grinde, *The Encyclopedia of Native American Biography,* 1997, pp. 205-206; Waldman, *Who Was Who in Native American History,* p. 192.

ca. 1940s Alvin Bearskin (Wyandot), an aerospace technician for NASA flight systems, participated in "Operation Eager Beaver," an experiment to test men and equipment in temperatures below -56 degrees in the Northern Yukon. A veteran of World War II and the Korean Conflict, Bearskin received a Good Conduct Medal; he also served in the Army Engineer Corps for more than five years.

Sources: *Biographical Dictionary of Indians of the Americas,* Vol. 1, p. 42.

ca. 1950 Bernard Anthony Hoehner (Standing Rock Sioux) was the first American Indian veterinarian. He was one of only five students in the United States chosen to intern at Angell Memorial Veterinary Hospital in Boston. Successful in his private practice, he was awarded Indian Businessman of the Year for Northern California in 1978. At the time of his death Hoehner was an accomplished amateur artist and sculptor, as well as a respected pipe carrier and Lakota elder.

Sources: *Airogram, American Indian Research Opportunities,* Vol. 2, No. 9 (December 1995); Medicine, Beatrice (anthropologist/educator; Mobridge, South Dakota), Personal communication to Karen Gayton Swisher, June 1996.

ca. 1950s Taylor McKenzie (Navajo) became the first Navajo physician after graduating from Baylor University, College of Medicine. McKenzie, the grandson of a medicine man, worked as director of the Indian Health Unit at the Indian Hospital in Shiprock on the Navajo Reservation.

Sources: *Biographical Dictionary of Indians of the Americas,* Vol. 1, p. 414.

ca. 1950s Edmund J. Ladd (Zuñi/Pueblo) was the first member of his tribe to earn a college degree in anthropology. He graduated from the University of New Mexico. His grandmother was one of the first teachers to teach the Zuñi. He served as an archaeologist for the National Park Service and has worked in Washington State and Hawaii.

Sources: *Biographical Dictionary of Indians of the Americas,* Vol. 1, p. 346; Gridley, ed., *Indians of Today,* p. 270.

1954 Evelyn Yellow Robe (Rosebud Dakota Sioux) was the first Native American to win a Fulbright scholarship. She used it to study the physiology of the larynx at the Faculté de Médecine in Paris. She attended school on the East Coast; and in high school, she was the first girl elected president of the honor society. While in Europe she lectured at several medical centers. In the United States Dr. Yellow Robe taught at Mt. Holyoke College and Vassar College and served on the staff of Northwestern University Medical School, where she taught and conducted research in audiology and voice disorders. In 1940, she was bestowed the French Government Award for Excellence; and in 1946, she was honored with the Indian Achievement Medal by the Indian Council Fire and an honorary lifetime membership.

Sources: *Biographical Dictionary of Indians of the Americas,* Vol. 2, p. 854; Dennis, *The American Indian, 1492–1976,* p. 146; Gridley, ed., *Indians of Today,* p. 481.

1956 George Blue Spruce (Laguna-San Juan Pueblo)became the first American Indian dentist as well as the first member of his tribe to enter the dental profession. He earned his degree from Creighton University. He has worked with public health facilities starting with the U.S. Navy Dental Clinic. He became involved in

Indian health and was active in Native American health organizations. He helped found the American Indian Dentists Association.

Sources: Gridley, ed., *Indians of Today*, pp. 136–37; "Indian Dentist Unites to Better Serve People," *Navajo Times*, Vol. 30, No. 21 (May 24, 1990), p. 8.

1956 Everett Ronald Rhoades (Kiowa; 1931–) was the first member of his tribe to receive a medical degree, earning it at the University of Oklahoma in 1956. In 1982 he became the first American Indian to be sworn in as director of the U.S. Indian Health Service in Washington, D.C. Following graduation, Rhoades specialized in infectious diseases as well as health administration and worked extensively with Indian health services, where he initiated several substance abuse and prevention programs. Active in children's health protection, he began the country's leading fetal alcohol syndrome prevention program. In 1991 he received the Public Health Service Distinguished Service Medal; in 1992 he was awarded the Surgeon General's Medallion and the President's Council on Physical Fitness Recognition Award; and in 1993 he earned the Indian Health Service St. Martin-Beaumont Award. Rhoades also served in the U.S. Air Force.

Sources: *Biographical Dictionary of Indians of the Americas*, Vol. 2, p. 609; Champagne, ed., *The Native North American Almanac*, p. 1143; Hirschfelder and Kreipe de Montaño, *The Native American Almanac*, p. 311; Malinowski, ed., *Notable Native Americans*, pp. 360–61.

1958 Herbert Burwell Fowler (Santee Sioux; 1919–1977), a psychiatrist specializing in Indian medicine, founded the first mental health clinic for Indians on the Fort Duchesne Ute Reservation in Utah. It was the first facility of its kind on any Indian reservation. Fowler received his B.S. from the University of Wyoming in 1942 and his M.D. from the University of Michigan in 1946. He became the first director of the Whitecloud Center at the University of Oregon, Health Sciences Center, which was supported by the National Tribal Chairmen's Association.

Sources: *Biographical Dictionary of Indians of the Americas*, Vol. 1, p. 227.

ca. 1960s Francis Quam (Zuñi) was the first Native American to become a pharmacist. Further, when he earned his B.S. from the University of Cincinnati, he became the first Native American to graduate from that institution's 110-year history. He worked on the Pine Ridge Indian Reservation and on the Turtle Mountain Reservation and has served as deputy chief at the Alaska Native Hospital in Anchorage, Alaska.

Sources: *Biographical Dictionary of Indians of the Americas*, Vol. 2; Gridley, ed., *The Indian Today*, p. 314.

ca. 1960s Richard French (Yakima; 1939–) was the first American Indian with a degree in forest management. French graduated with a B.S. from Washington State University. From 1963 to 1965, he served in the U.S. Army and attained the rank of staff sergeant.

Sources: *Biographical Dictionary of Indians of the Americas*, Vol. 1, p. 231; Gridley, ed., *Indians of Today*, p. 221.

1964 Beryl Blue Spruce (Laguna-San Juan Pueblo; 1934–1973) was the first Pueblo Indian physician. A graduate from the University of Southern California School of Medicine in 1964, Blue Spruce later became director of the Detroit

Maternal and Infant Care Project in 1973 after teaching at three medical schools and serving as president of the National Indian Physician's Association.

Sources: *Biographical Dictionary of Indians of the Americas,* Vol. 1, p. 80; Gridley, ed., *Indians of Today,* p. 138.

1973 Geneticist Frank C. Dukepoo (Hopi/Laguna Pueblo; 1943–) was the first (of two) Hopi to receive a Ph.D. in biology. He received his B.S., M.S., and Ph.D. from Arizona State University. In 1982, he founded the National Native American Honor Society, the first organization devoted exclusively to rewarding Native students for academic excellence.

Sources: *Biographical Dictionary of Indians of the Americas,* Vol. 1, p. 199; Malinowski, ed., *Notable Native Americans,* pp. 132–33; Ryan, Steve, "Dukepoo Organized Native American Honor Society," *Arizona Daily Sun,* April 22, 1990.

1992 Emigdio Ballon (Quechua) an agronomist from Cochambamba, Bolivia, began working with Seeds of Change, an organization in Santa Fe, New Mexico, dedicated to developing and reviving sustainable agriculture through organic methods. The program is particularly unique in that it collects heritage seeds from Indian tribes in the Southwest and uses polyculture (the use of a variety of seeds to ensure a harvest). This strategy assures a harvest from at least some of the seeds because some will adapt to crop difficulties such as dryness, heat, cold, insects, etc., allowing for the most adaptable seeds to be available for future planting. Ballon encourages Indian farmers to follow the rhythms of nature, and to avoid hybrid seeds so that they can remain independent of over commercialization of their farm products. Formerly Ballon was national director of high altitude crops in Bolivia. He has a degree in genetics and is considered an international expert on *quinoa,* a high altitude plant that is a staple food for Indians of the Bolivian highlands.

Sources: Ballon, Emigdio (agricultural director, Seeds of Change, Santa Fe, New Mexico), Personal communication to AnCita Benally, June 6, 1997; Witmer, Sharon, "Emigdio Ballon: Sowing the Seeds of Independence," *Tribal College,* Vol. 7, No. 2 (Fall 1995), p. 29.

SOCIAL SCIENCES

1881 Francis La Flesche (Omaha; 1857–1932) was the first American Indian anthropologist. La Flesche was the son of Joseph La Flesche, Omaha chief, and brother to Susan La Flesche, the first American Indian physician, and Susette La Flesche, the first American Indian to publish a work of fiction.

La Flesche began his career in the 1870s as a lecturer and an advisor and interpreter for the Bureau of Indian Affairs (BIA). He interpreted for Alice Fletcher in 1881, and in 1891, he collaborated with her to produce the publication entitled *A Study of Omaha Music.* They also wrote *The Omaha Tribe.* La Flesche primarily conducted the research, while Fletcher was responsible for the writing. La Flesche later wrote two books as sole author: *The Middle Five* (1900) and *A Dictionary of the Osage Language* (1932). La Flesche was also a member of staff of the U.S. Senate Committee on Indian Affairs in Washington, D.C. During his tenure there, he attended the National University School of Law and earned a bachelor of jurisprudence in 1892 and a master of law degree in 1893. In 1910, he joined the Bureau of American Ethnology, remaining there until he retired in 1930.

La Flesche demonstrated a strong interest in music other than Native American traditional forms. He composed an opera entitled *Da-o-ma, Land of Misty Waters* (1912) and worked with Charles Wakefield Cadman, who was the composer of "From the Land of Sky Blue Water." A widely acclaimed scholar, La Flesche was honored with several awards, including an honorary LL.D. by the University of Nebraska in 1926.

Sources: Champagne, ed., *The Native North American Almanac*, p. 1087; Dockstader, *Great North American Indians*, p. 144; Liberty, Margot, "Francis La Flesche: The Osage Odyssey" in her *American Indian Intellectuals*, pp. 45–59.

1939 Author, teacher, and councilor Louise Abeita Chewiwi (Laguna Pueblo; 1926–) received the first Robert P. Goodkin Award for her work in sociology. A woman of exceptional achievement, Chewiwi wrote *I Am a Pueblo Girl* at the age of thirteen; the book became a children's classic. She may be the youngest Native American ever to publish a storybook.

Sources: *Biographical Dictionary of Indians of the Americas*, Vol. 1, p. 125; Gridley, ed., *Indians of Today*, p. 120.

1950s Distinguished anthropologist and author, Frederick J. Dockstader (Oneida/Navajo; 1919–) was the first Native American employed as a staff ethnologist at the Cranbrook Institute of Sciences in 1950. In 1952, Dockstader became the curator of anthropology at Dartmouth College. He moved to assistant director of the Museum of the American Indian in New York City in 1955, then director in 1960. Dockstader also served as commissioner of the Indian Arts and Crafts Board for the Interior Department in 1955.

Sources: *Biographical Dictionary of Indians of the Americas*, Vol. 1, p. 190.

1952 Edward Pasqual Dozier (Santa Clara Pueblo) was the first member of his tribe to earn a Ph.D. in anthropology. He was also one of the first to advance the idea of developing a curriculum for American Indian studies. Dozier was also known as an advocate for Indian rights. He earned a B.A. and M.A. from the University of New Mexico, then a Ph.D. from the University of California, Los Angeles, in 1952. He specialized in Pueblo linguistics, having studied the language of the Tewa people who moved to the Hopi pueblos. He became interested in anthropology while serving in the U.S. Air Force during World War II.

During his career as a scholar, Dozier was employed in academic positions at several major universities, including the University of Oregon, University of Arizona, University of Minnesota, and the University of the Philippines. He published two major books: *Hano, a Pueblo Community in Arizona* and *Pueblo Indians in the Southwest*. His scholarly accomplishments were considered major contributions in providing a genuine account of Pueblo cultures and languages. In March 1970, Dozier participated in the First Convocation of American Indian Scholars at Princeton.

Sources: *Biographical Dictionary of Indians of the Americas*, Vol. 1, p. 195; Johansen and Grinde, *The Encyclopedia of Native American Biography*, p. 114; Markowitz, *American Indians*, Vol. 1.

1969 Maxine Paddock Reichert (Athabascan) was the first Alaska Native to earn a degree in psychology from Reed College. Daughter of Constance Harper, a noted leader, she has been active in Alaska Native issues, serving as assistant secretary of the Sealaska Corporation and working with the United Indian Planners Association. In 1977, Reichert coordinated the first caucus of Alaska Native Women at the Alaska Federation of Natives. In 1980, she produced a film entitled *Hoonah Symposium: A Village Model for Development.*

Sources: Anderson, ed., *Ohoyo One Thousand,* p. 97; *Biographical Dictionary of Indians of the Americas,* Vol. 1, p. 507.

SPORTS AND GAMES

BASEBALL

1897 Louis Sockalexis (Penobscot) was the first known American Indian athlete to sign with a major league baseball team, the Cleveland Spiders. Although he played only a short time, he was considered one of the greatest baseball athletes of his time. Purportedly, the Cleveland Indians team was so named in honor of his skills as a superb athlete.

Sources: Aaseng, *Athletes,* pp. 2–3, 151; Oxendine, *American Indian Sports Heritage,* pp. 251–52.

1903 Charles A. Bender (Ojibwa; 1884–1954), nicknamed "Chief," became a major league baseball player for the Philadelphia Athletics (A's). From 1903 to 1917, he was an outstanding pitcher and established a consistent record of sportsmanship and great skill in the development of baseball. While playing for the Athletics under Coach Connie Mack, Bender and his teammates won the World Series three times, and the American League pennant five times. In 1910, 1911, and 1914, he led the league in strikeouts. On May 12, 1910, he pitched a no-hitter against the Cleveland Indians. After leaving the Athletics, Bender played for Baltimore and then the Philadelphia Nationals. In his entire career he won two hundred games and lost 111. After retiring from baseball he was a coach at the U.S. Naval Academy and for two professional teams. In 1953, Bender was inducted into the Baseball Hall of Fame. Bender attended Carlisle Indian School during the heyday of its athletic program. and then went to Dickinson College where he earned a degree.

Sources: Aaseng, *Athletes,* pp. 1–14; *Biographical Dictionary of Indians of the Americas,* Vol. 1, p. 48; Davis, ed, *Native America in the Twentieth Century,* p. 613; Johansen and Grinde, *The Encyclopedia of Native American Biography,* p. 25; Oxendine, *American Indian Sports Heritage,* p. 243; Thompson, S. I., "The American Indian in the Major Leagues," *Baseball Research Journal,* Vol. 13, pp. 1–7.

Early 1930s Walter Perry Johnson (Paiute; 1887–1946) has been called the fastest right-handed pitcher in baseball history. While playing twenty-one seasons in the major leagues, Johnson set several records during his 414 winning games: most shutouts (113), most strikeouts (3,497), and most scoreless innings (56). In 1939, Johnson was one of the first men to be inducted into the Baseball Hall of Fame.

Sources: *Biographical Dictionary of Indians of the Americas,* Vol. 1, p. 319.

Walter Perry Johnson.

1951 Allie P. Reynolds (Creek) was a prominent pitcher for the Cleveland Indians and the New York Yankees. In 1943 and 1952, he led the American League in strikeouts and, in 1952, had the best earned-run average. In 1945 and 1952, he made the most pitching shutouts. In 1951, he became the first player in American League history to pitch two no-hit games. He was the second among contemporary players to have thirty-seven shutouts. He had seven world series wins.

Sources: *Biographical Dictionary of Indians of the Americas,* Vol. 2, p. 608; Oxendine, *American Indian Sports Heritage,* p. 278; Gridley, ed., *Indians of Today,* pp. 148–49.

1971 Austin Ben Tincup (Cherokee) was inducted into the Oklahoma Baseball Hall of Fame. He was one of the first professional American Indian coaches. He played major league baseball beginning in 1914.

Sources: Oxendine, *American Indian Sports Heritage,* pp. 253–54.

BASKETBALL

1924 Clyde James (Modoc) set school and conference scoring records playing basketball for Southwest Missouri State. He was inducted into the American Indian Athletic Hall of Fame in 1977.

Sources: Oxendine, *American Indian Sports Heritage,* p. 147

1996 Ryneldi Becenti (Navajo) became the first Navajo woman to be inducted into the American Indian Athletic Hall of Fame. Becenti is also the first Native American woman to play professional basketball for a foreign team—the Swiss team in 1995. At Arizona State University she played on the women's basketball team and established individual game records. She was ranked an outstanding player in 1992 and 1993 and was a member of the first-team All-Pacific 10 Conference. In her senior year at Arizona State University she was an honorable mention All-American.

Sources: Aaseng, *Athletes,* pp. 91–100; "Becenti Elected into Indian Hall of Fame," *Navajo Times,* Vol. 35, No. 19 (May 9, 1996), p. B-1; *Insight,* Arizona State University, May 24, 1996, p. 3.

BOXING

1939 Chester L. "Chet" Ellis (Seneca) was the first American Indian to win boxing championships at the national and international levels. In 1939, he won the national Golden Gloves Champion in the bantam weight division and later won the International Golden Glove Championship. He was inducted into the American Indian Athletic Hall of Fame in 1977.

Sources: Oxendine, *American Indian Sports Heritage,* p. 273.

CHESS

1990 Jason Stevens (Navajo) captured first place in the "B" section of the eighteenth Annual World Chess Open held in Philadelphia. He was the first Native

Opposite page:
Walter Perry Johnson, one of the first men inducted into the Baseball Hall of Fame, and perhaps the fastest right-hand pitcher in baseball history, is shown here in the 1927 World Series. Johnson pitched a four-inning shutout to help his team with a Game 7 victory.

American to win in any section in a World Open. He won eight of nine games to take top honors over three hundred other players.

Sources: "Stevens Wins First Place at Annual World Chess Open," *Navajo Times,* Vol 30, No. 28 (July 12, 1990), p. 9.

FOOTBALL

1897 Frank Hudson (Laguna Pueblo) was selected to football's Walter Camp All-American Second Team in 1897. He was the first recorded American Indian to be inducted.

Sources: Oxendine, *American Indian Sports Heritage,* p. 247.

1901 Martin F. Wheelock (Oneida) was selected for the football All-American Second Team in 1901. In 1902, he was placed on the All-University team by the *Philadelphia Inquirer.* In 1980, he was inducted into the American Indian Athletic Hall of Fame.

Sources: Oxendine, *American Indian Sports Heritage,* p. 255.

1907 Albert Andrew Exendine (Delaware; 1884–?), born in Bartlesville, Indian Territory, was a nationally known football coach, who accomplished several firsts. Exendine attended Carlisle Indian School, where he played six years of varsity football under Glenn "Pop" Warner. He made football history when the Carlisle team constructed the first recognized forward passing combination in modern football. In 1908, Exendine became the assistant football coach at Carlisle, under Pop Warner. During that time, he coached players who later became famous, including Jim Thorpe. Exendine graduated from Dickinson Law School in 1912. From 1913 to 1922, he was head coach at Georgetown University, probably the first Indian to become head coach of a college team. At Georgetown, Exendine led his team to its highest scoring record in 1916. He then became head coach at Washington State University, where he created more new techniques, such as the solid, deceptive passing attack. Exendine's last position as a university head coach was near his home territory, Oklahoma State University. He was inducted into the American Indian Athletic Hall of Fame in 1972.

Sources: *Biographical Dictionary of Indians of the Americas,* Vol. 1, p. 218; Oxendine, *American Indian Sports Heritage,* p. 245.

1919 Gustavus Welch (Ojibwa) served as head football coach at Washington State College, possibly the first American Indian to coach at a major college.

Sources: Oxendine, *American Indian Sports Heritage,* p. 254.

1920s The Oorang Indians, the first professional football team consisting of all American Indian players, was formed in the 1920s. It comprised mostly former athletes of the great Carlisle teams and achieved only modest success. The name "Oorang" was the name of dog kennels in La Rue, Ohio, where the team originated.

Sources: Oxendine, *American Indian Sports Heritage,* p. 224.

1930 Thomas "Wahoo" Yarr (Snohomish) played football on the national championship team in 1930, and was captain of the 1931 national team. In 1931, he was also selected as a member of the Associated Press All-American team as a center. He was inducted in to the American Indian Athletic Hall of Fame in 1982.

Sources: Oxendine, *American Indian Sports Heritage,* pp. 255, 299.

1966 Joseph N. Guyon (White Earth Chippewa; 1892–1971) was inducted into the National Professional Football Hall of Fame in 1966, possibly the first American Indian to be inducted. Guyon was one of the original inductees into the American Indian Athletic Hall of Fame in 1972. He attended Carlisle Indian School from 1911 to 1914 and Georgia Technical University from 1917 to 1918. Guyon's team was selected for the All Indian Football Team in 1917 and 1918. He played both professional football and professional baseball.

Sources: *Biographical Dictionary of Indians of the Americas,* Vol. 1, p. 258; Oxendine, *American Indian Sports Heritage,* pp. 192, 246.

GOLF

1974 Golfer Rod Curl (Wintu) won the Colonial National Open in 1974, edging Jack Nicklaus by one stroke. Curl was one of the first American Indians to compete at a national level in golf.

Sources: Oxendine, *American Indian Sports Heritage,* p. 273.

LACROSSE

1683 The sport of baggataway (lacrosse) was described by French missionaries for the first time. It is an Ojibwa sport filled with much ritual meaning.

Sources: Champagne, ed., *Chronology of Native North American History,* p. 74.

RODEO EVENTS

1881 Bill Picket (Cherokee/African American) originated the steer wrestling or bulldogging event in the sport of rodeo. He used a technique that he devised from observing a small dog bite the lips of a bull and thereby take total control of it. Picket thought if a dog could do it so could a human. By 1905 he was performing this technique, and other cowboys were beginning to adopt it. In the same year he joined the Miller Brothers' 101 Ranch Wild West Show and performed for audiences. In 1971 he was admitted to the select company of the National Cowboy Hall of Fame. In 1994 his image was to be used on a stamp series called "Legends of the West." A picture of his brother Ben was used instead; and by the time the mistake was discovered the stamp had already been printed. Rather than issue a stamp with the wrong information, the Post Office recalled the entire series, the first time such a move ever happened.

Sources: Slatta, *The Cowboy Encyclopedia,* pp. 278–80.

ca. 1902 Jackson Sundown (Nez Percé), also known as Waaya-Tonah-Toesits-Kahn, won the first world rodeo championship record in bronco riding. He was fifty years old when he became champion.

Sources: *Rodeo in America,* p. 13; *Western Horsemen,* September 1967, pp. 36–37.

1970s Dean Jackson (Navajo) founded the All-Indian Rodeo Cowboy Association and the Indian National Finals Rodeo. Jackson, himself a cowboy, was committed to advancing Navajo education as well as working to improve the treatment of Indians in rodeo. He was an educator who was a past president of Navajo Community College and the superintendent of Chinle Public School District at the time of his death. He served on the board of directors of the Native American Church of Navajoland.

Sources: Iverson, Peter, "The Road to Reappearance: Indians and Cattle Ranching in the American West," *Tribal College,* Vol. 7, No. 2 (Fall 1995), pp. 23–26; Iverson, *When Indians Became Cowboys,* pp. 191–96; Jackson, Jack (Phoenix, Arizona), Personal communication to AnCita Bennaly, February 1996.

SOFTBALL

1993 Ed Morrissette (Ojibwa) was the first Native American inducted into the Minnesota Softball Hall of Fame.

Sources: Champagne, *Chronology of Native North American History,* p. 494.

TABLE TENNIS

1972 At age seventeen, Angelita Rosul (Sioux) became the first American Indian woman to make the U.S. Women's Table Tennis National Team. Rosul was the first woman selected for the American Indian Athletic Hall of Fame in 1973.

Sources: Oxendine, *American Indian Sports Heritage,* p. 260.

TRACK AND FIELD

1861 Louis "Deerfoot" Bennett (Seneca; 1830–1896) was the first professional American Indian track athlete. He ran professionally in the United States and Great Britain. Bennett was considered one of the best professional runners of his time. He performed his most prominent running between 1861 and 1863, pacing close to five minutes a mile.

Sources: Oxendine, *American Indian Sports Heritage,* p. 242.

1876 Big Hawk Chief (Pawnee) was the first man to run the mile in under four minutes. His record, although unofficial, was recorded by two army officers in 1876. The officers meticulously measured the course. After they clocked Big Hawk at three minutes and fifty-eight seconds they remeasured the course and

timed him again, with the same results. This record held for more than seventy-five years.

Sources: Johansen and Grinde, *The Encyclopedia of Native American Biography*, pp. 31–32; Oxendine, *American Indian Sports Heritage*, pp. 243–44.

1907 Thomas Longboat (Onondaga) won the Boston Marathon in 1907. His win broke the previous record by five minutes with a time of two hours, twenty-four minutes, and twenty-nine and four-fifths seconds. He is considered the first "world's professional marathon champion."

Sources: Oxendine, *American Indian Sports Heritage*, pp. 87, 249.

1928 Andy Payne (Cherokee) won the transcontinental foot race known as "The Great Cross-Country Marathon Race" that marked the opening of Route 66. It extended from Los Angeles to New York City. Payne ran a distance of 3,422.3 miles in 573 hours, four minutes and thirty-four seconds. He later earned a law degree from Oklahoma City University and served as clerk of the Oklahoma Supreme Court for more than forty years.

Sources: *Give It Your Best Shot*, dedication page.

1930 Wilson "Buster" Charles (Oneida; 1908–) was a champion track and field, football, and basketball athlete. In 1930 he won the decathlon championships in both the renowned Kansas Relays and the National Amateur Athletic Union (AAU) competitions. In 1932 he was a member of the U.S. Olympic team, placing fourth in the decathlon.

Sources: *Biographical Dictionary of Indians of the Americas*, Vol. 1, p. 118.

In 1936 Ellison J. ("Tarzan") Brown won the Boston Marathon in two hours, 33 minutes, 40 4/5 seconds; he won the race again in 1939.

Wilson "Buster" Charles.

1936 Ellison "Tarzan" Brown (Narraganset) won the Boston Marathon in 1936 and 1939.

Sources: Oxendine, *American Indian Sports Heritage,* p. 88.

1978 Chuck Foster (Navajo) was the first Navajo to be inducted into the American Indian Athletic Hall of Fame for his excellence in track and field. He held the fastest cross-country time in the nation for junior college in 1993.

Sources: "Becenti Elected into Indian Hall of Fame," *Navajo Times,* Vol. 35, No. 19 (May 9, 1996), p. B-1.

1984 Al Waquie (Jemez Pueblo) won the Pike's Peak Marathon twice and set a record that lasted nearly a decade. In addition, in 1984, 1985, and 1986, he won the Empire State Building Race. Waquie specialized in long distance mountain running.

Sources: Aaseng, *Athletes,* pp. 85–92.

1992 Phillip Castillo (Acoma Pueblo) was the first Native American to win a collegiate cross country title. In 1992, he became the NCAA Division II National cross country champion. He also earned nine All-American honors in other cross country and track meets.

Sources: *Give It Your Best Shot,* p. 11.

TRAPPING

1989 Mike Halona (Navajo) was the first Native American to be awarded the "National Trapper of the Year Award." The award was given by the National Trappers' Association in recognition of Halona's efforts to establish programs related to predator animal control, animal damage control, and the proper use of pesticides for animal damage control, and his commitment in training individuals in the proper purpose and use of trapping techniques. His goal has been to work for the benefit of the people and resources of the Navajo Nation.

Sources: Arviso, Tom. "Halona Awarded National Trapper of the Year," *Navajo Times,* Vol. 27, No. 36 (September 7, 1989), p. B-4.

Lewis Tewanima.

THE OLYMPICS

1907 Lewis Tewanima (Hopi; 1879–1969) is considered one of the greatest long distance runners in U.S. track history. Originating from Shongopovi, Arizona, Tewanima attended Carlisle Indian School from 1907 to 1912. He was a member of the U.S. Olympic Team in 1908 and 1912. At the 1912 games, Tewanima set a U.S. record for the 10,000 meter race, winning a silver medal. This record was broken by Billy Mills (Oglala Lakota Sioux) in the 1964 Olympic Games. Tewanima also set the world record for the indoor ten mile at Madison Square Garden. In 1954, he was selected as the Helms Foundation member of the All-Time U.S. Track and Field Team. In 1972, he was inducted into the American Indian Athletic Hall of Fame.

Sources: Aaseng, *Athletes,* p. 87; Champagne, ed., *The Native North American Almanac,* p. 1175; Oxendine, *American Indian Sports Heritage,* pp. 89, 253.

JIM THORPE (1888–1953)

1912 Jim Thorpe (Sac-Fox; 1888–1953) won gold medals in the pentathlon and the decathlon at the 1912 Olympics in Sweden. Thorpe played All-American lacrosse, basketball, and football in college, professional baseball from 1913 to 1919, and then went on to play professional football. He was the first president of the American Professional Football Association. Thorpe was called the "greatest athlete in the world" by the King of Sweden and voted the greatest athlete of the first half of the century by the Associated Press in 1950. Although he held world records in track and field, his gold medals were taken from him based on a technicality—he had accepted money for playing sports. The medals were returned posthumously seventy years later on October 13, 1982.

Jim Thorpe.

Sources: Aaseng, *Athletes*, pp. 15–34; Champagne, ed., *The Native North American Almanac*, p. 1177; Davis, ed., *Native America in the Twentieth Century*, p. 613; Oxendine, *American Indian Sports Heritage*, p. 253.

1924 Clarence Able (Sault Ste. Marie Chippewa) captained the U.S. Olympic hockey team in 1924, becoming the first known American Indian to do so.

Sources: Aaseng, *Athletes*, p. 78.

1932 Charles Curtis (Osage/Kaw), as vice president of the United States in Herbert Hoover's administration, was sent to officially open the International Olympics held in Los Angeles. He has been the only Native American to officially open an Olympic Games.

Sources: Costas, Bob. Olympic Opening Ceremonies telecast commentary, NBC News, July 1996.

1948 Jesse B. "Cab" Renick (Choctaw) captained the U.S. Olympic basketball team, which won a gold medal at the 1948 Olympic Games. His basketball career included All-American honors in the late 1930s at Oklahoma A&M, National Amateur Athletic Union (AAU) basketball All-American in 1947 and 1948, and coach/player for the Phillips 66 Oilers, where he led the team during their first three seasons to a 153–3 record.

Sources: Aaseng, *Athletes*, p. 94; Mallon and Bock, *Quest for Gold*; Oxendine, *American Indian Sports Heritage*, p. 277.

1961 Successful businessman A. E. Hagberg (Inuit) co-founded the World Eskimo-Indian Olympics. Hagberg worked his way up from doing odd jobs to becoming vice-president of Wien Consolidated Airlines.

Sources: *Biographical Dictionary of Indians of the Americas*, Vol. 1, p. 259.

1964 Benjamin Nighthorse Campbell (Northern Cheyenne; 1933–), the only American Indian to become a member of the U.S. Olympic Judo team, captained the team to win the gold medal in the 1964 Olympics in Tokyo. During his association with the sport he won a number of honors. From 1960 to 1964, Campbell was the Pacific Coast judo champion six times, U.S. Open champion three times, and a gold medalist in the 1963 Pan-American Games. He taught judo and published a book entitled *Championship Judo: Drill Training*. In addition, he is an accomplished jeweler and a political leader, having served as the first Native American in the Colorado state legislature, and the first Native American since Charles Curtis in the U.S. House of Representatives and the U.S. Senate.

Sources: Aaseng, *Athletes*, p. xvi; Ballard, J. Kevin, "A Salute to Native American Olympians," *Native Peoples*, (Summer 1992), pp. 32–37; Hirschfelder, *Artists and Craftspeople*, pp. 97–102; Malinowski, ed., *Notable Native Americans*, pp. 64–65.

WILLIAM "BILLY" MILLS (1938–)

Billy Mills.

1964 William "Billy" Mills (Oglala Lakota Sioux; 1938–) won a gold medal for the 10,000 meter race at the 1964 Olympic games, breaking the previous record set by Lewis Tewanima (Hopi) in 1907 and setting the world's record. He was the first American Indian and first American to win a medal in an Olympic distance race. A virtual unknown at the time, Mills turned in a performance that is considered one of the greatest upsets in sports history. In 1965, Mills set a world record in the six-mile run. He was enshrined in two halls of fame: the National Track and Field Hall of Fame and the American Indian Athletic Hall of Fame.

Sources: Aaseng, *Athletes*, p. 45–54; Champagne, ed., *The Native North American Almanac*, p. 1108; Davis, *Native America in the Twentieth Century*, pp. 614–615; Oxendine, *American Indian Sports Heritage*, p. 277.

1969 Frank Medina (Cherokee) was the head trainer at the International Games for the Deaf Olympics in Finland and again in Belgrade, Yugoslavia. Medina was an athletic trainer who traveled the world, participating in the Olympics in London in 1948 and Mexico City in 1965, probably the first American Indian to do so.

Sources: *Biographical Dictionary of Indians of the Americas*, Vol. 1, p. 416.

1970 The first First Nations Arctic Winter Games were held in Yellowknife, Northwest Territories, on March 9–14, 1970.

Sources: Champagne, ed., *Chronology of Native North American History*, p. 369.

1991 Gary Begay (Navajo) was the only Native American member, out of sixty-six teammates, on the Arizona Special Olympics team. He captured first place honors in the 400 and 1,500 meter run at the Arizona Special Olympic Championships in Tempe. He was slated to participate in the 400 and 1,500 meter runs and in the 4x100 meter relay.

Sources: "Rock 'n' Roll Superstar Meets Special Olympian," *Navajo Times*, Vol. 31, No. 27 (July 3, 1991), p. 1.

1991 Benny Hathle (Navajo) was the only Navajo and the only Native American to represent Utah in the Special Olympics. Participating in the 1990 International Special Olympics as a runner, he won a gold medal.

Sources: "Running Is a Way of Life for Special Athlete," *Navajo Times*, Vol. 31, No. 28 (July 11, 1991), p. B-1.

Opposite page:
Billy Mills crossing the finish line to win the 1964 Tokyo Olympics 10,000-meter race. No American had won a medal in this event since Lewis Tewanima placed second in 1912.

1996 Phillip Castillo (Acoma Pueblo) carried the Olympic Torch on May 12, through Manitou Springs in Colorado. He was one of fifty-five hundred community heroes selected by the United Way for their leadership and role model qualities. In addition, he is the only Native American, to date, to win a collegiate cross country title. He and his teammates captured the NCAA Division II cross country championships in Slippery Rock, Pennsylvania, on November 21, 1992. It was the first meet in which the Adams State College team participated; they won the top five spots and the teammates ran within five seconds of each other. For his part, Castillo said that he ran for his grandmother who had died just a few days earlier. In November 1995 he was awarded the Giant Steps Award for Courageous Athlete of the Year.

Sources: "Carriers of the Torch," *Navajo Times,* Vol. 35, No. 19 (May 9, 1996) p. B-1; Fischbach, Steve, "Acoma Man Runs into Success and Shares it with Others," *Indian Country Today,* Vol. 12 No. 30 (January 21, 1993), p. B-4.

1996 Valencia Tilden (Navajo) was the only Navajo and Native American woman to carry the Olympic torch in the 1996 Olympic Torch Relay. She ran on May 12 through the Sac and Fox Nation near Prague, Oklahoma, the birthplace of Jim Thorpe. She was one of Coca-Cola's twenty-five hundred "Share the Spirit: Who Would You Choose?" torchbearers. These individuals were chosen from all walks of life. Tilden is also actively involved in the youth leadership development organization, Wings of America. In her senior high school year, Tilden won the New Mexico state cross country championship.

Sources: "Carriers of the Torch," *Navajo Times,* Vol. 35, No. 19 (May 9, 1996) p. B-1.

1996 Cheri Becerra (Omaha) was the first Native American to participate in the Paralympics, representing the United States. She set the world record in the 400 meter race and set four U.S. records in the 100, 200, 400, and 800 meter wheelchair racing events. Becerra received other medals for her participation in the Paralympics in Paris. She won silver medals in the 100 and 200 meter events, and bronze medals in the 400 and 800 meter events. At age four, she contracted an unknown virus that destroyed the ability to use her legs. Wheelchair-bound since then, she became involved in Special Olympics competition. With only two years of competition against other wheelchair-bound athletes, Becerra has had tremendous impact on the sport.

Sources: Coffen, Kimberly, "Paralympic Medalist Tells Stories, Signs Autographs," *Lincoln Journal Star;* Duggan, Joe, "Nebraska City Woman Eyes Paralympics Title," *Lincoln Journal Star;* State of Nebraska, Commission on Indian Affairs, Lincoln Nebraska *(for further information).*

BIBLIOGRAPHY

A

Aaseng, Nathan. *Athletes*. New York: Facts on File, 1995.

The American Indian: A Multimedia Encyclopedia, CD-ROM 2.0. New York: Facts on File, 1995.

Anderson, Owanah, editor. *Ohoyo One Thousand: A Resource Guide of American Indian/Alaska Native Women, 1982.* Wichita Falls, Texas: Ohoyo Resource Center, 1982.

B

Bataille, Gretchen M., editor. *Native American Women.* New York: Garland Publishing, 1993.

Bataille, Gretchen, and Kate Sands. *American Indian Women, Telling Their Lives.* Lincoln: University of Nebraska Press, 1984.

Biographical Dictionary of Indians of the Americas, two volumes. Newport Beach: American Indian Publishers, 1991.

Bird, Traveller. *Tell Them They Lie.* Los Angeles: Westernlore Publishers, 1971.

Bremser, Martha, editor. *International Dictionary of Ballet,* two volumes. Detroit: St. James Press, 1993.

C

Champagne, Duane, editor. *Chronology of Native North American History.* Detroit: Gale, 1994.

Champagne, Duane, editor. *Native America: A Portrait of the Peoples.* Detroit: Visible Ink Press, 1994.

Champagne, Duane, editor. *The Native American Almanac.* Detroit: Gale, 1994.

D

Danky, James P., editor, and Maureen E. Hady, compiler. *Native American Periodicals and Newspapers, 1828–1982.* Westport, Connecticut: Greenwood Press, 1984.

Davis, Mary B., editor. *Native America in the Twentieth Century.* New York: Garland Publishing, 1994.

Debo, Angie. *And Still the Waters Run.* New York: Gordion Press, 1966.

Debo, Angie. *The Road to Disappearance.* Norman: University of Oklahoma Press, 1941.

Dinéltsoi, Mazii, *Saad.* Princeton, New Jersey: Lenape Yaa Deez'a, 1995.

Dennis, Henry C. *The American Indian, 1492–1976.* Dobbs Ferry, New York: Oceana Publications, 1977.

Dockstader, Frederick J. *Great North American Indians.* New York: Van Nostrand Reinhold, 1977.

E

Edmunds, David. *American Indian Leaders.* Lincoln: University of Nebraska Press, 1980.

F

Ferris, Jeri. *Native American Doctor: The Story of Susan La Flesche Picotte.* Minneapolis: Carolrhoda Books, 1991.

Foreman, Carolyn Thomas. *Oklahoma Imprints, 1835–1907.* Norman: University of Oklahoma Press, 1936.

Fox, Isabella. *Solomon Juneau: A Biography with Sketches of the Juneau Family.* Milwaukee: Evening Wisconsin Press, 1916

Francis, Lee. *Native Time: A Historical Time-line of Native Americans*. New York: St. Mary's Press, 1996.

Furtaw, Julia C., editor, *Native Americans Information Directory*. Detroit, Gale, 1993.

G

Gettuso, John, editor. *Native America*. Singapore: Apa Publications, 1991.

Gilman, Carolyn, and Mary Jane Schneider, *The Way to Independence*. St. Paul: Minnesota Historical Society Press, 1987.

Gridley, Marion E., *American Indian Women*. New York: Hawthorn Books, 1974.

Gridley, Marion E., *Contemporary American Indian Leaders*. New York: Dodd, Mead, 1972.

Gridley, Marion E., editor. *Indians of Today*. Crawfordsville, Indiana: Lakeside Press, B. B. Donnellly & Sons, 1936; Chicago: Millar Publishing Company, 1947; Chicago: I.C.F.P., 1960.

H

Haury, Emil W. *The Hohokam, Desert Farmers and Craftsmen*. Tucson: University of Arizona Press, 1978.

Hirschfelder, Arlene. *Artists and Craftspeople*. New York: Facts on File, 1994.

Hirschfelder, Arlene, and Martha Kreipe de Montaño. *The Native American Almanac: A Portrait of Native America Today*. New York: Prentice Hall, 1993.

Hirshfelder, Arlene, and Paulette Molin. *The Encyclopedia of Native American Religions*. New York: Facts on File, 1992.

Hodge, Frederick Webb, editor. *Handbook of American Indans North of Mexico*. New York: Rowman and Littlefield, 1965.

Hoxie, Frederick E., editor. *Encyclopedia of North American Indians*. New York: Houghton Mifflen, 1961.

I

Iverson, Peter. *Carlos Montezuma and the Changing World of American Indians*. Albuquerque: University of New Mexico Press, 1982.

Iverson, Peter. *When Indians Became Cowboys*. Norman: University of Oklahoma Press, 1994.

J

Jimenez, Carlos M. *The Mexican American Heritage*. Berkeley: TQS Publications, 1992.

Johansen, Bruce E., and Donald A. Grinde, Jr. *The Encyclopedia of Native American Biography*. New York: Henry Holt, 1997.

K

Kane, Joseph Nathan. *Famous First Facts*. New York: H. W. Wilson, 1964.

Kappler, Charles J., editor. *Indian Affairs: Laws and Treaties*. Washington, D.C.: U.S. Government Printing Office, 1979.

Katz, William Loren. *Black Indians*. Atheneum: Ethnic Publications, 1982.

Keith, Mike. *Signals in the Air: Native Broadcasting in America*. Westport, Connecticut: Praeger, 1995.

Koegler, Horst. *Dictionary of Ballet*. New York: Oxford University Press, 1982.

L

Lamb, Jerome D., Jerry Ruff, and William C. Sherman, editors. *Scattered Steeples, the Fargo Diocese: A Written History of its Centennial*. Fargo, North Dakota: Burch, Londergan, and Lynch, 1988.

Leitch, Barbara A. *Chronology of the American Indian*. St. Clair Shores, Michigan: Scholarly Publishers, 1975.

Leitch, Barbara A. *A Concise Dictionary of Indian Tribes of North America*. Algonac, Michigan, Reference Publications, 1979.

Liberty, Margot, editor. *American Indian Intellectuals*. St. Paul: West Publishing, 1978.

Littlefield, Daniel F., Jr., and James W. Parins, editors. *American Indian and Alaska Native Newspapers and Periodicals, 1826–1924*. New York: Greenwood Press, 1984.

Littlefield, Daniel F., Jr., and James W. Parins, editors. *American Indian and Alaska Native Newspapers and Periodicals, 1925–1970*. New York: Greenwood Press, 1986.

Littlefield, Daniel F., Jr., and James W. Parins, editors. *American Indian and Alaska Native Newspapers and Periodicals, 1971–1985*. New York: Greenwood Press, 1986.

Livingston, Lili Cockerille. *American Indian Ballerinas*. Norman: University of Oklahoma Press, 1997.

M

Malinowski, Sharon, editor, *Notable Native Americans*. Detroit: Gale, 1995.

Mallon, Bill, and Ian Bock. *Quest for Gold.* New York: Leisure Press, 1984

Markowitz, Harvey, editor. *American Indians,* three volumes. Pasadena: Salem Press, 1995.

McBeth, Kate C. *The Nez Perce Indians Since Lewis and Clark.* New York: Fleming H. Revell, 1908.

Menchu, Rigoberta. *Let Me Speak.* London: Verso, 1984.

N

Nies, Judith. *Native American History.* New York: Ballantine Books, 1996.

O

O'Beirne, F., and E. S. O'Beirne. *The Indian Territory: Its Chiefs, Legislators, and Leading Men.* St Louis: C. B. Woodward, 1892.

Ortiz, Alfonso, editor. *Handbook of North American Indians,* Vol. 10: *History of Indian-White Relations.* Washington, D.C.: Smithsonian Institution, 1983

Oxendine, Joseph B. *American Indian Sports Heritage.* Lincoln: University of Nebraska Press, 1995.

P

Patterson, Lotsee, and Mary Ellen Snodgrass. *Indian Terms of the Americas.* Englewood, Colorado: Libraries Unlimited, 1994.

Paulson, T. Emogene, and Lloyd R. Moses. *Who's Who among the Sioux.* Vermillion: Institute of American Indian Studies, University of South Dakota, 1988.

Prucha, Francis Paul. *American Indian Treaties: The History of a Political Anomaly.* Berkeley: University of California Press, 1994.

R

Ray, Grace Ernestine. *Early Oklahoma Newspapers.* Norman: University of Oklahoma Press, 1928.

S

Schoolcraft, Henry R. *History of the Indian Tribes of the United States: 1793–1864.* Philadelphia: J.B. Lippincott, 1853–1857.

Self-Guiding Tour for The National Hall of Fame for Famous American Indians and Anadarko Visitors' Center, Anadarko, Oklahoma.

Slatta, Richard W. *The Cowboy Encyclopedia.* Santa Barbara, California: ABC-CLIO, 1994.

Smith, Thomas R. *Choctaw Indians: Americans, First Class.* Ventura, California: Teesmith Enterprises, 1988.

Sonneborn, Liz. *Performers.* New York: Facts on File, 1995.

Stoutenburgh, John L., Jr. *Dictionary of the American Indian.* New York: Philosophical Library, 1960,

Szasz, Margaret. *Education and the American Indian: The Road to Self-Determination since 1928.* Albuquerque: University of New Mexico Press, 1974.

Szasz, Margaret Connell, *Indian Education in the American Colonies, 1607–1783.* Albuquerque: University of New Mexico Press, 1988.

T

Thatcher, B. B. *Indian Biography; or, An Historical Account of those Individuals Who Have Been Distinguished.* New York: Harper and Brothers, 1840.

W

Waldman, Carl. *Who Was Who in Native American History.* New York: Facts on File, 1990.

Walker, Paul Robert. *American Indian Lives: Spiritual Leaders.* New York: Facts on File, 1995.

Washburn, Wilcomb E. *Handbook of North American Indians: History of Indian-White Relations.* Washington, D.C.: Smithsonian Institution, 1988.

Wearne, Phillip. *Return of the Indian: Conquest and Revival in the Americas.* Philadelphia: Temple University Press, 1996,

Weatherford, Jack. *Indian Givers: How the Indians of the Americas Transformed the World.* New York: Fawcett Columbine, 1988.

Wissler, Clark. *Indians of the United States: Four Centuries of their History and Culture.* New York: Doubleday, Doran, 1940.

Witalec, Janet, editor. *Native North American Literature.* Detroit: Gale, 1994.

Wiget, Andrew, editor. *Dictionary of Native American Literature.* New York: Garland Publishing, 1994.

Wooden, Wayne S. *Rodeo in America.* Lawrence: University of Kansas Press, 1996.

INDEX BY YEAR

GENERAL INDEX

A

ABC News, 125
ABC Television, 125
Abel, Clarence, 219
Abenaki
   language, 87
   leadership, 34
   Penobscot dialect, 87
   religious leaders, 162, 176
   writers, 106
Academy Award, 149
Academy of Variety and Cabaret Artists, 155
Acamapichtli, 84
Account of the Chippewa Indians, An 101
acid-etching of shells, 203
Acoya, Andrew, 47
acting troupes, 156
ACTION Drug Alliance, 41
activism, 24, 139, 189, 193–94
actors, 148–49, 154, 156–57
Adahooniligii, 119
"Address to the Whites, An" 99
adoption, 199
Affiliated Tribes of Northwest Indians, 58
affirmative action, 196
agronomy, 49, 63, 203, 208
Ahenakew, Edward, 171
Air Force Commendation Medal, 130–31, 138, 141
aka Grafitti Man, 155
Akers, Dolly Smith, 58
Akipa, 68
Akwesasne Freedom, 123
Alaska state legislature, 59, 61
Alaska Conservation Society, 192
Alaska Federation of Native Associations (AFN), 192
Alaska Human Rights Commission, 192
Alaska Methodist University, 192
Alaska Native Claims Settlement Act (ANCSA), 188, 192, 194
Alaska Natives
   education, 43
   rights, 192, 210
   women, 210

Alaska Public Radio Network, 124
Alaska State Community Action Program, Inc., 192
Albuquerque Indian School, 6
Alcatraz Island takeover (1969), 75, 139, 193, 196
Alchesay, 129
alcoholism, 99
Aleut
   education, 45
   land rights, 188
Alexander, Hartley Burr, 3
Algonquin language, 86, 87
All-American Indian Award, 75
All American Indian Days, 21, 37
All-Indian Calvalry Troop L, 138
All Indian Football Team, 215
All-Indian Long Distance Runners Training Camp, 25
All-Indian Rodeo Cowboy Association, 216
All-Time U. S. Track and Field Team, 218
Allan Houser Lifetime Achievement Award, 21
Allen, Elsie, 8
allotment, 118
Almanac of the Dead, 108
Almojuela, Thomas N., 131
Altaha, Wallace, 17
American Ballet Theatre, 145
American Board of Commissioners of Foreign Missions, 166
American Book Award, 106
American Federation of Arts, 15
American Indian Achievement Award, 6, 23
American Indian Arts Center (New York), 12
American Indian Athletic Hall of Fame, 213–15, 217–18, 220
American Indian Center (Los Angeles), 119, 121, 154
American Indian Cultural Group Newsletter, 121
American Indian Dentists Association, 207
American Indian Development Corporation, 105
American Indian Development Program, 72
American Indian Exposition, 58

X

Y

Z